Reconciling Nature

Frontispiece: Man wrestling a bear, ca. 1902 (Wikimedia Commons)

Reconciling Nature

Literary Representations of the Natural, 1876–1945

Robert M. Myers

Published by State University of New York Press, Albany

© 2019 State University of New York

All rights reserved

No part of this book may be used or reproduced in any manner whatsoever without written permission. No part of this book may be stored in a retrieval system or transmitted in any form or by any means including electronic, electrostatic, magnetic tape, mechanical, photocopying, recording, or otherwise without the prior permission in writing of the publisher.

For information, contact State University of New York Press, Albany, NY
www.sunypress.edu

Library of Congress Cataloging-in-Publication Data

Names: Myers, Robert M., 1959– author.
Title: Reconciling nature : literary negotiations of the natural, 1876–1945 / Robert M. Myers.
Description: Albany : State University of New York Press, [2019] | Includes bibliographical references and index.
Identifiers: LCCN 2018058275 | ISBN 9781438476797 (hardcover : alk. paper) | ISBN 9781438476780 (pbk. : alk. paper) | ISBN 9781438476803 (ebook)
Subjects: LCSH: Nature in literature. | American literature—History and criticism.
Classification: LCC PS163 .M94 2019 | DDC 810.9/36—dc23
LC record available at https://lccn.loc.gov/2018058275

10 9 8 7 6 5 4 3 2 1

Contents

List of Illustrations — vii

Acknowledgments — ix

Introduction
Resisting the Resistance Narrative — xi

Chapter 1
Civilizing Nature in Twain's *Adventures of Huckleberry Finn* — 1

Chapter 2
The Ecological City in Crane's *Maggie* — 21

Chapter 3
Therapeutic Nature in Chopin's *The Awakening* — 37

Chapter 4
Disciplining Nature in Sinclair's *The Jungle* — 55

Chapter 5
Progressive Conservation in Austin's *The Ford* — 73

Chapter 6
Surveilling Wilderness in Dreiser's *An American Tragedy* — 89

Chapter 7
Assimilative Nature in Hurston's *Their Eyes Were Watching God* — 105

CHAPTER 8
Environmental Stewardship in Faulkner's *Go Down, Moses*   121

EPILOGUE   141

NOTES   161

WORKS CITED   177

INDEX   205

Illustrations

Figure 1.1	Mississippi River improvements, 1882 (Wikimedia Commons)	4
Figure 1.2	Martha Maxwell's exhibit (Carnegie Library for Local History/Museum of Boulder Collection)	17
Figure 2.1	Jacob Riis, "Dens of Death," 1902 (Wikimedia Commons)	22
Figure 3.1	*Ladies Home Journal* cover, 1894 (Wikimedia Commons)	42
Figure 4.1	Immigrants arriving at Ellis Island, 1904 (Wikimedia Commons)	57
Figure 4.2	Chicago stockyards, 1909 (Wikimedia Commons)	58
Figure 5.1	LA Aqueduct construction, 1912 (Wikimedia Commons)	75
Figure 6.1	Big Moose Lake postcard, ca. 1929 (Wikimedia Commons)	91
Figure 7.1	Herbert Hoover Dike on Lake Okeechobee, ca. 1935 (Wikimedia Commons)	108
Figure 8.1	Roosevelt hunting bear in Mississippi (Harvard Theodore Roosevelt Collection)	122

Figure E.1 Hiroshima, 1945 (Wikimedia Commons) 151

Figure E.2 Edison, Burroughs, Ford, and Firestone camping, 1918 (The Collections of The Henry Ford) 158

Acknowledgments

I have many to thank for their help with this book. Lock Haven University provided me with grants to travel to conferences and research institutions, and I am especially grateful for a sabbatical in the fall of 2016 that enabled me to finish the manuscript. The staff at Stevenson Library was efficient and courteous, procuring the many books and articles I needed. When I visited the Adirondack Experience Library, director Jerold Pepper was generous with his time and the resources of the library (even producing a locket of Grace Brown's hair!). His successor, Ivy Gocker, was also very helpful. Mary P. Stripling, retired librarian of the Mississippi Museum of Natural Science, provided useful information about Mississippi game laws.

An earlier version of chapter 2 was originally published as "Crane's City: An Ecological Reading of *Maggie*," *American Literary Realism* 47.3 (Spring 2015): 189–202; chapter 6 was published as "'A Purely Ideational Lake': The Representation of Wilderness in Dreiser's *An American Tragedy*," *Interdisciplinary Studies in Literature and the Environment* 20.2 (Spring 2013): 377–95; and chapter 8 was published as "Voluntary Measures: Environmental Stewardship in Faulkner's *Go Down, Moses*," *Mississippi Quarterly* 66.4 (Fall 2013): 645–68. I appreciate the permission to republish this work, and I benefited much from the editors and anonymous readers who offered input on these articles.

I feel fortunate to have been published by SUNY Press. My editor Michael Rinella was supportive and helpful throughout the entire process, and my readers were exceptional: their prompt, useful reports made this a better book. Eileen Nizer's careful copyediting of the manuscript was extremely helpful, and Kate Seburyamo did a fine job with the promotions.

My dissertation director, James West, has remained a friend and an inspiration for more than twenty-five years. His comments on an early draft of this project were immensely helpful. When I write, I hear his voice counseling clarity and directness. My friends and family have patiently listened to my thoughts about literary nature, often while we were sitting around campfires in wilderness areas. My hiking buddy and colleague in physics, John Reid, was a good sounding board when I was writing the chapter on the atomic bomb. My colleague and friend Larry Lebin, who is responsible for me being at Lock Haven University, read the manuscript and offered many helpful suggestions a few months before he passed away. My son Michael Myers, Evan Reibsome, and Carrie Shirk all contributed thoughtful ideas as we were climbing Adirondack peaks and listening to loons at Lake Kushaqua.

But most of all, I owe this project to my colleague, my office-mate, my wife, Elizabeth Gruber. If it were not for her inspiration, I would not have taken on such a project at this point in my career, and her careful reading of multiple versions of the manuscript improved it tremendously. As with all other aspects of our life, she made writing fun.

Introduction

Resisting the Resistance Narrative

In the summer of 1876, the celebrated literary naturalist John Burroughs killed a loon. In his collection of essays, *Signs and Seasons* (1886), Burroughs notes that like hummingbirds, loons were exceptionally difficult to shoot given their alertness and quickness. But while fishing at Pleasant Pond in the Maine woods, Burroughs had the advantage of a breech-loading rifle, and he bagged his first loon. Burroughs was not hunting for meat—his motive was purely scientific. He exulted, "The bird I had killed was a magnificent specimen," and when he returned home, he took pains to display the loon in a realistic manner (67). Avoiding the mistake made by most taxidermists, who mount loons standing on their legs, Burroughs placed his specimen on a table "as upon the surface of the water, his feet trailing behind him, his body low and trim, his head elevated and slightly turned as if in the act of bringing the fiery eye to bear upon you, and vigilance and power stamped upon every lineament" (67–68).[1]

I suspect that many contemporary readers would find this episode surprising since Burroughs, or "John O' Birds" as he was called, is recognized as one of the early voices of avian conservation. In 2000, Frank Bergon argued, "Burroughs's awareness and sensitivity establish, even today, an essential standard for anyone aspiring to become a fully engaged environmentalist" (25). Indeed, in another essay in *Signs and Seasons* entitled "Bird Enemies," Burroughs denounces in vitriolic terms bird collectors, "men who plunder nests and murder their owners" (134). Distinguishing between "genuine" ornithologists and those "sham" ornithologists who are driven by vanity, affectation, and mercenary motives rather than the pure principles of science, Burroughs insists that killing species that have already been documented is wasteful: "Thus are our birds hunted and cut off, and all in the name of science; as if science had not long ago finished with these birds. She has weighed and measured and dissected and described them, and their nests and eggs, and placed them in her cabinet" (134–35). However, this distinction is problematic, if not disingenuous, when applied to Burroughs's loon. Although he was elected an associate member of the American Ornithology Union in 1883, Burroughs was not a professional scientist, and he never published the results of his analysis of the loon he killed. Furthermore, by 1876, the loon had already been scientifically documented in works such as Elliott Coues's *Key to North American Birds* (1872). As if aware of this problem, Burroughs admits that the "student of ornithology" must occasionally kill a bird to identify it (136). But he explains that "once having mastered the birds, the true ornithologist leaves his gun at home"; accordingly, the real enemy of the birds is the "closet naturalist" with "his piles of skins, his cases of eggs, his laborious feather-splitting, and his outlandish nomenclature" (136).[2]

The dismissive phrase "closet naturalist" and the reference to "outlandish nomenclature" place Burroughs's polemic in an interesting moment in the history of ornithology. In *A Passion for Birds*, Mark V. Barrow demonstrates that in contrast to other sciences, ornithology maintained into the early twentieth century a close alliance between professional ornithologists and amateur bird collectors. But that alliance was not without tensions. Amateurs were likely to see professional scientists as effetes, divorced from the rugged outdoor life of collecting, and they were especially troubled by scientists' use of trinomial nomenclature to indicate subspecies. Barrow points out that this new emphasis on subspecies variation reflected the influence of evolutionary theory and resulted in a massive increase in the specimens taken because collectors now needed examples of each variation rather than the traditional male and female pair of each species.

In the Spring of 2015, while watching a pair of nesting loons on an Adirondack lake, I recalled Burroughs's loon hunt, and it struck me that his ability to reconcile a deeply felt love of nature with the senseless killing of such a magnificent bird complicates the story of the rise of environmentalism in America. The textbook version is that in the nineteenth century, when Americans saw nature as nothing more than a resource to be used, voices began to speak up for the nonhuman world. The vanguard of this resistance consisted of figures such as George Marsh and Henry David Thoreau, and they were followed by the great conservationists of the Progressive Era: Theodore Roosevelt, John Muir, Gifford Pinchot, and John Burroughs. In the introduction to *American Earth* (2008), Bill McKibben explains, "After the prophetic explosion that was Thoreau, American environmental writing and thought continued, even if at a more deliberate pace and sometimes at extended intervals, to drive the movement forward" (xxiv). In his history of American environmentalism, Benjamin Kline notes, "By the beginning of the twentieth century a new view of nature appeared in America" (51). Kline argues that this reformist movement continued through Franklin Delano Roosevelt's New Deal in the 1930s, so "much of the philosophy and most of the methods needed to construct an active environmental movement had been well formed during the first half of the twentieth century" (67). In this version, the early resistance to the culture of domination blossomed into contemporary environmentalism with the publication of Rachel Carson's *Silent Spring* in 1962, or perhaps on the first Earth Day in 1970. This story is an example of what William Cronon has called a "progressive narrative," a story in which "the plot line gradually ascends toward an ending that is somehow more positive—happier, richer, freer, better—than the beginning" ("Place for Stories" 1352).³

In *Reconciling Nature*, I complicate the resistance narrative through ecocritical readings of eight major American novels written in the decades surrounding the turn of the century. A close analysis of these works contributes to a cultural history of the contested ideologies of nature embedded in the development of modern environmental thought between the Civil War and World War II.

Since its development in the early 1990s, ecocriticism has steadily grown in popularity, producing academic appointments; its own journal, *Interdisciplinary Studies in Literature and the Environment* (*ISLE*); and the professional organization the Association for the Study of Literature and the Environment (ASLE), which sponsors biennial conferences. In the introduction to *The Ecocriticism Reader* (1996), Cheryl Glotfelty defines ecocriticism as "the study of the relationship between literature and the physical environment," a broad definition that suggests the diversity of the approach (xviii). Glotfelty links its future direction to the stages of feminist criticism outlined by Elaine Showalter in *Toward a Feminist Poetics* (1979), arguing that the feminist critique of misogyny in male-authored works parallels ecocritical critiques of anthropocentric representations of nature; and that gynocriticism, or the recovery and interpretation of writing by women, parallels the rediscovery of nature writing that has been excluded from the traditional canon (xxii–xxiv).

Two and a half decades later, ecocritics have indeed recovered an impressive body of previously ignored nature writing, but it is not as clear that they have fully explored the first of Glotfelty's stages, the ecocritical critique. A review of anthologies published between 1996 and 2003 suggests that early ecocritics were drawn to contemporary rather than classic American literature, perhaps because the representations of nature in those texts are more closely aligned with the values of contemporary environmentalism. I analyzed five ecocritical anthologies to determine the authors and texts that were studied: *The Ecocriticism Reader* (Glotfelty 1996), *Reading the Earth* (Branch 1998), *Reading Under the Sign of Nature* (Tallmadge 2000), *Beyond Nature Writing* (Armbruster 2001), and *The ISLE Reader* (Branch 2003). My admittedly unscientific results suggest a presentist bias within early ecocriticism. Approximately 63 percent of the essays deal with post-1900 literature; 37 percent are on literature written after 1970. My analysis did not suggest an undue emphasis on what David Mazel has called the "core nature-writing canon": Carson, Muir, Thoreau, Austin, Leopold, Dillard, and Lopez ("Ecocriticism" 41). Nevertheless, the authors discussed most in these anthologies are Dillard (four chapters) and Abbey (three chapters); there was no chapter on Shakespeare, Faulkner, Dickinson, or Hurston. An examination of scholarly articles in ten recent issues of *ISLE* (2014–2016) reveals that an even higher percentage of the articles are focused on post-1900 literature (77 percent) and post-1970 literature (45 percent).

In their anthology *Beyond Nature Writing* (2001), Karla Armbruster and Kathleen R. Wallace argue that if ecocriticism is to avoid marginalization, critics need to expand the ecocritical canon in order to demonstrate "the field's true range and its power to illuminate an almost endless variety of texts" (3).[4] This call has been answered by a growing number of studies that look at previously unexamined authors, but the tendency has often been to present them as voices of dissent against the mainstream exploitation of nature. For example, in *Shifting the Ground* (1997), Rachel Stein sees the work of Emily Dickinson, Zora Neale Hurston, Alice Walker, and Leslie Marmon Silko as "boldly polemic subversions" of "the traditional mythos of America as a nation lodged in the wilderness" (4). Likewise, Lawrence Buell, in *Writing for an Endangered World* (2001) reads "an incipient environmental ethic" in Faulkner (171). Terrell F. Dixon (2001) concludes that Mary Wilkins Freeman's short stories "present an expansive, evolving ecofeminist vision—one that avoids essentialism and that creates green women and green men who love and defend nature while engaged in ordinary life" (173). Likewise, Stefan Schöberlein (2016) sees Melville's "Paradise of Bachelors and the Tartarus of Maids" as "a politically conscious, environmentally perceptive work of art" that "has the potential to speak to socioecological concerns today in a way few texts from his time can" (747, 731).

Resistance to ideologies of domination is also embedded in attempts to define the purpose of ecocriticism. In their anthology *Reading the Earth* (1998), Michael Branch, Rochelle Johnson, and Daniel Patterson insist, "Ecocriticism is not just a means of analyzing nature in literature; it implies a move toward a more biocentric world-view, an extension of ethics, a broadening of humans' conception of global community to include nonhuman life forms and the physical environment" (xiii). Consistent with this agenda, James Perrin Warren (2000) explains that his analysis does not exonerate the vision of Whitman, "which is clearly not ecocritical" (175). But defining "ecocritical" as sympathetic alignment with nonhuman nature seems to reduce ecocritics to environmental police who point out anthropocentric attitudes towards nature and celebrate those who resist such attitudes. As Anne Milne (2012) warns, the activist impulse of ecocriticism could result in a "prescriptive mode" that "constricts inquiry and may even be seen to sanction a particular orientation of writers to and in nature" (141). Similarly, Robert Kern (2003) argues that ecocriticism "becomes reductive when it simply targets the environmentally incorrect, or when it aims to evaluate texts solely on the basis of their adherence to ecologically sanctioned standards of behavior" (260). In his brilliant, if acerbic, critique of ecocriticism, Dana Phillips (2003) questions its excessive praise for nature writing and poetry, "as if ecocriticism were to be organized and run as a sort of fan club" (138). He argues that undue respect for mimetic realism by ecocritics such as Lawrence Buell limits the texts that can be studied and reduces the role of the critic to an umpire, "squinting to see if a given depiction of a horizon, a wildflower, or a live oak tree is itself well-painted and lively" (164).

In contrast to this constrained scope, *Reconciling Nature* complicates the teleological implications of the resistance narrative by mapping the complex, often contradictory representations of the human relationship to the nonhuman that emerge in eight important American novels written between 1876 and 1945. Moving beyond the resistance narrative opens up ecocritical readings of texts that had not previously been read from this perspective, thereby demonstrating that ecocriticism is a remarkably flexible methodology that can produce fresh and significant readings of texts that have been thoroughly interpreted by more traditional approaches.

As the nineteenth century ended, many Americans began to realize that nature was not inexhaustible. By then the old-growth forests of New England, the Middle Atlantic, the Midwest, and the South were almost completely cutover. The massive herds of American bison had been reduced to a few hundred survivors, and in 1914 the last surviving passenger pigeon, sole remnant of a species that had numbered in the billions just decades earlier, died in a Cincinnati zoo. Exotic bird species were being decimated by the millinery business, and trapping had all but eliminated the beaver from its natural range.

Meanwhile, Americans felt that they had become increasingly distanced from the natural world. In 1870, 26 percent of the population lived in cities; by 1920, that figure had reached 51 percent (Carter et al. 103–04). Furthermore, the number and size of cities increased dramatically: in 1870 there were 663 cities with at least 2,500 people; by 1940, there were 3,485, including five cities of over a million people (Carter et al. 1–102). Turn-of-the-century cities were nightmares of pollution and overcrowding as nonhuman nature was eliminated to make room for factories, railroads, and tenement buildings. In 1883, economist Henry George noted that city dwellers "never, from year's end to year's end, press foot upon mother earth, or pluck a wild flower, or hear the tinkle of brooks, the rustle of grain, or the murmur of leaves as the light breeze comes through the woods. All the sweet and joyous influences of nature are shut out from them" (317). In response to these changes, Americans sought to restore the felt presence of nature to their lives. Transportation improvements made it possible for many to live in the suburbs and commute to work. Authors churned out fictional and nonfictional nature books that were eagerly consumed, and educators made nature study a part of the curriculum. Urban progressive reformers concerned about the migration of farmers to the city attempted to improve the conditions of rural life, while others left the city and returned to the farm.[5]

But if nature could be seen as threatened, it could also be viewed as threatening. Ted Steinberg proposes that in the fifty years between 1880 and 1930 more people died from natural disasters than in any other period in American history (*Acts of God* 69). Indeed, seven of the ten most deadly natural disasters in US history occurred between 1871 and 1928. In the late 1880s, blizzards killed hundreds in the Plains, and heavy rains collapsed a dam and killed over two thousand people in Johnstown, Pennsylvania.

Between 1893 and 1928, thousands died from hurricanes that hit Louisiana, Georgia, Texas, and Florida; meanwhile, forest fires killed hundreds more in Wisconsin, Michigan, Idaho, and Montana. Six magnitude 6 or higher earthquakes occurred between 1886 and 1940, including the 1906 San Francisco earthquake, which killed more than three thousand people. In this period, the boll weevil destroyed crops in the South and sustained droughts devastated farms in the Great Plains. Given these violent eruptions of the natural world, it is not surprising that naturalist writers such as Stephen Crane and Jack London wrote works depicting nature as dangerous and indifferent to human desire. Likewise, turn-of-the-century fear of nature can be seen in Coney Island's recreations of natural disasters such as the Johnstown Flood and the Galveston Hurricane, as well as in the popular attraction "The End of the World," a dramatization of the destruction of mankind as predicted in the Bible.[6] If nature is a threat to survival, one response is to turn to human ingenuity to mitigate that threat and render nature useful. In "The Moral Equivalent of War" (1910), William James proposed conscripting young people into an "army enlisted against *Nature*" (1291). He insisted that working in mines, building roads and tunnels, and constructing skyscrapers would eliminate childishness as youths played their part "in the immemorial human warfare against nature" (1291)

Such a war could be profitable. Gifford Pinchot observed that when he returned from France in 1890, "[t]he American Colossus was fiercely intent on appropriating and exploiting the riches of the richest of all continents—grasping with both hands, reaping where he had not sown, wasting what he thought would last forever" (*Breaking* 23). Max Oelschlaeger's magisterial *The Idea of Wilderness* (1991) traces the development of this dominance paradigm from the Paleolithic era to the present. He argues that the mastery of nature implied in the mechanistic philosophy of Bacon and Descartes led to modernism, "that combination of the power of science and technology with political and economic ideologies modeled on the machine metaphor" (97). Oelschlaeger points out that by the early twentieth-century, Americans became aware of the limits of natural resources, and governmental policy began to see nature in the utilitarian terms of conservation resourcism; accordingly, "the wilderness in whatever guise is effectively reduced to an environment, a stockpile of matter-energy to be transformed through technology, itself guided by the market and theoretical economics, into the wants and needs of the consumer culture" (286–87). Samuel P. Hays sees the conservation movement as a commitment to "rational planning to promote efficient development and use of all natural resources" (*Conservation*

2). In the decades surrounding the turn of the century, national forests were created, rivers were dammed, predators were eliminated, deserts were reclaimed, and wetlands were drained. Pinchot, the architect of American conservation, insisted that "the first duty of the human race is to control the earth it lives upon" (*Fight* 45).

The progressives were also committed to controlling those humans whom they deemed more closely linked to nature than themselves. Darwinian thought blurred the distinction between human and animal and made it possible to justify a racialized hierarchy of evolution. The Civil War resulted in the sudden citizenship of 4 million African Americans, who were perceived by many as less evolved than whites. In 1906 Ota Benga, a Congolese man, was exhibited in the American Museum of Natural History and at the Monkey House of the Bronx Zoo. Women were also seen as closer to nature, and thus their increasing demands for full inclusion into society posed a threat. Likewise, the waves of immigration in the late nineteenth century, especially from southern and eastern Europe, caused many Americans to feel that the new immigrants threatened the older, "Nordic" groups with "race suicide." To control these groups, progressives relied on a combination of education and repressive legislation, including such extreme measures as eugenics. Indeed, Charles R. McCann Jr. has argued that paternalistic coercion of the individual by the state is the "true legacy" of progressivism (224).[7]

The tension between these views of nature—vulnerable, threatening, or useful—is manifested in the cultural productions of this period. In 1876, as Mark Twain was beginning to write *Huckleberry Finn*, Americans gathered in Philadelphia for the nation's centennial. The authorizing act of Congress specified the purpose as "an Exhibition of the natural resources of the country and their development, and of its progress in those arts which benefit mankind" (qtd. in Giberti 24).[8] However, that same year a less optimistic note was sounded with the publication of J. A. Allen's *The American Bisons*, the first book to raise awareness about anthropogenic extinction of species. Likewise, the detonation of the atomic bombs that ended World War II in 1945, three years after the publication of William Faulkner's *Go Down, Moses*, represented both the apotheosis of scientific mastery of nature and a heightened fear about the apocalyptic implications of that mastery. Burroughs's use of science to justify his loon hunt illustrates just one of the ways that Americans in this period constructed various strategies to reconcile their desire to protect a diminishing nature with their fears of a threatening nature and their confidence in human ability to reshape the nonhuman world. As these novels negotiated these tensions, they both resisted and reinforced the culture of dominance over nature.

⁂

To untangle the representations of nature in turn-of-the-century American literature, I examine a diverse group of novels. In "From Wide Open Spaces to Metropolitan Places" (2003), Michael Bennett notes the relative neglect by ecocritics of eastern, urban literature, a trend he links to the disproportionate number of ecocritics who were associated with universities in the American West (302). Likewise, the environmental justice movement has challenged ecocritics to address literature that depicts urban life. The novels I discuss are set in the Mississippi River Valley, the Adirondacks, New York City, the Everglades, New Orleans, Mississippi, Chicago, and southwest California, thus representing more fully the environments of modern America. The novels are likewise written by authors of diverse backgrounds and perspectives: several saw themselves as part of the social reform movements of the era; others were more indifferent or even reactionary in their politics. But despite their differences, these eight novels are unified by efforts to reconcile concerns about a threatened nature with an ideology of domination that rendered nature safe or useful. Collectively, these reconciliations offer a more complete map of environmentalism in the period between the Progressive Era and the New Deal.

The Progressive Era has been the subject of much debate. Recent historians have challenged the idea of a coherent progressivism, given the diversity of those associated with the reform movements. Daniel T. Rodgers proposes that instead of an overall unifying principle, the progressives loosely organized around three clusters of ideas: "the first was the rhetoric of antimonopolism, the second was an emphasis on social bonds and the social nature of human beings, and the third was the language of social efficiency" ("In Search" 123). Historians also differ significantly on the question of when the movement began and ended. Charles R. McCann Jr. defines the Progressive Era as extending from 1885 to 1925, but he admits that "no clear-cut designation is possible, given the protean nature of Progressive thought" (10). Indeed, a recent anthology edited by Stephen Skowronek, Stephen M. Engel, and Bruce Ackerman addresses the "Progressives' Century," beginning with the 1912 election and ending with Barak Obama's election in 2012. Similarly, recent historians of the New Deal have recognized its continuity with progressivism: in *Atlantic Crossings*, Daniel T.

Rodgers sees the New Deal as a "culmination" of progressivism and argues that "to a striking degree the New Deal enlisted its ideas and agenda out of the Progressive past" (415).[9]

Certainly, the period between the Civil War and World War II was important in American environmentalism. Discounting outliers such as Thoreau and Marsh, before the 1870s, few Americans expressed any reservations about the ideology of domination. The environmental crises of the late nineteenth century did indeed inspire challenges to this attitude and led to progressive conservation. Benjamin Heber Johnson defines conservation as "a robust political program with different but overlapping principles," including respect for the transcendent beauty of wild nature and the need for efficient use of natural resources; he notes that to achieve their ends, conservationists relied on state power, scientific knowledge, and grassroots support (55). In his study of continuities and discontinuities between the progressives and the New Dealers, Otis L. Graham notes that progressives were more likely to support New Deal conservation than other issues (*Encore* 207–08). The end of World War II ushered in a new phase of American environmentalism, a response to what J. R. McNeill and Peter Engelke have called "the Great Acceleration," the rapid postwar increase in energy usage and population growth (208). Encompassing the origins and the eclipse of the conservation movement, these novels suggest continuities in the environmental attitudes of this period. Despite the half century that divides their careers, John Burroughs and Aldo Leopold have more in common than either has with contemporary, biocentric environmentalists. The strategies that turn-of-the-century Americans developed to reconcile their anxieties about a threatened nature with the older domination paradigm persisted until the late twentieth century, when new anxieties over human domination of the natural world led to the emergence of contemporary environmentalism.

Reflecting the diversity of liberal reform in this period, several patterns will be traced in this study. First, as middle- and upper-class Americans encountered the psychological pressures caused by the harsh realities of life in the industrial city, a strong anti-urban impulse drove them to seek temporary escape in both real and literary nature. Second, as the implications of Darwinian theory percolated through the culture, Americans attempted to control a threatening external world and direct evolutionary progress through technology and scientific management. Third, a growing awareness of the need to protect a nature threatened by industrialization dovetailed with the progressive expansion of the regulatory state; however, by the 1930s, reaction against what was seen as the excesses of this new federalism resulted in a revival of individualism. Finally, the newly emerging disciplines of ecology, psychology, sociology, and anthropology seemed to present effective strategies to manage and protect nature; these disciplines also offered useful ways to control the problematic nature represented by women, immigrants, and nonwhites.

Chapter 1 argues that Mark Twain's *Adventures of Huckleberry Finn* (1885) displays antimodern anxiety about the environmental crisis caused by the rise of industrial capitalism. Huck's excursion into nature on the frontier is encumbered by the manufactured objects that he acquires, suggesting that any effort to escape civilization is always entangled with consumer culture. Furthermore, Huck's efforts to assimilate Jim into human society reveal the threat of an untamed nature. Ultimately, Twain's response to the nineteenth-century environmental crisis is a nostalgic realism that attempts to preserve a disappearing nature.

Chapter 2 situates Stephen Crane's *Maggie* (1893) into late nineteenth-century debates over the growing problem of the city. The new disciplines of sociology and ecology intersected with progressive urban reform to emphasize the importance of the environment and the interdependence of the various elements of the city. Focusing on the ways in which the material conditions of the city warp the mental states of the characters in *Maggie* reveals the threats that the urban poor represent to the upper classes and the need for the police powers of the government.

Chapter 3 complicates the late nineteenth-century view of the socializing value of nature, especially its role in the education of young women. In Kate Chopin's *The Awakening* (1899), Edna Pontellier's outdoor experiences develop an individualistic desire to transcend external nature and social convention; however, she is destroyed by an intractable nature that opposes her desires and reinforces her status as a nineteenth-century wife and mother. Her failure suggests the need for experts in psychology who can reconcile the conflict between the inner desires of women and the harsh realities of nature and society.

Chapter 4 examines competing views of Darwin in Upton Sinclair's *The Jungle* (1906). Situated in the middle of the Progressive Era, Sinclair's novel represents socialist cooperation as a more efficient strategy for evolutionary progress than capitalist competition. Rather than repressing the nature of the immigrant workers, socialism carefully manages it through Progressive Era education and eugenics. That utilitarian view of nature is likewise represented in the novel's evasive engagement with questions of animal rights.

Chapter 5 looks at Mary Austin, a central figure in the ecocritical resistance narrative, arguing that she is more closely aligned with domination ideology than has been assumed. In her novel *The Ford* (1917), Austin represents the California "Water Wars" as a struggle between urban acquisitiveness and the need for an efficient agriculture that uses nature productively. The novel privileges a progressive "wise use" of nature through cooperation, scientific efficiency, and an understanding of human psychology.

Chapter 6 connects Theodore Dreiser's *An American Tragedy* (1925) to conservationist efforts to protect threatened wilderness areas, such as the Adirondack setting of the novel. The preservation of the Adirondacks required the legal erasure of people who had been living in the area and led to a network of surveillance and coercive mechanisms of control. Clyde Griffiths attempts to transform the external reality of the Adirondacks into an empty space where he can enact his desires without detection. However, his arrest and conviction demonstrate that the wilderness is not outside of the disciplinary surveillance of the state.

A central concern of the New Deal was the assimilation of African Americans into mainstream American society, a project left unfulfilled by the progressives. Chapter 7 explores Zora Neale Hurston's *Their Eyes Were Watching God* (1937) from the perspective of twentieth-century anthropological theories that attempted to manage the problematic nature represented by African Americans. As she struggles to define herself against the natural, Janie Crawford develops a scientific objectivity that demonstrates her potential for assimilation into white culture.

Chapter 8 places William Faulkner's *Go Down, Moses* (1942) in the Depression-era debates over the role of the government in forestry and sport hunting. Reacting against the progressive–New Deal expansion of the regulatory state, Faulkner's novel presents the individual who acts ethically without external control as a constructive alternative to both rapacious individualism and governmental regulation. Ike McCaslin's failure to become that responsible individual can be attributed to his escapist immersion in atavistic wilderness nostalgia, an escapism that is in contrast to those who struggle to maintain the land and the people living on it on a sustainable basis.

The effort to control the forces of nature reached its apotheosis in the Manhattan Project; accordingly, the epilogue to this book synthesizes the themes of *Reconciling Nature* by focusing on the rhetoric of the creation and use of the first atomic bomb and the nuclear age's influence on the development of contemporary environmentalism. Turn-of-the-century ideologies of nature surface in the rhetoric surrounding the construction of the bomb, justifications of its use, and efforts to relieve the fear of nuclear war. In turn, anxiety over the threat of nuclear holocaust helped to shape the contemporary environmental movement.

⁂

In their 2001 anthology, Armbruster and Wallace urged ecocritics to draw from disciplines such as environmental history for "insights into the relationship between natural and cultural environments" (5). More recently, in 2015 Hannes Bergthaller argued that the promise of an environmental humanities has remained unfulfilled, and he called for a "closer engagement" between ecocriticism and environmental history (6). *Reconciling Nature* employs the work of environmental historians to trace ideologies of nature in works of literature through a key moment in American environmental history, a period that encompasses both the Progressive Era and the New Deal. By situating these novels in the context of the cultural conflicts that shaped modern views of nature, I present revisionist readings of these literary works and rereadings of some of the major issues of environmental history. Although I incorporate history, my approach focuses on the literariness of these texts and thus differs from an environmental history that uses literature as illustrations of how people thought at a given historical moment. If Greg Garrard is correct in seeing culture as "the production, reproduction and transformation of large-scale metaphors," then careful attention to how cultural ideologies are refracted through those metaphors as well as through the characters and the plots of literature seems to represent a unique opportunity for a historically grounded ecocriticism (7).[10]

My approach is an eclectic mix of historicism, feminism, and psychology, as well as the close reading strategies of formalism, but I am most directly influenced by cultural studies or the "New Historicism" (the title of which is now nearly as anachronistic as that of the "New Criticism"). I am especially drawn to the assumption that literary and nonliterary texts "circulate": in other words, they reveal similar ideological constructions of the world. Likewise, the work of Michel Foucault has shaped my thinking about environmental history, especially his analysis of the rise of biopolitics and the disciplinary state.

While cultural studies has been a dominant trend in American literary studies, it has been less influential in ecocriticism. However, I do expand upon the work of several recent Americanist ecocritics who have taken a historicist approach. Lawrence Buell's *Writing for an Endangered World* (2001) looks at the development of "the environmental unconscious" in American literature from the late 1700s to the present (18). David Mazel's *American Literary Environmentalism* (2000) explores the "genealogy of the environment" in such pretwentieth century authors as Mary Rowlandson, James Fenimore Cooper, and Theresa Yelverton (xxiii). Lloyd Willis, in his *Environmental Evasion* (2011), cogently discusses the failure of American literature "to spur along a vigorous and sustained environmental movement" (17). Indeed, my work could be seen as a continuation, albeit with a different focus, of his "attempt to explain the forces that have regulated environmental discourse in American literature since the early nineteenth century" (14). Other critics have historicized the relationship of views of nature to ideologies of gender and race in American literature. In *Undomesticated Ground* (2000), Stacy Alaimo discusses what feminism and nature "have meant within specific historical moments" in literature written by women (21). Paul Outka's *Race and Nature from Transcendentalism to the Harlem Renaissance* (2008) explores "the intersection between the construction of racial identity and natural experience" (4).

⁓

Of course, my sense of the loon as a "magnificent bird" is itself historically and culturally produced just as much as Burroughs's representation of it as a "magnificent specimen" (or as a "magnificent dinner"). An issue that has bedeviled ecocriticism from the beginning has been its relationship to poststructuralist thought, which problematizes such oppositional concepts as "nature" and "civilization." Especially since the publication of William Cronon's anthology *Uncommon Ground* (1996), ecocritics have debated the question of to what extent our concepts of nature are socially constructed. Much like Samuel Johnson kicking a rock to refute George Berkeley's idealism, essentialist ecocritics often confront poststructuralists with various illustrations of the "reality" of nature; indeed, they do this with a frequency only surpassed by those critics of Thoreau who charge that he went home to his mother's house for cookies, doughnuts, or pie.[11] Thus, Edward Abbey proposes a variation of Johnson's proof: if you throw a rock at the head of "the solipsist or the metaphysical idealist" and he ducks, "he's a liar" (97). Richard Dawkins quipped, "Show me a cultural relativist at thirty thousand feet and I'll show you a hypocrite" (31–32). And Terry Gifford confronts the poststructuralist students in his classes by pointing to his "balding head" and explaining that "daily, post-modernists have to use an active, if tentative, concept of ageing, or of justice, or of environmentalism, however these concepts have been socially constructed" (15).

But these representations of poststructuralist ecocriticism seem oversimplified, if not actual straw man/woman arguments. Most recent ecocriticism adopts a middle ground, acknowledging the reality of the natural world but recognizing the difficulty of apprehending that world except through culture. Thus, Stacy Alaimo in *Undomesticated Ground* concludes, "While nature cannot be understood apart from its discursive construction, it may *act* in ways that jostle or jolt that very construction" (12). Likewise, David Mazel, in *American Literary Environmentalism*, draws upon Judith Butler's feminist theory to insist that "the key is not in arguing over whether everything is a construct"; instead, the focus should be the "processes of exclusion, erasure, foreclosure, and abjection" that have constituted both the environment and the subject that perceives that environment (xvi). Indeed, in a discussion of the consensus that was reached during the writing of *Uncommon Ground* (which has become to the essentialists what E. M. W. Tillard's *Elizabethan World Picture* was to the New Historicists), Richard White noted, "There was considerable agreement that the natural world was more than a representation and that we could learn meaningful things about it—not just about our representations of it. There was also considerable agreement that, whatever else nature was, it was a representation" (qtd. in Cronon, *Uncommon Ground* 457).

A recurring question among ecocritics is the value of such criticism from an environmentalist perspective: in other words, is it worth the trees that were cut down to publish this book? Indeed, ecocriticism has often struggled with the question of praxis. Glotfelty notes that for environmentally conscious literature professors, "as environmental problems compound, work as usual seems unconscionably frivolous. If we're not part of the solution, we're part of the problem" (xxi). In an intriguing analysis of the environmental implications of ecocriticism, David Mazel concluded that there was no empirical evidence that "students who read and write about green texts turn into more thoughtful and effective environmentalists than they might have been otherwise" ("Ecocriticism" 42). Nevertheless, I would argue that focusing on the ways in which American writers creatively imagined strategies to reconcile nature is instructive for the present since many of these strategies have proven long-lived. For example, recently, sustainability, which is frequently linked to Progressive Era conservation, has emerged as an alternative to traditional environmentalism. Sustainability's focus on the relationship between ecological health, economic welfare, and social empowerment has added important questions of justice to the environmentalist agenda. But, as Leslie Paul Thiele points out, sustainability also can be used by businesses and governments as greenwashing to mask practices that destroy the environment (5–8).

Furthermore, some argue that the legislation and regulatory agencies that were the high achievement of postwar environmentalism have had limited effectiveness and thus raise questions about the future direction of the movement to protect the nonhuman. In a defense of Burroughs's lack of engagement with legislative environmentalism, Justin Askins notes, "Thoreau and Muir's legacy of battling within the Western legal and political system has done little to change the terrible shape the planet is in, even though the spirit of confrontation within that system remains stronger than ever" (263). If politics has proven inadequate, perhaps a cultural change is the only hope for amelioration of worsening environmental conditions. Garrett Hardin's "The Tragedy of the Commons" (1968) begins with a discussion of problems that have no technical solution; accordingly, they require "change in human values or ideas of morality" (1243). The value of environmental humanities (environmental history and ecocriticism) seems to lie in its potential to explore the implications of alternatives to the dominant culture. As Michael Branch notes, we "need to study earlier American conceptions of nature in order to better understand how certain misguided and destructive ideas gained prominence in our culture" ("Before Nature" 93). Or, as Sylvia Mayer observes, "ecocritical studies try to create knowledge that contributes to our understanding of the causes of environmental degradation as well to the search for effective strategies of amelioration" (4).

If our only way to approach nature is through representation, it nevertheless seems clear that some representations are more sustainable than others. In "The Trouble with Wilderness" Cronon observes, "If living in history means that we cannot help leaving marks on a fallen world, then the dilemma we face is to decide what kinds of marks we wish to leave" (88). In Barbara Kingsolver's *Prodigal Summer* (2000), the wildlife biologist Deanna Wolf explains to a coyote hunter that while living always involves taking life, "it can be thoughtful. A little bit humble about the necessity, maybe. You can consider the costs of your various choices. Or you can blow big holes in the world for no better reason than simple fear" (323). But thoughtful choice requires a full understanding of the tensions embedded in any alternatives to the culture of dominance. As American authors reconciled the desire to dominate nature with concerns about the threats to a diminished natural world, they suggested potential solutions to the human/nature relationship, solutions that might represent hope for our future.

Chapter 1

Civilizing Nature in Twain's *Adventures of Huckleberry Finn*

In "The Boy and the River," his introduction to a 1950 edition of *Adventures of Huckleberry Finn*, T. S. Eliot praised Twain's depiction of the Mississippi River. Declaring the novel a "masterpiece," Eliot insisted that "the River makes the book a great book. As with Conrad, we are continually reminded of the power and terror of Nature, and the isolation and feebleness of Man. . . . Mark Twain is a native, and the River God is his God" (285, 287). Eliot's reference to the River God is an allusion to his own "The Dry Salvages" (1941), which begins with a tribute to the Mississippi:

> I do not know much about gods; but I think that the river
> Is a strong brown god—sullen, untamed and intractable,
> Patient to some degree, at first recognised as a frontier;
> Useful, untrustworthy, as a conveyor of commerce;
> Then only a problem confronting the builder of bridges.
> The problem once solved, the brown god is almost forgotten
> By the dwellers in cities—ever, however, implacable,
> Keeping his seasons and rages, destroyer, reminder
> Of what men choose to forget. Unhonoured, unpropitiated
> By worshippers of the machine, but waiting, watching and
>   waiting. (1–10)

In both the introduction and the poem, Eliot represents the Mississippi, which he knew from his childhood in St. Louis, as a powerful force that cannot be tamed by humans. Furthermore, by depicting the river as a forgotten "brown god" that threatens to vent his rage upon the urban worshippers of technology, Eliot seems to link the threat of an uncontrollable nature with Western nightmares of the pent fury of subjugated races.[1]

Recent ecocritics have had little to say about *Huckleberry Finn*, which is somewhat surprising since earlier critics celebrated Twain's representation of nature in a manner consistent with the resistance narrative. Leo Marx notes that after the "idyll" of Jackson's Island, Huck and Jim "continue to enjoy many of the delights they had known earlier, above all a sense of the bounty, beauty, and harmony made possible by an accommodation to nature" (*Machine* 327). Similarly, Robert Schulman argues that "in the great, idyllic moments on the river, Huck fully if briefly realizes his individuality in the context of a human community with Jim and a natural community with the surrounding world" (33). However, other critics have complicated this reading. Sacvan Bercovitch points out that the lyrical description of the river occupies "less than one percent of the book," and he challenges the sentimentalism of the positive reading, noting that "the river is the source of storms and water snakes, it calls up the fog that keeps Huck and Jim from reaching Cairo; it is 'dangersome' to those on it and those who live near it" (111, 110). Likewise, Jocelyn Chadwick-Joshua rejects Eliot's claim that the river is what makes the novel great; instead, it is an "ambiguous symbol" that is both "a source of tremendous upheaval" and the "quiet center" where Huck is enlightened (90).

Placing *Huckleberry Finn* in the context of environmental history reveals the ambivalence of nineteenth-century Americans who hoped to reconcile their concerns about a threatened nature with their fears of a powerful nature that resists domination. The novel is set in the 1840s, when attempts were being made to bring the Mississippi under control, a process that had reached a critical moment by 1885, when the novel was published. Furthermore, Twain began writing *Huckleberry Finn* in 1876, at a time when Americans had begun to realize the damage to the natural world caused by a century of efforts to dominate nature. Twain's novel traces the late-nineteenth-century environmental crisis to its roots in the American frontier experience, but it also grapples with the potentially unmanageable nature represented by African Americans. Ultimately, these anxieties are reconciled by commodifying the disappearing natural world as wilderness nostalgia.

In 1936, President Franklin Roosevelt dedicated the Mark Twain Memorial Bridge in Hannibal, noting that "Mark Twain and his tales live, though the years have passed and time has wrought its changes on the Mississippi" (qtd. in Hearn cxxxviii). Those changes to the Mississippi River valley had already begun in Twain's lifetime. One of the earliest transformations was the system of levees that was constructed to limit the damage caused by flooding. In 1870, Louisiana senator John S. Harris called for new levees to change "a watery waste into a smiling expanse of cultivated lands unequaled in fertility" (qtd. in C. Morris 153). Christopher Morris points out that between 1840 and 1944, a series of flood-control acts shifted responsibility for levee construction and maintenance from the individual states to the federal Army Corps of Engineers (140–68). Much of this legislation was in response to particularly severe floods that occurred in 1874 and 1882, bracketing the composition of *Huckleberry Finn*. In fact, two of the four appendices in Twain's *Life on the Mississippi* (1883) deal with the destructive effects of the 1882 flood and the need for federal involvement in levy construction.

In addition to flood control, attempts were made to harness the power of the river. As late as 1907, the progressive hydrologist W. J. McGee saw the river "as lawless as a monster of the jungle and not yet brought under human control" (qtd. in Scarpino 63). Philip Scarpino points out that in the nineteenth century, the white pine industry, which required an unobstructed river to transport lumber, dominated the economies of river towns such as Twain's Hannibal (19–22, 36). But. after the decline of lumbering in the 1890s, industrial development demanded that the unpredictable river be made navigable. Channels were improved, meandering loops were straightened, and locks and dams were built to regulate the flow of the river and to produce hydroelectric power for industry. Scarpino notes that by the turn of the century, the river was forced to submit to "industrial discipline"; he quotes a journalist who boasts that the 1913 completion of the dam at Keokuk, Iowa, meant that "the mighty Mississippi River has been hitched to the machinery and devices of civilization" (7, 12). By the 1920s, these improvements had become so extensive that they were being contested by groups such as the Izaak Walton League and the Bureau of Fisheries. Scarpino reprints a 1923 cartoon supporting a proposed upper Mississippi wildlife refuge: as the ghosts of Huck and Tom look at a sad modern boy, Tom says, "Say Huck! Ain't you glad we lived before the country began to be civilized all out of shape?" (145).

In 1882, as he was struggling to complete *Huckleberry Finn*, Twain took a month-long trip on the Mississippi. His subsequent book, *Life on the Mississippi*, compares the river that Twain saw in 1882 with the one he remembered from the 1850s when he was a steamboat pilot. Reflecting on his training, Twain depicts the "science" of piloting as a difficult book that he eventually mastered, but at the cost of losing "the grace, the beauty, the poetry" of the river (286, 284). He contrasts his memory of a beautiful sunset with his perception of the same sunset after he had developed a pilot's perspective: "All the value any feature of it had for me now was the amount of usefulness it could furnish toward compassing the safe piloting of a steamboat" (285). But, on the 1882 trip, Twain realized that the navigational improvements made by the government had rendered much of this knowledge obsolete. He admits that artificial lighting, snag removal, and charts have reduced the dangers of the river, but he complains that they have "knocked the romance out of piloting" (397). He scorns the efforts by the engineers of the US River Commission to remake the Mississippi through dams, dikes, and other improvements, pointing out that the "abstruse science" of engineers "cannot tame that lawless stream, cannot curb it or confine it, cannot say to it, Go here, or Go there, and make it obey" (398). The untamable power of the river could be seen in the lingering effects of the most recent flood, which inundated the valley just a few months before Twain's trip. He describes the "flood-wasted land" with its "signs, all about, of men's hard work gone to ruin" (414, 413).

Figure 1.1. Mississippi River Improvements, 1882. Willow branches were fashioned into "mattresses" to protect the bends from erosion. (Wikimedia Commons)

Twain's ambivalence over efforts to control the river in "these modern times" suggests the antimodernism discussed by T. J. Jackson Lears in his brilliant *No Place of Grace*. Lears explains that in the late nineteenth century, many cultural elites sought alternatives to the rationalized complacency of modernism. A sense of human finitude, especially in the face of a threatening nature, led them to seek more authentic experience through premodern craftsmanship, militarism, and religion. Lears argues that this search for authenticity and therapeutic self-fulfillment "eased their own and others' adjustments to a streamlined culture of consumption" (xiv).

Antimodernism is an important motif in *Life on the Mississippi*. As Twain travels down the river, he frequently notes the economic and industrial progress of the towns. His home town of Hannibal "is no longer a village; it is a city," and he reflects that "nearly all the river towns, big and little, have made up their minds that they must look mainly to railroads for wealth and upbuilding" (553, 449). He hopes that the growth of these cities will be accompanied by "intellectual advancement and the liberalizing of opinion," and he predicts that such progress will help the South escape the pernicious influence of the romanticism of Sir Walter Scott that has left the region "modern and mediaeval mixed" (449, 501). Nevertheless, it is difficult to read without irony his praise of "the wholesome and practical nineteenth-century smell of cotton-factories and locomotives" or his putative celebration of "the plainest and sturdiest and infinitely greatest and worthiest of all the centuries the world has seen" (468–69). Twain is also uneasy with such efforts to imitate or transform nature as ice factories, artificial lights, and oleomargarine (396, 464, 523, 466). Meanwhile, the river itself is represented as a powerful force that literally undermines the confident belief in progress of those living along it: Twain marvels that the "self-complacent" town of Napoleon, Arkansas, has been completely destroyed by the erosive effects of the river (436).

One alternative to the banality and overcivilization of modernism for many late-nineteenth-century Americans was an excursion into wild nature. W. Douglas McCombs explores the development of the wilderness vacation as a response to the pressures of civilization. He notes that William Murray's 1869 guide to the Adirondacks, *Adventures in the Wilderness*, initiated a rush of people seeking escape from the unhealthy environment of the city as well as therapy for psychological enervation (414). In 1878, Charles Dudley Warner, Twain's friend and co-author of *The Gilded Age* (1873), published *In the Wilderness*, a series of sketches about vacationing in the Adirondacks; in part, they were intended as a parody of Murray, who presented the north woods as a welcoming place. For Warner, the "impassive, stolid brutality" of the "pitiless" Adirondack wilderness mocks any belief in "man's superiority to Nature; his ability to dominate and outwit her" (20). This untamed nature is the reason why civilized people take temporary excursions into the wilderness: "it is the unconquered craving for primitive simplicity, the revolt against the everlasting dress-parade of our civilization" (78). Twain had both the magazine and book versions of Warner's Adirondack essays in his library, and he included two of the sketches in *Mark Twain's Library of Humor* (1888).[2] Accordingly, it seems useful to begin by focusing on Huck's excursion into the wilderness. Reading the novel from an ecocritical perspective confounds the opposition between civilization and nature: Huck's flight into the wild nature of the 1840s frontier is thoroughly imbricated in the culture of industrial capitalism.

༼ঞ༽

The novel opens with Huck in an uneasy relationship with those who are trying to "sivilize" him (1). At first, he finds living with the Widow Douglas and Miss Watson difficult because he must wear confining clothing, follow a structured schedule, and be subjected to educational and religious instruction. But after several months, he learns to tolerate civilized life, and when he needs a temporary escape, he slips out and camps in the woods (18). Huck's gradual assimilation into middle-class culture is cut off by the arrival of his father. Disgusted by his son's starchy clothes and education, Pap condemns Huck as an overcivilized effete, "a sweet-scented dandy," before kidnapping him and taking him to the wilderness, a place "where the timber was so thick you couldn't find it if you didn't know where it was" (24, 29).

At first, Huck is content with this reversion to the wild, but Pap's abuse soon makes him decide to run away. His initial plan is simple: he will take only a gun and fishing lines and "tramp right across the country" (32). But after he finds a drifting canoe, he decides to "camp in one place for good, and not have such a rough time tramping on foot" (38). To outfit this permanent camp, he takes "everything that was worth a cent" from the cabin:

> I took the sack of corn meal . . . then I done the same with the side of bacon; then the whisky jug; I took all the coffee and sugar there was, and all the ammunition; I took the wadding; I took the bucket and gourd, I took a dipper and a tin cup, and

my old saw, and two blankets, and the skillet and the coffee-pot. I took fish-lines and matches and other things. (39)

Not satisfied that his outfit was complete, Huck decides to stop at Jackson's Island, where he could paddle over to town "and pick up things I want" (41). As Leo Marx has pointed out, this passage suggests that Huck is clearly not "an expositor of primitivist values"; indeed, his list is comparable to the extensive wilderness outfits described in Murray and other guidebooks (*Machine* 326).

Huck's experience on Jackson's Island begins as a moment of immersion into sublime nature. When he awakes, he is surrounded by "big trees"; he watches a friendly squirrel; and he admires the "pretty" river (45). But Huck quickly displays the desire to control nature that was central to late nineteenth-century excursions into the wilderness. He makes a "nice camp" and begins to feel a sense of ownership over the island: he boasts, "I was boss of it; it all belonged to me" as he surveys it for anything that would "come handy" (48). Later, Huck regrets that he cannot sell the giant catfish he catches, noting that "he would a been worth a good deal, over at the village" (66).

Huck continues to encumber his simple life by acquiring both practical camping gear and worthless possessions. The catalog of his finds from the floating house includes such potentially useful supplies as a lantern, knives, candles, a tin cup, a hatchet, and a fishing line with hooks (62). But the passage quickly turns into a parody of wilderness outfits with such worthless items as "a leather dog-collar, and a horseshoe, and some vials of medicine that didn't have no label on them; and . . . a ratty old fiddle-bow and a wooden leg" (62). After a similar "rummaging" expedition on the wrecked steamboat, Huck boasts that he and Jim "hadn't ever been this rich before, in neither of our lives" (81, 93). Far from the simple hunter-gatherer escape into nature that Huck first imagined, his trip has increasingly become encumbered with the possessions of civilization. Warnings against carrying excessive gear were commonplace in nineteenth-century wilderness guides: Warner mocks those who introduce "artificial luxuries" into camping excursions and thereby "reduce the life in the wilderness to the vulgarity of a well-fed picnic" (75).[3]

As Huck travels down the river, he periodically goes ashore, where he encounters a series of frontier communities that are corrupted both by the influences of consumer culture and the ruthless individualism of life on the edge of the wilderness. The Grangerford house is filled with the cheap goods of industrialization, such as chalk parrots, lithographic reproductions, and plaster fruit, which Huck sees as "much redder and yellower and prettier than real ones" (137). Twain's unromantic critique of frontier life continues in Bricksville, Arkansas. The houses are "old shackly dried-up frame concerns," and the gardens are repositories for the detritus of civilization: "[T]hey didn't seem to raise hardly anything in them but jimpson weeds, and sunflowers, and ash-piles, and old curled-up boots and shoes, and pieces of bottles, and rags, and played-out tinware" (181). The people of Bricksville are equally "played-out" and violent: their greatest excitement is "putting turpentine on a stray dog and setting fire to him, or tying a tin pail to his tail and seeing him run himself to death" (183). In *Landscapes of Fear,* Yi-fu Tuan challenges the myth of the peaceful rustic, noting that "proneness to violence and readiness to kill have been a part of the frontier tradition" (139). The selfish individualism of the people in these towns makes them easy marks because they lack the protection that communalism provides. The Royal Nonesuch scam is successful because the King and the Duke know that the townspeople will be drawn in by a suggestion of a titillating performance and that they will then allow their fellow townspeople to be conned rather than be humiliated as the only dupes. The easy successes of the King and the Duke in the river villages make Huck "ashamed of the human race" (210).

Whenever civilization explodes into violence or corruption, Huck is eager to return to the raft and the natural world of the river. In chapter 19, after he has fled from the violence of the Grangerford-Shepherdson feud, Huck describes the sights, sounds, and smells of a sunrise on the river, concluding, "It's lovely to live on a raft," a passage that has been frequently quoted by critics who praise Twain's appreciation of nature (158). But it is important to note that Huck's vision of nature is not free from the taint of human culture. Twain's revisions to the manuscript set up a pattern of alternation between the beauties of nature and the environmental degradations caused by civilization.[4] Huck begins with the sound of the bullfrogs "a-cluttering" and the sight of the horizon gradually emerging from the mists of the river (156). But then he sees the trading scows and the log rafts associated with the river's commercial development, and as the sky reddens, he distinguishes a wood-yard "piled by them cheats so you can throw a dog through it anywheres" (157). Even the olfactory image of the breeze, "so cool and fresh, and sweet to smell, on account of the woods and the flowers," is corrupted by humans who have "left dead fish laying around" (157). As the description of a typical day on the river continues, the human presence on the river dominates Huck's description: his sleep is often interrupted by raftsmen chopping wood and by steamboats belching sparks. Furthermore, the temporary nature of pastoral idylls is reinforced later in the same chapter when the Duke and the King commandeer the raft. Leo Marx argues that once these two arrive, Twain "sets up a rhythmic alternation between idyllic moments on the river and perilous escapades on shore," but this reading distorts the actual proportion of time spent on the raft (336). After chapter 19, 88 percent of the novel takes place on the shore, including all of chapters 22, 25–28, and 32–43. Furthermore, even while he is on the raft, Huck's experience of nature is entangled with discussions of royalty, Shakespearian rehearsals, and schemes to con the rubes.

Huck's excursion into nature stops at the Phelps plantation, but at the end of the novel, the boys plan to "get an outfit" and spend a few weeks in the Territory having "howling adventures amongst the Injuns" (361). Importantly, Huck decides to escape civilization even sooner: he will "light out for the Territory ahead of the rest, because aunt Sally she's going to adopt me and sivilize me and I can't stand it. I been there before" (362). But by this point it is clear that Huck cannot escape the corruptions of civilization by fleeing deeper into the frontier; indeed, the term "territory," as opposed to "wilderness," implies a place already marked and in the process of being transformed by culture. And the reader should understand, even if Huck does not, that any antimodern quest for a simpler life is doomed by the same factors that complicated his earlier attempt at escape. Indeed, before he learns that Pap is dead, Huck is worried that he does not have the money to buy the outfit necessary for Tom's recreational trip into the wilderness; going off with just a gun and fishing lines is no longer an option (361). Like his earlier flight into nature, Huck's escape is already corrupted by civilization.[5]

Twain's depiction of the entanglement of the frontier with consumer culture parallels issues raised in discussions by turn-of-the-century progressives of the European settlement of North America. In his famous essay, "The Significance of the Frontier in American History" (1893), Frederick Jackson Turner saw the pioneer experience as the source of the American character, which developed from "its continuous touch with the simplicity of primitive society" (2–3). Significantly, for Turner, the key figure in the "social evolution" from the hunter to the manufacturing city is the trader who provided guns to the Indians and thus introduced "the disintegrating forces of civilization" into the wilderness (11, 13). Likewise, Lewis Mumford's *Golden Day* (1926) is a powerful critique of the acquisitive pioneers and their environmental devastation. Mumford saw the American experience on the frontier as a mix of the romantic return to primitive nature and the perfectionist confidence in progress. As they moved westward, the settlers abandoned "the traditions of a civil life," and the result was a war against nature in a pursuit of comfort: "[U]ninfluenced by peasant habits or the ideas of an old culture, the work of the miner, woodman, and hunter led to unmitigated destruction and pillage" (62, 58).

Turner and Mumford also echo Twain's unromantic depiction of the violence and corruption of the pioneers. Turner admits, "I have refrained from dwelling on the lawless characteristics of the frontier, because they are sufficiently well known," and he notes the potential for governmental and business corruption that develops from the individualism that is at the center of the pioneer experience (32–33). Similarly, Mumford contrasts the heroism and social gains of the frontier experience with "the crudities of the pioneer's sexual life, his bestial swilling and drinking and bullying, and his barbarities in dealing with the original inhabitants," and he notes that wherever the covered wagon went, it left behind "deserted villages, bleak cities, depleted soils, and . . . sick and exhausted souls" (79).[6]

For Twain, the frontier is at the intersection of primitive nature and modern consumer culture, a bleak place where pristine nature is degraded by the individualistic acquisitiveness that was a target of the progressives. In contrast to Leo Marx, who sees the ending as embodying the tragic realization that a "refuge" in the pastoral frontier no longer existed, I argue that Twain recognizes that it never did exist, at least in post-Columbian America (340). Thus, the novel anticipates Pudd'nhead Wilson's comment on Columbus Day: "It was wonderful to find America, but it would have been more wonderful to miss it" (1055).

As he comprehends the selfishness of the frontier, Huck turns away in disgust and develops a more communal ethic: against his better judgment, he works to protect the Wilks orphans from the Duke and the King, and he commits to helping Jim escape. But unlike the relatively easy decision to protect the white Wilkses, helping Jim requires that Huck must first establish the place of the African American in the human community.

Turner recognized that the frontier, the "meeting point between savagery and civilization," had the potential for reverse assimilation, where the civilized becomes the savage (3). He notes that "the environment is at first too strong for the man," and the pioneer begins to adopt Indian ways (4). However, Turner remained confident that the pioneer soon "transforms the wilderness" and becomes American (4). While Twain was writing *Huckleberry Finn*, the question of how to assimilate nonwhites into mainstream culture emerged as a central problem for white Americans. In the summer of 1876, the defeat of Custer at the Little Big Horn inspired critics of the reservation system to demand that Native Americans be fully assimilated into American society—or exterminated. That fall, the contested presidential election eventually resulted in the withdrawal of federal troops from the South, signaling the official end of Reconstruction and leaving the status of the former slaves very much undetermined.

The late nineteenth-century debate over what to do with racial others was shaped by increasingly racist ideologies within the scientific community and the larger society. Anthropologists argued that Indians and blacks represented different, inferior, species from whites, and thus their subjugation was inevitable and attempts to educate them futile. In an essay that appeared in the *Atlantic Monthly* a few months before *Huckleberry Finn* was published, Harvard geologist Nathaniel Shaler noted that upon reaching adolescence, "the animal nature generally settles down like a cloud" on African Americans ("Negro Problem" 700). Furthermore, since they were so little removed from animality, nonwhites were seen as incapable of developing the resources of the natural world. In 1880 Vanderbilt geology professor Alexander Winchell insisted that the Negro "has built no cities; erected no durable monuments; excavated no canals; transformed no topography, nor removed any natural obstacles to the efficient cultivation of the soil" (256–57). Francis E. Leupp, Theodore Roosevelt's commissioner of Indian affairs, wrote, "All primitive peoples are, from our economic point of view, grossly wasteful of their natural resources"; accordingly, he opened up tribal lands to mining, lumbering, and irrigation projects (93). Huck's evolving relationship with Jim demonstrates the deep ambivalence felt by late nineteenth-century whites about the potential assimilation of African Americans.[7]

At the beginning of the novel, Huck sees Jim as property, more specifically, chattel or livestock. He introduces him as "Miss Watson's big nigger, named Jim" (6). When they meet on Jackson's Island, Huck assumes that Jim is incapable of mastering nature. He immediately displays his sense of superiority by mocking Jim's diet of "strawberries and such truck"; he notes that when Jim sees Huck's civilized provender (meal, bacon, and coffee), "the nigger was set back considerable" (52). But soon a different relationship emerges as Jim's connection with nature enables him to make

Huck's excursion more comfortable. Jim interprets the habits of birds and recommends moving their camp to the cave to escape the thunderstorm; later he makes a wigwam on the raft to protect them (60, 78). Thus, like the guides who accompanied wealthy tourists in the Adirondacks, Jim is a transitional figure between nature and civilization. Seen by Huck as a mixture of the human and the animal, Jim helps to control the threat of nature.[8]

As the excursion continues, Jim himself becomes threatening because his increasingly obvious humanity confounds the nature/civilization binary. After he witnesses Jim crying about his separation from his children, Huck realizes that Jim has human emotions: "I do believe he cared just as much for his people as white folks does for theirn. *It don't seem natural*, but I reckon it's so" (201, italics mine). Huck's gradual realization of Jim's humanity continues to the well-known climax of the novel. Fully realizing his complicity in the theft of "a poor old woman's nigger," Huck's conscience torments him until he writes a letter to Miss Watson telling her where Jim is. But then he thinks of a series of incidents that illustrate Jim's humanity, until finally he decides, "All right, then, I'll *go* to hell," as he destroys the letter and commits to helping Jim escape (271). Thus, Twain's famous description of the novel as a conflict between "a sound heart and a deformed conscience" turns on the question of whether Huck sees Jim as an animal or as a human (qtd. in Hearn 154).

If Jim is human, Huck is forced to wrestle with the question of how to assimilate him into the community. Throughout the novel, Huck attempts to educate Jim, but with little more effect than the Widow's and Miss Watson's efforts to educate Huck. As Carl Wieck notes, Twain "often shows teaching, even by parents and their proxies, to be a frustrating and frequently disappointed endeavor" (151). At the conclusion of a failed lesson on why people speak French, Huck despairingly concludes, "[Y]ou can't learn a nigger to argue. So I quit" (98). Even more troubling are Tom's efforts to teach Jim about the literature of prison escapes. When Jim complains about the difficulty of adhering to Tom's literary models, Tom "lost all patience with him" and forces Jim to meekly apologize (328). Huck's and Tom's failures are consistent with the even more pessimistic critique of the "white man's burden" in Twain's *Connecticut Yankee*. When the church turns society against Hank Morgan's efforts to uplift the common people, his assistant, Clarence, points out his folly: "Did you think you had educated the superstition out of those people? . . . Well, then, you may unthink it" (418). Charles Carroll's *The Negro a Beast* (1900) cites a source who sees blacks as uneducable, arguing that their "coarse nature is easily aroused, and they have never heard tell of such a thing as self-control" (65).[9]

If education was problematic, perhaps candidacy for citizenship could be established by displaying desirable behavior. In 1898, Albert Beveridge, who would later become a progressive senator and key supporter of conservation, delivered a speech, "The March of the Flag," in support of US imperialism. He dismissed those "triflers with nature's laws" who would reject this opportunity to create new markets by conquering nature, noting that there were "so many real things to be done" (56). In response to critics who would argue that we cannot govern the Filipinos without their consent, Beveridge argued that "the rule of liberty that all just government derives its authority from the consent of the governed, applies only to those who are capable of self-government" (49). In other words, being civilized meant the ability to control both external nature and the internal self.

The widow Douglas's efforts to "sivilize" Huck early in the novel are necessary because he has become wealthy due to the fortune he and Tom found at the end of *Tom Sawyer*. To assume his place in society, he must demonstrate his ability to manage nature and himself. The canoe, raft, and camping equipment that he appropriates from others enable him to control external nature; thus, for example, in chapter 20, he is entertained rather than frightened by the violent lightning storm (167–68). As was the case with the wealthy elites who vacationed in the Adirondacks, Huck's ability to master nature suggests his fitness for managing property. To protect his money from Pap, Huck shrewdly signs it over to Judge Thatcher (19–20). When Peter Wilks's money is given to the Duke and the King, Huck steals it to make sure that it is returned to the Wilks orphans even though he is worried that he might be "catched with six thousand dollars in my hands that nobody hadn't hired me to take care of" (231).

Of course, the most significant property that Huck must manage is Jim. When he first escapes from Miss Watson, Jim thinks, "I owns myself," but it soon becomes clear that his ownership is being negotiated by others (57). At first, Huck feels guilt over his complicity in the theft of Miss Watson's property (124). But after he commits to helping Jim escape, he begins to see himself as Jim's owner. Huck tells the Duke that he was afraid that they had stolen "my nigger, which is the only nigger I've got in the world, and now I'm in a strange country, and ain't got no property no more" (272). One might argue that Huck is dissembling to the Duke—as some have claimed that he is when he responds "No'm. Killed a nigger" to Aunt Sally's question about whether anyone was hurt by the steamboat explosion (279).[10] But Huck's sense of proprietorship over Jim is even more clearly displayed when he explains to Tom that if he decides to steal a slave, "I ain't no ways particular how it's done, so it's done. What I want is my nigger" (307). Huck has no reason to pretend with Tom; indeed, when he first learns of Tom's willingness to help him steal Jim out of slavery, he is privately shocked: "Tom Sayer a *nigger stealer!*" (284).

Meanwhile, of course, Jim has already been freed by Miss Watson, but that does not protect him from being enslaved again. In 1876, William Dean Howells was troubled by Francesco Pezzicar's bronze statue, "The Freed Slave," which he saw at the Philadelphia Centennial Exhibition. Fearing the insurrectionist spirit depicted in the statue, Howells confessed that "one longs to clap him back into hopeless bondage" (93). Perhaps the same impulse explains the re-enslavement of Jim. As Toni Morrison has trenchantly argued, the ending of *Huckleberry Finn* "becomes the elaborate deferment of a necessary and necessarily unfree Africanist character's escape, because freedom has no meaning to Huck or to the text without the specter of enslavement, the anodyne to individualism; the yardstick of absolute power over the life of another" (309). Caught up in enthusiasm over his project of enslavement/emancipation, Tom evokes the gradualism of post–Civil War reformers: "[W]e would keep it up all the rest of our lives and leave Jim to our children to get out; for he believed Jim would come to like it better and better the more he got used to it. He said that in that way it could be strung out to as much as eighty year, and would be the best time on record" (310).

But, it is not just Tom who prolongs Jim's enslavement. Throughout the novel, Huck sees Jim's desire for freedom as subhuman. When Jim first expresses excitement at the possibility of helping his children escape, Huck is disappointed: "I was sorry to hear Jim say that, it was such a lowering of him" (124). Even after his celebrated decision to risk hell by helping Jim escape, Huck expects Jim to demonstrate self-government even if it means remaining a slave. When he must decide whether to help the wounded Tom, Jim is forced to choose between his individualistic desire for freedom and a recognition of his social obligation. Confident that Jim has the potential for assimilation, Huck knew that he would stay with Tom: "I knowed he was white inside, and I reckoned he'd say what he did say" (341). Thus, Jim demonstrates his whiteness by controlling his own nature. At the end, Jim is freed (again), reimbursed for his difficulties, and invited to join the boys on the excursion to the Territory. Accordingly, the novel seems to suggest that African Americans were capable of the self-governance required of progressive citizenship.

But the ending also suggests that the nature that is represented by Jim might remain frustratingly unmanageable. Shortly after he learns of his new freedom, and thus is no longer in need of Huck's help to escape, Jim reveals that Huck's father is dead (361–62). Jim's revelation means that Huck had no reason to flee St. Petersburg and raises the possibility that Jim has been manipulating Huck from the beginning and makes his expressions of love and trust in Huck seem Machiavellian (a reading that deeply troubles my students). Intriguingly, Huck does not respond to Jim's announcement, instead shifting abruptly into the final paragraph, where he indicates that he will try to escape civilization. Like the Mississippi River, the African American might prove difficult to control.[11]

In 1962, Henry Nash Smith could describe the river excursion of Huck and Jim as a pastoral paradise: "Projected into the natural setting, the love of the protagonists for each other becomes the unforgettable beauty of the river when they are allowed to be alone together. It is always summer, and the forces of nature cherish them" (123). Recent critics of the novel have been more critical of Huck, especially of his presumed growth in racial understanding. Bercovitch argues that Huck does not develop and remains "the racist, death-haunted, would-be conformist he was before he set out on his adventures" (114). Focusing on Huck's relationship with the natural world extends this revisionist reading in a new direction. Far from being an innocent child of nature, Huck is deeply complicit in the consumerism responsible for the environmental degradation of the frontier, and he is no less involved in the project of managing the nature represented by nonwhites than is Hank Morgan, who tries to reshape the "white Indians" of *Connecticut Yankee* (20). Given this critique of the human role in the exploitation of nature, Twain seems to represent a voice of resistance against the culture of domination; ultimately, however, his concerns for a diminished nature are reconciled by an escape into nostalgia.

When Twain began working on *Huckleberry Finn* in 1876, the nation was celebrating the one hundredth anniversary of the signing of the Declaration of Independence at Philadelphia. Wieck suggests that Twain probably attended the Centennial Exhibition, but he was overwhelmed and quickly left (4).[12] The dizzying modernism of the Centennial appealed to William

Dean Howells, who saw the gigantic Corliss engine as a symbol of America's "national genius" (96). Other visitors to Philadelphia were drawn to exhibits that looked back nostalgically to a lost American past and a diminishing natural world. J. S. Ingram's 1876 guide to the Centennial highlights the New England log house with its quaint utensils, "whose very simplicity made them incomprehensible to the victim of modern improvements," and the Hunter's Camp, "a complete illustration of the life of a Western hunter" (707–08, 718). The Hunter's Camp was constructed by *Forest and Stream* magazine, which was edited by George B. Grinnell, an early leader in the wildlife conservation movement. An editorial in *Forest and Stream* praised the exhibit as an opportunity for "quiet, rest, and contemplation" amidst the Centennial's celebration of instrumental uses of nature: "It is a reminder of the world's youth when it was content to play and be happy. Then the streams were for pleasure and not for power; the savannas were for strolling and not for tilling; the forests were storehouses of game and nuts, and rarest flowers" ("Hunter's Camp" 333).

Another popular exhibit that evoked a sense of nature nostalgia was Martha Maxwell's stuffed animals. A pioneer in taxidermy, Maxwell displayed her extensive collection of skillfully preserved western birds and mammals on an ersatz mountain, complete with a stream, waterfall, and cave, thus anticipating the technique of realistic habitat exhibition that would soon become popular through the work of William Temple Hornaday. (The same technique is now featured in natural history museums and outdoor stores such as Cabela's.) As a woman doing work that was traditionally associated with men, Maxwell herself became a curiosity and was subjected to endless questioning. She resisted the characterization of herself as an Amazonian huntress, explaining her killing as a form of memorialization: "All must die some time; I only shorten the period of consciousness that I may give their forms perpetual memory; and I leave it to you, which is the more cruel? to kill to eat, or to kill to *immortalize*?" (qtd. in Benson 137).[13]

The popularity of Maxwell's mountain of immortalized dead animals suggests the ambivalence that Americans felt about their domination of the natural world. In the year of the Centennial, J. A. Allen, a curator at Harvard's Museum of Comparative Zoology, drew attention to the plight of the buffalo in a series of articles that were later published as *The American Bisons* (1876). In *Nature's Ghosts*, Mark V. Barrow points out that Allen challenged the American belief in "the myth of inexhaustibility" by demonstrating that a bison population that had numbered in the millions had been reduced by market hunting and disease to a few hundred sur-

Figure 1.2. Martha Maxwell's Exhibit (Carnegie Library for Local History/Museum of Boulder Collection)

vivors (78–84). Even Theodore Roosevelt could feel "a half melancholy feeling" over shooting "the last remnant of a doomed and nearly vanished race" when he killed one of the few remaining bison in 1889 (*Hunting the Grisly*, 34). In *Hunting Trips on the Prairie* (1885), he expresses regret over the "veritable tragedy" of the buffalo's extermination even though it was a necessary condition for "the advance of white civilization in the West" (108, 119). But if bison were nearly extinct in 1876, they were well represented at the Centennial Exhibition: stuffed bison could be seen at Maxwell's mountain and at the US government's exhibit; live bison could be observed at the Zoological Gardens; and W. J. Hays's painting "Bison at Bay" was displayed at Memorial Hall.[14]

The nostalgic exhibits at Philadelphia and Twain's *Huckleberry Finn* can be seen as part of a larger attempt to preserve the memory of an earlier time when nature was not threatened. To blur the distinction between a disappearing reality and her artificially preserved animals, Maxwell used realist techniques of representation such as including live animals in the foreground. Maxine Benson points out that Maxwell's taxidermy was so lifelike that spectators drank from her mountain stream and prodded the specimens with canes to determine if they were truly dead (133–34). Likewise, Twain muddies the difference between fiction and reality in his writings about the Mississippi. Many of the incidents and descriptions from the autobiographical *Life on the Mississippi* end up in *Huckleberry Finn*, and he begins his novel with an explanatory note that insists upon the accuracy of his dialects and Huck's assurance that Twain could be trusted to tell the truth "mainly" (1). Furthermore, like Maxwell's exhibit (or Burroughs's stuffed loon, for that matter), Twain's realism is contextual: he was intensely concerned with capturing the dialect, the scenery, and the mannerisms of the Mississippi Valley in the 1840s.

Twain's nostalgia is far from uncritical: as my reading demonstrates, he does not romanticize the human culture of the frontier "forty to fifty years ago" (vii). Nevertheless, as the response of Twain's critics suggests, the lyrical descriptions of a less-degraded nature (especially those in chapter 19) have had a powerful effect on readers, transcending their relative importance to the novel as a whole. The popular success of Maxwell's exhibit and Twain's novel suggests that as industrial capitalism was in the process of consuming the resources of the natural world, nostalgic nature realism emerged as a product of the same consumer economy. As David Mazel points out in *American Literary Environmentalism*, "the idea of wilderness has always been weakest when 'real' wilderness has abounded, and strongest when it has been perceived to be on the brink of disappearance" (31). Or, as Dana Phillips notes, nature writing is a "commodity" that is "almost always nostalgic" (211, 233).[15]

The consumerism embedded in this nostalgia is best expressed at the end of James Dickey's *Deliverance* (1970) when the narrator, Ed Gentry, reflects on the river, which has been destroyed by a hydroelectric dam: "The river and everything I remembered about it became a possession to me, a personal, private possession, as nothing else in my life ever had. Now it ran nowhere but in my head, but there it ran as though immortally. . . . It pleases me in some curious way that the river does not exist, and that I have it" (275). As long as pristine nature is available to be consumed recreationally or imaginatively, its inevitable loss can be accepted. Thus, Progressive Era preservation efforts in places such as the Adirondacks or Yosemite National Park, or in the nature writing of John Burroughs or Mark

Twain made bearable the continued environmental devastation of industrial capitalism. Indeed, Twain's wilderness nostalgia seems consistent with Leslie Fiedler's reading of the novel as an iteration of the white American fantasy that oppressed peoples will always forgive their oppressors. Despite Twain's sensitivity to the environmental degradation of industrial civilization, his nature is always waiting to welcome Huck and the reader back to the pre-industrial pastoral of the raft.[16]

Chapter 2

The Ecological City in Crane's *Maggie*

In 1890, Eugene Schieffelin, the chairman of the American Acclimatization Society, released sixty European starlings into Central Park in an effort to populate America with all of the birds mentioned in Shakespeare. By 1900, Schieffelin's starlings had spread beyond New York City, and by the twenty-first century, their population had grown to an estimated 200 million. However, the success of the starlings has resulted in serious environmental problems. Large flocks congregate in cities and produce tremendous amounts of feces, which pose health risks for humans. Furthermore, starlings are exceptionally aggressive birds, taking over the nests of native species such as woodpeckers and bluebirds. Perhaps Schieffelin should have considered Shakespeare's context: in *Henry IV Part I*, Hotspur considers using the call of the starling to drive the king mad.[1]

This intersection of the urban, the literary, and the environmental suggests a potentially fertile site for ecocriticism. Ecocritics have virtually ignored Stephen Crane's New York City novel *Maggie* (1893), perhaps because of its urban setting, which makes it difficult to see the novel as part of the resistance narrative. But the absence of a wilderness setting should not preclude an ecocritical reading. Since the 1980s, environmental historians have focused on the interface between the natural and the human in urban environments. Martin Melosi defines urban environmental history as the story of how "the physical features and resources of urban sites (and regions) influence and are shaped by natural forces, growth, spatial change and development, and human action" (2). Urban environmental historians are especially interested in such issues as sanitation, pest control, pollution, and the segregation of space in cities. More recently, literary ecocritics have also begun to engage with the environment of the city. The essays in Michael Bennett and David Teague's groundbreaking 1999 anthology,

The Nature of Cities, focus on "the process by which cultural production is implicated in human adaptation to urban habitats" (10). The essays in Bennett and Teague's anthology are important contributions to ecocritical cultural studies, but few of them discuss literary texts, as opposed to such topics as public parks, films, and contemporary cosmetics discourse. In this chapter, I examine the role of the environment of *Maggie* by situating it in the contexts of progressive urban reform and the newly developed science of ecology.[2]

Between 1890 and 1900, the population of New York City increased from 2.5 million to 3.4 million people, largely due to immigration (Carter et al. 1:110). The poor were crowded into tenements in lower Manhattan that lacked adequate sunlight and air; accordingly, diseases such as cholera and tuberculosis were rampant. The streets were unpaved, and sewage disposal was inefficient. In 1892, progressive reformer Jacob Riis described the characteristics of the tenement environment as "Dirt, Discomfort, and Disease" (159). Many of the tenements served as sweatshops, and unregulated industries such as tanneries, slaughterhouses, and varnish factories were located in poor neighborhoods. Furthermore, in contrast to the wealthier sections of New York, lower Manhattan had few public parks or playgrounds.[3]

Figure 3.1. Jacob Riis, "Dens of Death," 1902 (Wikimedia Commons)

The rapid growth of the slums coupled with class tensions caused by a series of economic depressions in the 1890s produced anxiety among the native-born middle and upper classes, who began to view the city as a threat to the American ideal of a homogenous society. In 1903, progressive socialist Kate Holladay Claghorn attributed the degeneration of people in the slums to Darwinian evolution: "A sort of selective process, always going on, forces out or kills off those of the immigrant population who are not satisfied with or not able to endure tenement conditions, leaving behind a peculiar 'type,' that is the despair of those who are working for social betterment today" (78). In the face of such perceived difference, some Americans turned to nativism and sought a ban on further immigration. Others, however, retained confidence in the assimilative power of American culture.[4]

As they searched for strategies of social control that would Americanize the immigrants, middle-class urban reformers began by quantifying and mapping the problem. In the 1870s, the Charity Organization Society compiled centralized records of those seeking relief, and in 1900, it organized a Tenement Exhibition that presented the problems of the slums through detailed disease and poverty maps. George Kneeland's *Commercial Prostitution in New York City* (1913) includes 134 pages of statistical tables and graphs that analyze the demographics of prostitution. Meanwhile, journalists and novelists provided more intimate views of the life of the poor through an outpouring of nonfictional and fictional representations of slum life.[5] A primary concern was mapping the shifting ethnic boundaries of the city: in 1890 Riis noted that the eastern European Jew "having overrun the district . . . east of the Bowery, to the point of suffocation, is filling the tenements of the old Seventh Ward to the river front, and disputing with the Italian every foot of available space in the back alleys of Mulberry Street" (22).

To deal with the problems of the slum, various technologies of social control emerged. In *Urban Masses*, Paul Boyer documents how late nineteenth-century reformers shifted from an ideology that blamed poverty on the moral failings of the poor to a recognition of the shaping power of environment. According to Boyer, by the 1890s, progressive reformers had developed two different, but complementary, strategies of reform. Negative environmentalists focused on eradicating the evils of the slums, especially prostitution and alcohol. On the other hand, the positive environmentalists pursued tenement reform, city planning, and the construction of parks and playgrounds as a way to inculcate virtue among the poor by improving their environment. Boyer argues that this new emphasis on the urban environment suggests a larger shift of focus within the social sciences from the individual to the group, a shift that "reflected not merely an interest in *studying* social groups, but also in *controlling* them through the benevolent manipulation of their physical and social environment" (224). Charles R. McCann Jr. links this trend to the influence of Darwinism, which suggested that only humans possess the ability to change their environment; accordingly, progressive reformers believed that "technological advancements and social cooperation offered man the greatest ability to overcome the challenges of nature" (4).

The shift from focusing on the individual to an awareness of group dynamics led to what could be called an "ecological" view of the city since it emphasized the interrelatedness of its elements. Benjamin Heber Johnson notes that despite the very different lives of city dwellers, "the urban landscape revealed the inescapable connections that bound them together: diseases bred in the ponds of household garbage and human waste easily spread from their neighborhoods of origin; the miserly wages of the workers who slaughtered the livestock whose offal fouled the water fueled the prosperity of their employers" (33). In 1893, progressive reformer Benjamin O. Flower acknowledged "the great basic truth, that in a complex life like ours the interests of all are so interwoven that anything which injures one, sooner or later injures all, and that which elevates one elevates all" (230). Accordingly, while some reformers continued to focus on individual problems such as the saloon or the Tammany boss, most progressives recognized the role that these institutions played in the life of the slum and instead sought more socially-desirable substitutes. In 1901, temperance activist Raymond Calkins argued that "to destroy the social functions of the saloon without making any provision for the social needs of the people would be unjust" (25–26).

This focus on the interrelatedness of the city suggests parallels between progressive urban reform and the new science of ecology. In 1866, Ernst Haeckel coined the term "oekologie," defining it as "the whole science of the relations of the organism to the environment (qtd. in Flader 5). But it was not until the 1890s that ecology began to emerge as a self-conscious discipline, complete with college courses, textbooks, established academic chairs, and doctoral dissertations. In 1893, the year *Maggie* was published, the Madison Botanical Congress officially established the modern spelling of "ecology."[6]

The post-1970s sense of ecology as a subversive science that challenges human domination of the natural world has obscured the extent to which early ecologists participated in the control of nature, as well as the reshaping of their fellow humans. Peter J. Bowler argues that many early ecologists were interested in "sustainable exploitation" through the efficient use of natural resources (362). Similarly, Sharon Kingsland sees an "ideology of domination and control" in early ecology (98–99). Some ecologists wanted to extend the implications of their research to the control of human populations. Ellsworth Huntington, the founder and second president of the Ecological Society of America, was a strong advocate for both human ecology and eugenics. His *Civilization and Climate* (1915) is based on questionnaires he sent to 213 people, asking them to rank the world's countries on such characteristics as initiative, self-control, and "the power to lead and to control other races" (150). He then correlated the relative "civilization" of countries with maps of the world's climates. Ultimately, he dreamed of improving the world by controlling climate and manipulating plant evolution.

Huntington's desire for a human ecology helped to shape the emerging discipline of sociology. In 1892, the year before *Maggie* was published, the first sociology department was founded at the University of Chicago. Influenced by the plant succession theories of Frederic Clements, in the 1920s, the Chicago School created what became known as urban ecology by arguing that in cities competition for land led to the development of ecological niches, dividing the city into distinct zones. The Chicago School represents an intriguing nexus of the literary and the sociological. Martin Bulmer recounts that students in the program were encouraged to read such authors as Theodore Dreiser and Sherwood Anderson to fill in the gaps in the literature on urban problems, and he notes that the Chicago School's distinctive research methods included intensive field work or "participant observation" similar to Crane's experiments in which he posed as a tramp in order to understand the environment of the Bowery more accurately (96–98).

In 1893, Crane wrote in Hamlin Garland's copy of *Maggie* that the novel "tries to show that environment is a tremendous thing in the world and frequently shapes lives regardless" (*Correspondence* 1:53). However, despite Crane's insistence on the significance of environmental determinism, many critics have downplayed the role of the physical environment in the novel. In 1965 Donald Pizer established what has become an interpretative trend, arguing that *Maggie* "is not so much about the slums as a physical reality as about what people believe in the slums and how their beliefs are both false to their experience and yet function as operative forces in their lives" (169). He notes that "Maggie is thus destroyed not so much by the physical reality of slum life as by a middle-class morality imposed on the slums by the missions and the melodrama, a morality which allows its users both to judge and to divorce themselves from responsibility from those they judge" (172–73). While Pizer is correct in noting the importance of false beliefs and morality, his effort to distance Crane from literary naturalism mystifies the ways in which the physical reality of the city is connected to the moral attitudes of those living in the slums. By focusing on the physical and psychological threats posed by the urban environment of the novel, I will demonstrate how Crane's sensitivity to the ecological nature of the city is linked to the progressive expansion of the police powers of the state.[7]

∽

After she has been to the theater, Maggie wonders whether the "culture and refinement" she has just seen "could be acquired by a girl who lived in a tenement house and worked in a shirt factory" (28). This passage suggests the centrality of environment, but it is also significant because it represents one of the few moments when we see into Maggie's mind. In perhaps the first critical response to the novel, John D. Barry, editor of the *Forum*, complained in an 1893 letter to Crane, "I have little idea of Maggie's personality; she is not much more than a mere figure to me" (*Correspondence* 1:50). Subsequent critics have essentially agreed with Nell's view of Maggie as "A little pale thing with no spirit" (49). For example, Keith Gandal argues that Maggie's struggle "is not a battle with temptation and sin . . . but a battle with doubts and a feeling of inferiority" (102). Significantly, this dismissal of Maggie's interiority is consistent with how progressive reformers discussed prostitutes. Ruth Rosen notes that reformers often linked prostitution to "feeble-mindedness," which they defined as passivity, suggestibility, and a lack of shame and remorse or, in other words, "refusal or failure to conform to middle-class values and behavioral patterns" (23).

What has not been recognized is the extent to which Maggie's lack of self is the result of the constructed environment of New York City. Michael McGerr notes that the overcrowding of working-class homes made it difficult for children "to develop a sense of their individuality and autonomy (18). In these circumstances, the privacy necessary to distinguish the self from others simply does not exist. In an early passage, Crane captures the claustrophobic environment of a crowded tenement building:

> Eventually they entered into a dark region where, from a careening building, a dozen gruesome doorways gave up loads of babies to the street and the gutter. . . . In the street infants played or fought with other infants or sat stupidly in the way of vehicles.

> Formidable women, with uncombed hair and disordered dress, gossiped while leaning on railings, or screamed in frantic quarrels. Withered persons, in curious postures of submission to something, sat smoking pipes in obscure corners. A thousand odors of cooking food came forth to the street. The building quivered and creaked from the weight of humanity stamping about in its bowels. (6)

In this crowded environment, Maggie is seldom alone and thus has no opportunity for reflection. Lee Clark Mitchell has argued that realistic novels are distinguished from naturalistic ones by "scenes that enact a process of deliberation—a weighing of alternative actions through a consideration of consequences" ("Naturalism" 530). Maggie does not debate the wisdom of succumbing to Pete's seduction or her decision to become a prostitute. However, unlike Huck Finn, Isabel Archer, and Silas Lapham, Maggie is constantly surrounded by her violent, drunken family; by her neighbors in the tenement; by her boss and coworkers at the sweatshop; and by the patrons of the beer halls and theaters that she visits with Pete. Without private space, Maggie's environment offers her little chance of developing the interiority that critics sense is missing.

The physical environment of the tenement also contributes to the conventional morality of the slums that Pizer and others have pointed to as the center of the novel. In the crowded slums, all private acts are public, exposed to the gaze of the community. When Maggie returns home after she has been abandoned by Pete, she is immediately surrounded by watching neighbors: "Through the open doors curious eyes stared in at Maggie. Children ventured into the room and ogled her, as if they formed the front row at a theatre" (48). Aware that she is being watched, Maggie's mother, Mary, is compelled to demonstrate that she shares the moral standards of the neighborhood, so she denounces her daughter, "addressing the doorful of eyes, expounding like a glib showman at a museum. Her voice rang through the building" (48). Likewise, after Maggie's death, a crowd of neighbors gathers around Mary, "staring in at the weeping woman as if watching the contortions of a dying dog. A dozen women entered and lamented with her" (57). Again, the presence of these spectators limits the range of Mary's response. One of the mourners, with a vocabulary "derived from the mission churches," rehearses the conventional reassurances of grief, repeatedly saying, "Yeh'll forgive her," and, "She's gone where her sins will be judged," until Mary adopts these banalities as her own (57–58). In the urban ecology of the slum, individual psychology is determined by interactions with others.

The importance of the physical environment can also be seen in Maggie's work in the sweatshop. As Maggie becomes older, she is increasingly exposed to the gaze of the men in the neighborhood. Accordingly, Jimmie presents her with a choice: go to work or go to hell—that is, become a prostitute (16). In lower Manhattan, Maggie's only alternative to prostitution is work in one of the sweatshops located in the growing garment district.[8] Lawrence E. Hussman Jr. complains that "Crane misses the opportunity to describe in detail the brutalizing labor which Bowery residents endured in the sweatshops" (94). However, this reading ignores the precise, if compressed, details of the environmental conditions of Maggie's workplace that Crane does provide: "The air in the collar and cuff establishment strangled her. She knew that she was gradually and surely shriveling in the hot, stuffy room. The begrimed windows rattled incessantly from the passing of elevated trains. The place was filled with a whirl of noises and odors" (25). In addition to the physical conditions of the room, the employees must endure the verbal abuse of the owner, for "his pocket-book deprived them of the power of retort" (26). The narrator notes that the working conditions of such industries are reified, so that the collars that are produced bear a name that "could be noted for its irrelevancy to anything in connection with collars" (17).

The ecology of the sweatshop modifies those who work there. Maggie worries that working in such "a dreary place of endless grinding" was destroying her youth, which she had begun to recognize as "valuable" (20, 25). The reformer Jane Addams noted that the fear that they were "rapidly losing health and charm" led many factory girls to become prostitutes (77). When she first arrives, Maggie notices the "yellow discontent" of her coworkers, and increasingly she is concerned that she will become "a scrawny woman with an eternal grievance," a fusion of her fears of the physical and psychological effects of such work (17, 25). The conditions of the sweatshop make Maggie vulnerable to the seductions of Pete, who represents a potential escape: on their date, "no thoughts of the atmosphere of the collar and cuff factory came to her" (24).

The lives of the characters are also shaped by the spatial stratification of the city, a central concern of environmental historians. After Pete abandons her, Maggie wanders aimlessly, but she soon realizes that a single woman in this neighborhood is assumed to be a prostitute, as "men looked at her with calculating eyes" (51). This emphasis on surveillance is replicated when Maggie walks into an upper-class neighborhood, where the houses themselves seem to have eyes that read her as someone who is in the wrong place: she "passed between rows of houses with sternness and stolidity stamped upon their features. She hung her head for she felt their eyes grimly upon her" (51). She is forced to return to her home, but the response of her family is equally hostile. Mary is baffled that her daughter could "bring disgrace upon her family," and Jimmie is concerned that his sister's fall "queers us" (40). Their response is a reflection of the social stratification of the city. As Timothy Gilfoyle points out, turn-of-the-century prostitution was confined to poor neighborhoods, where it could be hidden from the middle and upper classes; accordingly, those living in the tenements felt pressure to distance themselves morally from the pervasive prostitution in their midst.[9] Thus, when Mary becomes aware that the neighbors are gossiping, she must demonstrate her outrage by becoming "terrific in denunciation of the girl's wickedness" (40). Before her fall, even Maggie shares her culture's repulsion at sexual immorality: at one of the beer halls she visits, she passes some prostitutes and "with a shrinking movement, drew back her skirts" (39).

The ecological stratification of the city into distinct niches is most clearly evident in Maggie's progression to her death in chapter 17. As critics such as Fredson Bowers have noted, this chapter seems to be a "symbolic compression" of Maggie's declining career as a prostitute (lxxxvi).[10] The chapter begins in the theater district (presumably the Tenderloin), a transitional zone where the classes intersect. As the wealthy emerge from the theaters, they pass a park with "wet wanderers, in attitudes of chronic dejection" (52). Named only as "a girl of the painted cohorts of the city," Maggie tries unsuccessfully to attract one of the men in the theater district before she moves to the restaurants, saloons, and concert halls of the Bowery, which are full of slummers from the upper class. A sophisticated man considers Maggie, but he loses interest "when he discerned that she was neither new, Parisian, nor theatrical" (52). Maggie continues to the "darker blocks" of lower Manhattan and is spurned by several men whose refined speech indicates that they are not from this neighborhood (52). Then she descends to the industrial district, "where the tall black factories shut in the street and only occasional broad beams of light fell across the pavements from saloons" (53). After rejection by an immigrant, who presumably lives in this neighborhood, she enters "the blackness of the final block," where she is surrounded by tall buildings that "seemed to have eyes that looked over her, beyond her, at other things" (53). At last (in a passage deleted from the 1896 edition), she meets the grotesque man who follows her to the river, an industrial niche where a "hidden factory sent up a yellow glare, that lit for a moment the waters lapping oilily against timbers" (53). In addition to depicting the pollution and claustrophobic confinement of lower Manhattan, Maggie's final walk makes it clear that the city has been thoroughly, if unofficially, zoned into distinct spaces: uptown is the site of respectable residences, and lower Manhattan is the place of entertainment, vice, and industry. As Andrew Lawson points out, Maggie "has navigated an urban geography of decreasing taxable values, to end in a space of industrial production and debased consumption" (610).

Maggie's ability to pass through these zones, as well as the mix of classes present in the various neighborhoods, demonstrates that the boundaries that stratify the city are permeable. The novel frequently depicts interactions between the different ecological niches of the city. The gnarled woman who lives with the Johnsons does her begging on Fifth Avenue, perhaps in the Tenderloin district. Most of the money she receives is given "by persons who did not make their homes in that vicinity," presumably visitors from wealthier neighborhoods (10). In the "hilarious hall," Nell's companion, Freddie, is clearly crossing urban boundaries: he has money to spend and dismisses Pete as a "Bowery jay" (44). He explains to Maggie that "Freddie" is the alias he uses when he is slumming: "I always tell these people some name like that, because if they got onto your right name they might use it sometime" (45). Chad Heap notes that, in the late nineteenth century, the fad of slumming became possible only because of "the increasing geographic segregation of U.S. cities along class lines" (19). In addition to being a place where the classes and genders mingle, the concert theaters also elide the ethnic boundaries of the city. On their first date, Pete takes Maggie to a beer garden where "the nationalities of the Bowery" are peacefully gathered (22). The evening's entertainment climaxes with a call for the national anthem, and "instantly a great cheer swelled from the throats of the assemblage of the masses. . . . Eyes gleamed with sudden fire, and calloused hands waved frantically in the air" (24).

This social permeability indicates that in contrast to those reformers who were mapping the city into distinct zones, Crane recognized its ecological interdependence. The eponymous Maggie is not developed in any depth until chapter 5, thereby indicating her dependence on the other characters, and her fall into prostitution is overdetermined by multiple factors: a dysfunctional family, limited work opportunities, and cultural views of women's sexuality. Indeed, the structure of the novel is ecological, with the authorial gaze uniting the stories of remotely connected characters. Crane's use of repeated incidents as a structural device (such as Jimmie's and Pete's rejections of former lovers) establishes the interconnected nature of Bowery life.[11] The health threat posed by such consanguinity is suggested by the skin blotches on Mary, Pete, and the grotesque man: Gerard M. Sweeney argues that this detail indicates the pervasiveness of syphilis in the city.

The possibility of social permeability represents other potential threats to the upper classes. On one of their outings, Pete and Maggie go uptown to Central Park, which was designed by Frederick Law Olmsted in 1858 to help civilize and Americanize the lower classes of New York.[12] In an 1870 speech before the American Social Sciences Association, Olmsted noted that despite concerns that lower-class thugs would be drawn to the park, it has had a "distinctly harmonizing and refining influence upon the most unfortunate and most lawless classes of the city" (34). Nevertheless, Benjamin Heber Johnson points out that by the turn of the century, many elites had become troubled by what they saw as inappropriate uses of the park by the lower classes (189–91). Clearly, the disciplinary park has little effect on Pete. While in the Metropolitan Museum of Art, Pete resents the observation of the guards and attempts to stare down "the appalling scrutiny of the watch-dogs of the treasures" (26). As Howard Horwitz observes, Pete "fails to grasp the moral mission of the museum" (621). He is, however, fascinated by "the spectacle of a very small monkey threatening to thrash a cageful because one of them had pulled his tail" (26). He can identify with this resistance to authority, and on subsequent visits he winks at the monkey and tries to encourage him to fight with the others.

Pete's identification with the monkey suggests that the lower classes have the potential to turn the urban environment into a dangerous wilderness.[13] The novel opens with a Darwinian struggle between children who yell with "triumphant savagery" (4). When Jimmy defends the family's honor by fighting Pete, the novel stacks up bestial symbols: "He snarled like a wild animal"; "they bristled like three roosters"; the bravery of bull-dogs sat upon the faces of the men" (35–36). Their violence spills over to affect others: the "quiet stranger" is entangled with the combatants and thrown out onto the sidewalk (37). Even the gnarled woman who is kind to Jimmy in chapter 3 is capable of surprising violence: when she was arrested for stealing a purse, "she had cursed the lady into a partial swoon, and with her aged limbs, twisted from rheumatism, had almost kicked the stomach out of a huge policeman whose conduct upon that occasion she referred to when she said, "The police, damn 'em" (10).

This breakdown of discipline suggests the need for more effective mechanisms of social control. Daniel T. Rodgers notes that progressive urban reformers increasingly sought legislation that relied on the doctrine of the "police powers" of the government as "the legal expression of the interdependencies of city health and living conditions" (*Atlantic* 202). In 1904, legal scholar Ernest Freund defined police powers as "promoting the public welfare by restraining and regulating the use of liberty and property" (iii). Freund discusses the state's right to intervene in such areas as prostitution and child rearing when the health, safety, or morals of society were at risk. The disturbing world of *Maggie* presents a prima facie case for the need for more extensive social control.

The novel suggests that the police have been largely successful in establishing control over the residents of the Bowery. William Dean Howells described Jimmy as "an Ishmaelite from the cradle, who, with his warlike instincts beaten back into cunning, is what the B'hoy of former times has become in our more strenuously policed days" (qtd. in Dowling 54). From an early age, Jimmie is in conflict with the police, whom he sees as "always actuated by malignant impulses" (14). When he fights Pete, Jimmy tries to evade arrest because "on his feet he had the same regard for a policeman that, when on his truck, he had for a fire engine" (37). Progressive police power transcended law enforcement to include any agency involved in regulating undesirable behavior. In the first chapter, the narrative gaze moves outward from Jimmie's fight in Rum Alley to include "the Island," where "a worm of yellow convicts came from the shadow of a grey ominous building and crawled slowly along the river's bank" (3–4). Crane's first apartment in New York was across the East River from Blackwell's Island (now Roosevelt Island), a cluster of nineteenth-century disciplinary machinery, which by the 1890s included a penitentiary, a workhouse for petty violators, a lunatic asylum, a smallpox hospital, and a charity hospital.[14]

Maggie might seem an unusual choice for an ecocritical study because so little of the natural world appears in the novel. I would argue that Crane's sensitivity to the ways in which the built ecology of the city warps the psychological responses of those living in it intersects with the concerns of contemporary environmental history and ecocriticism. Furthermore, we should not ignore the small, yet significant role that the nonhuman does play in the novel. Maggie's escapist longings are expressed in pastoral imagery drawn from the Bible: "Her dim thoughts were often searching for far away lands where, as God says, the little hills sing together in the morning. Under the trees of her dream-gardens there had always walked a lover" (19). As she considers improving the apartment to impress Pete, she is concerned about the "almost vanished flowers in the carpet-pattern" and tries to compensate with the "flowered cretonne" that she fashions into the lambrequin (20). Even Jimmie, the Bowery tough, is capable of moments of nature appreciation: "[H]e had, on a certain star-lit evening, said wonderingly and quite reverently: 'Deh moon looks like hell, don't it?'" (16).

Crane's representation of nature as an absence suggests a link to late-nineteenth-century concerns about life in the city. Michael J. Thompson argues that during this period anti-urbanism emerged as a reaction to the perceived unnaturalness of the metropolis: "Cities became viewed as collections of rootless individuals characterized by competition, the impersonal, and conflict. It was a place not for man's development, but for his corruption, his debasement" (3). Crane himself regularly sought relief from the city: Paul Sorrentino notes that in 1891, at the same time that he was exploring the tenements of Manhattan to gather background information for *Maggie*, Crane began a yearly ritual of camping trips to Sullivan County, New York, and Pike County, Pennsylvania (87–89). Crane's excursions were part of a larger back-to-nature movement, as Americans sought psychological relief in the outdoors from the crowding, interdependence, and vice that they associated with the city.

Crane's irony-infused text resists easy placement in the progressive urban reform tradition. In 1896, he denied any overt ideology, insisting, "Preaching is fatal to art in literature. I try to give to readers a slice out of life; and if there is any moral or lesson in it I do not point it out" (*Correspondence* 1:230). Nevertheless, his claim that "environment is a tremendous thing" is sustained by the role played by the materiality of the city. Crane recognized that the crowding of the tenements, the conditions of the sweatshop, and the geographic stratification of Manhattan all determine the psychological and moral attitudes of those who live in the slums. In an 1896 letter, Crane expressed skepticism about efforts to improve the Bowery, but he praised the relocation work of the Children's Aid Society: "The missions for children are another thing and if you will have Mr. Rockefeller give me a hundred street cars and some money I will load all the babes off to some pink world where cows can lick their noses and they will never see their families any more" (*Correspondence* 2:671). The Children's Aid Society originated the "orphan trains" that eventually relocated more than two hundred thousand children from cities to farms in the western states between 1854 and 1929. Similar fears of the urban and confidence in therapeutic nature inspired the Fresh Air Fund, which since 1877 has arranged free summer vacations in the country for poor urban children.[15] Thus, separation from parents and forced immersion into nature might be the best hope for an urban girl who "blossomed in a mud puddle" (16). But, for those who must remain in the interdependent environment of the city, the novel suggests that more effective means of social control might be necessary.

∞

The novel's focus on the materiality of lower-class environments has implications for the contemporary environmental justice movement, which seeks to expand the focus of environmentalism to include problems faced by the poor and minorities, especially those living in urban areas. In July 1964, the year before Pizer's study of *Maggie* was published, riots broke out in several New York City neighborhoods when a fifteen-year-old African American student was killed by a police officer. After six days of conflict between police and rioters, the uprising came to an end, leaving one rioter dead, 118 injured, and 465 arrested.[16] Over the next three years, there were hundreds of riots in American cities, leading to President Lyndon Johnson's call in July 1967 for a National Advisory Commission on Civil Disorders. In his address to the nation, Johnson pointed to the material conditions of the slums: "The only genuine, long-range solution for what has happened lies in an attack—mounted at every level—upon the conditions that breed despair and violence. All of us know what those conditions are: ignorance, discrimination, slums, poverty, disease, not enough jobs."

But not everyone agreed with Johnson's analysis. In *The Unheavenly City* (1970), a classic text of anti-urbanism, Harvard political scientist Edward C. Banfield attributed the riots to psychological factors: youthful spirits and the desire for pillage. Indeed, he insisted that those who would link the riots to material conditions were exacerbating the problem: "Explanations that find the cause of rioting in the rioter's environment are bound to be taken as justifications, or at any rate extenuations, of their behavior and therefore tend to reinforce the irresponsibility that is characteristic of the age and class culture from which the rioters are largely drawn" (200–01). An ecocritical reading of *Maggie* suggests the problematic nature of downplaying the material roots of the psychological. Environmental justice demands that we acknowledge the role of the material reality of the city in the psychological health of those living in it. By the same token, awareness of the power of material conditions, especially when coupled with confidence in the potential of environmental manipulation, can justify the expansion of coercive mechanisms of social control.

Chapter 3

Therapeutic Nature in Chopin's *The Awakening*

In the 1870s, Kate Chopin frequently vacationed at Grand Isle, a Gulf Coast resort for middle-class New Orleans Creoles. Emily Toth notes that Chopin saw Grand Isle as "a wholesome escape from a city that was mercilessly hot and disease-ridden in the summer" (137). This paradise was destroyed in 1893 when the Gulf Coast was hit by "the Great October Storm," a hurricane that killed an estimated two thousand people and devastated five hundred miles of the coast. Six years after the storm, Chopin's *The Awakening* was published; the novel opens and closes at Grand Isle. Accordingly, Toth suggests that it "was an elegy for a lost way of life" (139).[1]

The destruction of the resort at Grand Isle was not Chopin's first experience of the vulnerability of human efforts to tame an intractable nature. In 1855, when she was five, her father was killed near St. Louis when his train plunged into the Gasconade River after heavy rains caused a temporary trestle to collapse. Between 1870 and 1884, while she was living in Louisiana, Chopin would have experienced no fewer than ten tropical storms or hurricanes. In the late 1870s, excessive rain limited the Louisiana cotton crop and forced her husband, Oscar Chopin, to close his New Orleans cotton brokerage. The family moved to Cloutierville, in northwestern Louisiana, where Oscar died of malaria in 1882.[2]

Chopin's experiences with an unmanageable nature exemplify the environmental history of the region. As Craig Colten argues in *An Unnatural Metropolis*, the people of New Orleans have always had to "struggle to make a habitable city, to transform the flood-prone, ill-drained, mosquito-infested site into a metropolis" (6). Colter notes that in response to these environmental challenges, the residents of New Orleans have attempted to control nature by constructing an elaborate system of levees, by draining the swampy ground with canals and pumps, and by fleeing the city during the summer to resorts such as Grand Isle. But, as Chopin's own experiences suggest, nature periodically demonstrates the inadequacy of such efforts.

Ecofeminist critics have argued that the effort to control a threatening nature is strongly gendered. Noël Sturgeon defines ecofeminism as "the theory that the ideologies that authorize injustices based on gender, race, and class are related to the ideologies that sanction the exploitation and degradation of the environment" (23). Accordingly, ecofeminists have explored literary alternatives to the culture of domination. In *Undomesticated Ground* (2000), Stacy Alaimo examines the ways that American women writers have "negotiated, contested, and transformed the discourses of nature that surround them" (1). Alaimo argues that rather than denigrating nature by representing it as overdetermined by culture, these writers depict nature as an actor that is beyond human control: "Nature, then, is undomesticated both in the sense that it figures as a space apart from the domestic and in the sense that it is untamed and thus serves as a model for female insurgency" (16).

In this chapter, I would like to complicate this ecofeminist resistance narrative. Seeing nature as uncontrollable does not inevitably result in a challenge to either the culture of domination or the patriarchy. Instead, *The Awakening* demonstrates the need for experts in psychology to help women reconcile the destructive potential of nature with its therapeutic value.

∽

At the end of the nineteenth century, middle- and upper-class Americans who were distressed by the complexities of urban life increasingly turned to nature for therapy. In 1886, John Burroughs insisted, "A nation always begins to rot first in its great cities, is indeed perhaps always rotting there, and is saved only by the antiseptic virtues of fresh supplies of country blood" (*Signs* 140). In his classic *Wilderness and the American Mind*, Roderick Frazier Nash discusses the rise of a turn-of-the-century "wilderness cult" that celebrated primitive virility and appreciation of the aesthetic and spiritual values of wild places (141–60). Peter J. Schmitt sees the back-to-nature movement as an attempt to seek temporary relief from the pressures of urban life through suburban homes, nature literature, and hunting and camping excursions in the wilderness.

Evidence of this turn to nature can be seen in the nature-study movement. Between 1890 and 1920, progressive educators championed the value of introducing children, especially urban children, to the principles of science through hands-on experiences with nature. Kevin C. Armitage argues that the nature-study movement was an attempt "to embrace scientific modernity while simultaneously recoiling from the narrow, instrumental, and ugly society engendered by industrial civilization" (2). In *Nature Study for the Common Schools* (1891), Wilbur Jackman explains that ecological education connects students to reality: "The life, health, and happiness of the individual is dependent upon his knowledge of the things about him, and upon the understanding that he has of their relations to each other and to himself" (1).

The back-to-nature movement also contributed to a revival of interest in the nature-infused transcendentalism of Ralph Waldo Emerson and Henry David Thoreau. Beginning in the 1880s, biographies and new editions of Emerson and Thoreau were published, and Concord became a destination for literary tourists. Len Gougeon observes that by the 1903 centennial of Emerson's birth, the Sage of Concord was seen "as a spiritual idealist whose philosophy offered a vaguely conceived alternative to the conspicuous materialism of the times" (61). Likewise, Randall Stewart attributes the rise of Thoreau's reputation in the late nineteenth century to "the urbanization of American life" and the threat to individualism posed by "the modern aggrandizement of the state" (211, 213). The tensions embedded in this revival of transcendentalism are evident in Henry Ford, the father of modern industrial capitalism and an enthusiastic fan of both Emerson and Thoreau, whom he discovered through the writings of John Burroughs. In 1913, Ford and Burroughs traveled to Concord in a fleet of Ford vehicles to visit the sites associated with the transcendentalists.[3]

Ford's interest in the transcendentalists suggests that as much as American elites might have been attracted to nature, civilization still represented evolutionary progress and racial superiority. Indeed, by the early twentieth century, many commentators were critiquing the back-to-nature movement as regressive. In 1907, the *Nation* saw the fad as a recurring response to the problems of urbanization: "We begin to study our falling birth-rate, our increasing slum and criminal population, the iniquities of the food adulterer and of the yellow press, and become convinced that we are well on the way to ruin, and that the city is responsible for it all" ("Hobbling" 259–60). However, the writer insisted that such flights to the country are escapist and ignore the fact that "the city is as natural a place of habitation as a farm on Long Island or a cabin in the Adirondacks" (260). In 1912, American literature professor Norman Foerster contrasted the "Puritan earnestness" of Thoreau with the popular nature writers of his day, who possess "a great deal of sensuousness and a negligible degree of spirituality" (358). By 1934

Lewis Mumford would describe attempts to return to primitive conditions as "a bedraggled retreat" from modernity (*Technics* 299).

One way to reconcile the tensions between culture and nature was recapitulation theory. First articulated by the German biologist Ernst Haeckel, who coined the phrase "ontogeny is a recapitulation of phylogeny," recapitulation is the belief that individuals pass through the evolutionary stages of the species (5). In the social sciences, recapitulation is most commonly associated with G. Stanley Hall, a founder of American psychology. In 1878, Hall became the first American to receive a PhD in psychology; in 1883, he created the first American psychology lab; and in 1892, he was elected the first president of the American Psychological Association.[4] His most significant book, *Adolescence* (1904), draws upon recapitulation theory, even though by that time it had been largely discredited by the scientific community. Hall sees adolescence as a period when the extremes of our racial history are recapitulated in the individual: "The individual can never again expand his nature to so nearly compass the life of the species. The voices of extinct generations, sometimes still and small, sometimes strident and shrill, now reverberate, and psychic development is by leaps and bounds" (2:90). Gail Bederman notes that Hall believed that allowing boys to experience the primitive stages of the race inoculated them against the emasculating effects of overcivilization: "As adults they could be safely civilized, refined, and cultured—but only if they had fully lived and outgrown a temporary case of savagery as small boys" (97).

Recapitulation provided useful theoretical support for the "boy experts," those professionals who sought to build character in white, middle-class boys through outdoor experience. In *The Outdoor Handy Book* (1896), Daniel Carter Beard, who contributed to the founding of the Boy Scouts, contemptuously dismisses the boy represented in Francis Hodgson Burnett's best-seller *Little Lord Fauntleroy* (1886) as "a gentle little 'sissy' aristocrat, who would never have been tolerated by the 'Huck' Finns and Tom Sawyers inhabiting the valleys of the Mississippi" (10). Reflecting contemporary concerns that women had too large a role in childrearing, Beard warns, "This is a rough world, and it requires experiences outside of a gentle, loving mother's care or the sweet lady-like tuition of a governess to fit a lad for the battle of life" (10). Similarly, George Walter Fiske, in *Boy Life and Self Government* (1910), which was published by the YMCA, argues that parents will be confused by the "*duality* of boyhood" until they recognize that all boys are both James, "the prim little pink-and-washed Puritan," and Jimmy, who is "a good deal of a savage" (12, 14). Ultimately, however, if both James and

Jimmy are allowed to have full expression, Jim emerges as "a manly boyish fellow, frank of face and sound of heart" (13). Recapitulation theory can be seen in the opening scene of *Maggie*, where the boys fight "in the modes of four thousand years ago" (5).

The situation was different for turn-of-the-century girls. Crista Deluzio concludes that "Hall's final assessment of the girl's development was that she was both quintessential *and* perpetual adolescent" (112). Hall believed that adolescent boys passed through a feminine stage of moodiness and emotional strife before emerging with mental unity and settled character, but he insisted that girls remained stuck in this state: "Woman at her best never outgrows adolescence as man does, but lingers in, magnifies and glorifies this culminating stage of life with its all-sided interests, its convertibility of emotions, its enthusiasm, and zest for all that is good, beautiful, true, and heroic" (2:624). Repositories of adolescent idealism and emotionalism, women could uphold the refined culture and morals of civilization. Accordingly, they had no need for a primitive stage: as Anthony Rotundo notes, nineteenth-century men "preferred to think of women as completely civilized creatures, free of passion and full of moral sensitivities" (230).

But by the turn of the century, some were arguing that girls should be exposed to nature. Steven Mintz discusses the increased freedoms available to girls through bicycling, team sports, and the Girl Scouts, and he notes that parents were increasingly encouraging their daughters "to be 'real girls,' a phrase signifying wholesome vitality and energy" (193). Leslie Paris points out that by 1915, there were an estimated one hundred summer camps for girls (49). Hall himself, in a discussion of the ideal education of adolescent girls, prescribed an environment with hills for climbing; water for boating and swimming; gardens and forests; and opportunities for walking, biking, golf, and tennis (2:636). Above all, there should be "plenty of nooks that permit each to be alone with nature, for this develops inwardness, poise, and character" (2:637).

An idealized vision of the role of nature in the socialization of adolescent girls can be seen in the best-selling novels of Gene Stratton-Porter, who described her life's work as an attempt to lead women "back to the forest" ("My Life" 13). The heroine of her bestseller *A Girl of the Limberlost* (1909) pushes conventional gender roles by exploring the Limberlost swamp by herself. Yet Elnora's experience in nature does not unleash any primitive passions; indeed, she is perhaps the most emotionally untroubled adolescent in literature. She explains to her future suitor that the trees have taught her the truths of life: "To be patient, to be unselfish, to do unto others as

Figure 3.1. *Ladies Home Journal* cover, 1894 (Wikimedia Commons)

I would have them do to me"; likewise, the oaks teach her to "'be true,' 'live a clean life,' 'send your soul up here and the winds of the world will teach it what honour achieves'" (298). Meanwhile, her young friend Billy manifests the primitive instincts expected of boys by torturing cats.

This highly gendered belief in the developmental value of outdoor experience invites an ecocritical analysis of the role of nature in the socialization of the young in Chopin's *The Awakening*. Between 1871 and 1879, Chopin gave birth to five sons and one daughter. Pamela Knights, one of the few critics to discuss childrearing in the novel, argues that *The Awakening* "presents an extended sequence of arguments, explicit and implicit, about the role of the mother, the relationship of child and adult and the most appropriate way of raising the young" (49). I would extend Knight's analysis by arguing that while Edna's boys clearly benefit from exposure to the natural world, Edna's own experiences with nature suggest that the value of outdoor activity for young women is much more problematic and thus demands expert guidance.

One of the complaints Léonce Pontellier has about his wife is that she is not one of the "mother women," who flutter about "with extended, protecting wings when any harm, real or imaginary, threatened their precious brood" (10). Yet, in the absence of an overly protective mother, Raoul and Etienne become sturdy, independent youths. The narrator notes, "If one of the little Pontellier boys took a tumble whilst at play, he was not apt to rush crying to his mother's arms for comfort; he would more likely pick himself up, wipe the water out of his eyes and the sand out of his mouth, and go on playing" (9). Indeed, the Pontelliers dominate the more coddled children, battling "with doubled fists and uplifted voices, which usually prevailed against the other mother-tots" (9). The hardiness of the boys is reinforced by frequent exposure to nature. Léonce's mother takes them to her home in the country because "She did not want them to be wholly 'children of the pavement.' . . . She wished them to know the country, with its streams, its fields, its woods, its freedom, so delicious to the young" (72).

But Raoul and Etienne are not the only children in the novel. As Christina Giorcelli points out, Edna is twenty-eight, but she is consistently represented as a child (140). When Edna learns to swim at Grand Isle, she is compared to "the little tottering, stumbling, clutching child, who of a sudden realizes its powers, and walks for the first time alone, boldly and with over-confidence" (28). Adéle tells her, "In some way you seem to me like a child, Edna. You seem to act without a certain amount of reflection which is necessary in this life" (95). At the end of the novel, Doctor Mandelet calls her "my dear child" as he dispenses fatherly advice, explaining that "youth is given up to illusions" (109–10).

At Grand Isle, Edna moves toward adulthood as she begins to perceive the conflict between her newly developed sense of self and her social obligations. She struggles to "realize her position in the universe as a human being, and to recognize her relations as an individual to the world within and about her" (14–15). Donald A. Ringe argues that *The Awakening* is "a powerful romantic novel" that engages with "the relation of the individual self to the physical and social realities by which it is surrounded, and the price it must pay for insisting upon its absolute freedom" (587–88). Certainly, Edna's awakening invokes transcendentalism as she immerses herself in nature and pursues freedom from social restraint. Staring at the ocean, she recalls the limitlessness she experienced as a child, and the roar of the surf calls her soul "to lose itself in mazes of inward contemplation" (15). When she returns to New Orleans, Edna reads Emerson and takes long Thoreauvian walks by herself (73).[5] But previous critics have not recognized the Progressive Era concerns about uncontrolled individualism in Chopin's depiction of Edna's transcendental awakening.

A central component of progressivism was a focus on the interdependency of society; Daniel T. Rodgers argues that progressivism was "an assault on the idea of individualism itself" ("In Search" 124). Not surprisingly, then, the turn-of-the-century revival of interest in the transcendentalists was accompanied with warnings about the potential effect of Emersonian individualism on naive readers. Charles E. Mitchell notes that after Emerson's death in 1882, critics and biographers developed an interpretative consensus that praised his character but dismissed his writings as "either inconsequential or, if taken too seriously, dangerous" (19). In 1883 Edmund Clarence Stedman warned that Emerson's "chief peril is that of nurturing a weaker class that cannot follow where he leads"; he feared that such enthusiasts might "set too high a value upon their personal impulses" (875). Passages such as the conclusion of *Nature* were potentially subversive since readers might be empowered by Emerson's suggestion that the individual inner self can dominate external realities:

Build, therefore, your own world. As fast as you conform your life to the pure idea in your mind, that will unfold its great proportions. A correspondent revolution in things will attend the influx of the spirit. So fast will disagreeable appearances, swine, spiders, snakes, pests, madhouses, prisons, enemies, vanish; they are temporary and shall be no more seen. (48)[6]

For the progressives, such thinking represented the fundamental problem with American society: an individualistic discourse that rejected communal values. Furthermore, aspiring transcendentalists might discover that nature is obdurate to our desires.

Edna's awakening leads to a recognition of disjunctions between her internal and external worlds, but rather than transforming the outside world, Edna's inner consciousness is more frequently determined by unmanageable externalities. When Robert Lebrun leaves for Mexico, "her whole existence was dulled, like a faded garment which seems to be no longer worth wearing" (46). After a fight with Léonce, she looks at the world and realizes that everything is different: "The street, the children, the fruit vender, the flowers growing there under her eyes, were all part and parcel of an alien world which had suddenly become antagonistic" (54). When she goes outside to cry over the frustrations of her marriage, Edna is driven indoors by mosquitoes, which "succeeded in dispelling a mood which might have held her there in the darkness half a night longer" (8). A few nights later, Edna stays in the hammock as an act of rebellion against Léonce, but she eventually feels "the realities pressing into her soul. The physical need for sleep began to overtake her; the exuberance which had sustained and exalted her spirit left her helpless and yielding to the conditions which crowded her in" (32).

Edna's sense of power and autonomy is further subverted by her internal nature, her moods and impulses, which are represented as a force beyond her control. During her party, "she felt the old ennui overtaking her; the hopelessness which so often assailed her, which came upon her like an obsession, like something extraneous, independent of volition" (88). Edna experiences euphoric states when "she was happy to be alive and breathing, when her whole being seemed to be one with the sunlight, the color, the odors, the luxuriant warmth of some perfect Southern day" (58). On other days, however, "life appeared to her like a grotesque pandemonium and humanity like worms struggling blindly toward inevitable annihilation" (58). Often, her internal state is correlated with the weather, almost as if she were suffering from what today we would diagnose as Seasonal Affective Disorder: Edna is unable to paint when the weather is "dark and cloudy," and she is depressed by "the murky, lowering sky" (73, 81).[7] Her rebellion is also shaped by her animalistic passions. Alcée Arobin detects Edna's "latent sensuality" and appeals "to the animalism that stirred impatiently within her" (103, 78). When he kisses her, "It was the first kiss of her life to which her nature had really responded" (83).

The ultimate check on Edna's individualism is the turn-of-the-century ideology of motherhood that reinforced cultural assumptions about women's nature. In 1896, economist Francis Walker alarmed Americans by demonstrating with statistics that the older, Anglo-Saxon population had not been increasing as rapidly as that of immigrants, thereby initiating eugenic concerns about the threat of race suicide. In a speech to the 1905 Mothers' Congress, President Roosevelt praised those women "able and willing to perform the first and greatest duty of womanhood, able and willing to bear, and to bring up as they should be brought up, healthy children, sound in body, mind, and character, and numerous enough so that the race shall increase and not decrease" ("Before" 577). Hall, who shared Roosevelt's fears about race suicide, insisted that "woman's body and soul are made for maternity and she can never find true repose for either without it" (2:610).

Early in her awakening, Edna is able to reject this maternal ideology. She tells the perfect mother-woman, Adèle, "that she would never sacrifice herself for her children" (48). When Doctor Mandelet attempts to contain her desire for escape from marriage with his story of a woman's love that is tempted to stray but eventually returns to "its legitimate source," Edna is unimpressed and responds with an impromptu story of a woman who disappears with her lover, never to return (70). She admits to Alcée that according to all the "codes" of womanly behavior, "I am a devilishly wicked specimen of the sex" (82).

But Edna's rebellion is brought up short when she witnesses Adèle's childbirth. She resists the scene "with an inward agony, with a flaming, outspoken revolt against the ways of Nature" (109). The "Nature" that she is rebelling against is the biological maternal bond—what Adèle invokes when she implores her, "Think of the children, Edna. Oh think of the children!" (109). Carroll Smith-Rosenberg discusses the deterministic scientific-medical discourse that was used to subjugate women by connecting them to nature: woman was "a complex network of reproductive organs that controlled her physiology, determined her emotions, and dictated her social role" (183). During the night before Edna leaves for Grand Isle, her "children appeared before her like antagonists who had overcome her; who had overpowered and sought to drag her into the soul's slavery for the rest of her days" (113). But she discovers "a way to elude them," and, in a final effort to resist the cultural construction of her inner self, Edna returns to the sea, the incubator of her transcendental individualism (113).

A central issue in the critical discussion of the novel is whether Edna's suicide should be read as a heroic, feminist gesture. Elizabeth Nolan sees the ocean as "a site of freedom and possibility for the heroine—an alternative space, beyond the reaches of those who seek to define her" (125). On the other hand, Janet Beer argues that "Chopin's new woman, unable to locate an autonomous space in the city, accepts defeat in a return to nature, in death" (97). I argue that reading Edna's suicide in the context of progressive anxieties about excessive individualism suggests that, far from being a heroic gesture, Edna's decision indicates her failure to accept the limits imposed by the external world. Despite Edna's desire for Emersonian domination, the language of the ending makes it clear that she is mastered by nature. As she stands on the beach, she is symbolized by "a bird with a broken wing" that was "reeling, fluttering, circling disabled down, down to the water" (113). When she takes off her clothes, she is "at the mercy of the sun, the breeze that beat upon her" (113). The off-season water is both "chill" and "deep," and, unable to stay afloat, she sinks into the ocean. As in the fiction Alaimo discusses, nature is indeed an actor that intrudes into the human world, but rather than creating a separate space where feminist revolt might be possible, this nature is destructive of any woman who tries to imagine an alternative reality.

Put another way, psychologically, Edna's inability to accept the limits of nature could be seen as pathological, a diagnosis at odds with those who would read Edna as heroic. Stephen Whicher interprets *Nature* as Emerson's "effort to assimilate nature into himself, to reduce the NOT ME to the ME" (52). But Whicher argues that Emerson moved from his youthful confidence in the unlimited power and freedom of the individual soul to a mature recognition of deterministic limits and an acquiescence to Fate: "With time Emerson became sharply aware of the contrast between the transcendental Self and the actual insignificant individual adrift on the stream of time and circumstance" (171). Gretchen Legler suggests that one of the "emancipatory strategies" of an ecofeminist literary criticism might be an Emersonian "[e]rasing or blurring of boundaries between inner (emotional, psychological, personal) and outer (geographic) landscapes, or the erasing or blurring of self-other (human/nonhuman, I/Thou) distinctions" (230).

Certainly, such a desire for fusion drives Edna's quest for freedom, but without a mature recognition of social and natural limits, she is doomed. Cynthia Griffin Wolff interprets Edna's failure to accept the limits that the external world imposes as evidence of her "schizoid personality" and links her condition to Freud's discussion of the "oceanic feeling," the persistence in some adults of "desires for limitless fusion with the external world" (453, 463). She notes that Edna cannot be satisfied with any human relationship, for her desire is "a limitless void whose needs can be filled, finally, only by total fusion with the outside world, a totality of sensuous enfolding. And this totality means annihilation of the ego" (464). Accordingly, her only option is self-destruction.

Michael Gilmore has argued that *The Awakening* rejects the idolatry of nature that dominated late nineteenth-century culture as it turns "toward the anti-naturalist, self-referential agenda of modernism as a liberating mode of behavior in life and art" (60). However, I would argue that rather than rejecting late nineteenth-century naturalism, Chopin reflects the progressives' skepticism about the ability of the individual to transform the external world. Instead, Chopin represents nature as a powerful force that is indifferent to the desires of the individual, a view similar to the naturalism of Stephen Crane's "The Open Boat" (1897) or Jack London's "To Build a Fire" (1908).

⁂

Although they recognized the danger that immersion in nature represented, progressives still desired to make it useful in the socialization process. In 1901, John Muir celebrated the therapeutic potential of wilderness, noting, "Thousands of tired, nerve-shaken, over-civilized people are beginning to find out that going to the mountains is going home; that wildness is a necessity; and that mountain parks and reservations are useful not only as fountains of timber and irrigating rivers, but as fountains of life" (*National Parks* 1). At an 1897 meeting of the National Congress of Mothers, the group that eventually became the Parent Teacher Association, Hall noted, "Unity with Nature is the glory of childhood, and unity with Nature and with childhood is the glory of motherhood" ("Some Practical" 171). Hall's comments reflect the confidence of many turn-of-the-century elites that nature could be used to socialize women, as well as children, the poor, and racial and ethnic others. Colten points out that in the 1890s progressive planners developed large public parks in New Orleans "that would both offer healthful settings for recreation and provide a refining moral influence for their users" (74).

Indeed, Chopin herself turned to nature to ease her relations with society. In 1894, shortly after the publication of her first book, *Bayou Folk*, Chopin went through a period of moodiness. In her diary, she admitted that she found many things difficult to bear, but "my love and reverence for pure unadulterated nature is growing daily" (*Private Papers* 187).

However, the fate of Edna suggests that employing nature as therapy could be as problematic as building levees to tame the wetlands around New Orleans. In one of the most insightful readings of the role of nature in the novel, Tara Parmiter argues that *The Awakening* uses "Edna's vacation by the seaside to comment both on the limitations of the domestic sphere and on the assumption that the summer place can offer a cure for a woman's malaise" (2). She notes that while the summer vacation was designed "to renew one for life back home," Edna's vacation leads her to reject social conventions about a woman's role (9). Thus, Parmiter argues that Chopin subverts the therapeutic value of the summer resort by refusing "to 'cure' Edna if that cure requires Edna to suppress her individuality" (9). However, I would argue that Chopin is more troubled by Edna's individualism than Parmiter suggests and that the socializing value of immersion in nature is conserved, but only through the progressive confidence in the ability of experts. The novel suggests that an expert in psychology might have enabled Edna to integrate her experiences in nature with her social roles of wife and mother.

In response to their fears about the increasing heterodoxy of America, the progressives searched for effective methods of social control that would be less coercive than police power. Sociologist Edward Ross, whose opinions about eugenics and immigration restriction were so controversial that they led to his dismissal from Stanford University, explored technologies of socialization in his book *Social Control* (1901). Dorothy Ross describes his central premise as "the idea that there was a fundamental conflict between individual and social interests. In order to maintain itself, society had to modify individual feelings, ideas, and behavior to conform to the social interest" (*Origins* 230). Edward Ross used a conservation simile to establish the reasons why social control is necessary: "The elementary personal struggle threatens the general prosperity just as the swollen river or the wildfire. And if men raise levees and fire-brakes [sic] against the natural forces, why not against the human passions? (59). He recognized that "legal compulsion" will always be necessary, but he was much more interested in the subtle methods of "moral engineering," including social suggestion and education (124, 6).

A similar progressive response to the social crisis can be seen in the writings of John Dewey. In "The School as Social Centre" (1902), Dewey insists that "our pressing political problems cannot be solved by special measures of legislation or executive activity, but only by the promotion of common sympathies and a common understanding" (82). For Dewey, the school is a necessary response to the "relaxation of the bonds of social discipline and control" caused by the "comingling of classes and races" in the cities (85–86). This social degeneration even threatens the family: "The domestic ties themselves, as between husband and wife as well as in relation to children, lose something of their permanence and sanctity" (86). Accordingly, the school must serve as a socializing agent, providing "continuous instruction" (89). In "My Pedagogic Creed" (1897), he describes the teacher as "a social servant set apart for the maintenance of proper social order and the securing of the right social growth" (95). But, while it was relatively easy to shape children to social ends, progressives recognized that nonconforming adults represented a greater challenge.

When Edna objects to the extravagance of Léonce's desire for new fixtures in the library, he replies, "The way to become rich is to make money, my dear Edna, not to save it" (53). Their discussion reflects a shift to what T. J. Jackson Lears has called the therapeutic ethos, a pursuit of self-realization as the central goal of life. He argues that the older Victorian culture that emphasized "perpetual work, compulsive saving, civic responsibility, and a rigid morality of self-denial" was released by "a new set of values sanctioning periodic leisure, compulsive spending, apolitical passivity, and an apparently permissive (but subtly coercive) morality of individual fulfillment" ("From Salvation" 3). Lears attributes the therapeutic ethos to fears of unreality and overcivilization caused by urbanization and an interdependent economy; accordingly, Americans longed "for bodily vigor, emotional intensity, and a revitalized sense of selfhood" (10). Lears notes that this quest for self-fulfillment was accompanied by doubts and nostalgic escapism, even among the therapists who administered it: their discontent was evident in "their distrust of the modern city, their admiration for the healthiness of rural life, their yearnings for a childlike state of nature" (16). The destruction of Edna by an external nature that she cannot transform registers Chopin's own ambivalence about therapeutic culture and especially the role of nature in that search for self.

For the progressives, women's closeness to nature demanded special attention lest they fail to maintain a proper balance of the natural and the civilized. Reflecting the era's confidence in experts, the key figures in this therapeutic socialization of women were usually their doctors.[8] Smith-Rosenberg points out that turn-of-the-century doctors served as therapists "to counsel and to comfort" troubled women by reconciling their rebellions against social conventions to the demands of nature (185). In the novel, that role is performed by Dr. Mandelet, who seems to have been inspired by Frederick Kolbenheyer, a St. Louis physician who delivered several of Chopin's children and, after the death of her husband, encouraged her to write.[9]

When Léonce first consults Dr. Mandelet about Edna's condition, he asserts that woman "is a very peculiar and delicate organism" and notes that dealing with women requires "an inspired psychologist" (66). Dr. Mandelet believes that he is such an expert since he "knew his fellow-creatures better than most men; knew that inner life which so seldom unfolds itself to unanointed eyes," but he is reluctant to get involved because he had reached the point in his career when he "did not want the secrets of other lives thrust upon him" (71). Accordingly, he only observes Edna once, covertly, as an invited dinner guest.

After Adèle's childbirth, Doctor Mandelet detects Edna's psychological instability and attempts to soothe her. He notes that "youth is given up to illusions. It seems to be a provision of Nature; a decoy to secure mothers for the race" (109–10). In other words, evolutionary biology tricks young women with the illusion of the permanence of romantic feelings because a realization of their temporary nature might keep women from committing to childbirth and lead to the extinction of the species—or at least the "suicide" of the less-fecund races. He continues, "And Nature takes no account of moral consequences, of arbitrary conditions which we create, and which we feel obliged to maintain at any cost" (110). Having secured its mothers, nature is indifferent to the psychological conflicts that develop from the ideological constructions that society establishes upon those transient romantic feelings—namely, marriage and monogamy. By the time the illusion of love passes, women are already trapped. Rather than the empowerment that nature offers to nineteenth-century men, Doctor Mandelet makes it clear to Edna that the biological imperative to have children ties women to the conventions of the social structure. Struggling to maintain her individualist rebellion, Edna insists, "I don't want anything but my own way," but she has already begun to acknowledge the power of the external community, admitting, "[T]hat is wanting a good deal, of course, when you have to trample upon the lives, the hearts, the prejudices of others" (110).

Before Edna leaves, Dr. Mandelet urges her to seek his confidence, assuring her, "I know I would understand, and I tell you there are not many who would (110). But by then the damage has been done. Shortly before she drowns, Edna thinks, "Perhaps Doctor Mandelet would have understood if she had seen him—but it was too late" (114). Previous critics have been mostly dismissive of Dr. Mandelet's offer of counsel, seeing him as a foil to Chopin's putative feminism.[10] Admittedly, he is not successful in socializing Edna. However, her mental turn toward him at the end does suggest the potential role that the expert therapist could play in reconciling women with society.

Throughout the early twentieth century, the discipline of psychology would increasingly focus on treating the problems of women, and these experts frequently employed nature as a useful technology. S. Weir Mitchell is today best known as the doctor who administered his Rest Cure to Charlotte Perkins Gilman in 1887. Gilman had been suffering from a nervous disorder for two years before she went to Mitchell's sanitarium for a month. In her autobiography, she quotes Mitchell's prescription: "Live as domestic a life as possible. Have your child with you all the time. . . . Lie down an hour after each meal. Have but two hours' intellectual life a day. And never touch pen, brush or pencil as long as you live" (96). Gilman tried to follow his instructions until she "came perilously near to losing" her mind" (96). Interestingly, Mitchell might have proposed a very different cure to his patient. In 1888, the year after he treated Gilman, he published *Doctor and Patient*, a collection of essays on the prevention and treatment of nervousness in women. The final chapter is a revision of his 1874 essay "Camp Life"; in this version, he proposes that women could also experience the "joys" and "advantages" of camping (155). He insists that life in the outdoors leads to a proper accommodation of the individual to reality: "[N]othing so dismisses the host of little nervousnesses with which house-caged women suffer as this free life. Cares, frets, worries, and social annoyances disappear, and in the woods and by the waters we lose, as if they were charmed away, our dislikes or jealousies, all the base, little results of the struggle for bread or place" (161).[11]

Surprisingly, given his infamous ban on Gilman's writing, in *Doctor and Patient* Mitchell extols the therapeutic value of "word-sketches" of nature (168). But for this to be a useful therapy, careful instruction by an expert is necessary. He explains that if you take a young girl out in a canoe and ask her what she sees, she will respond with imprecise emotional feelings: "She says it is beautiful and has a vague sense of enjoyment, and will carry away with her little more than this" (166). Accordingly, it is necessary for the guide to instruct her on the realistic and aesthetic details of the scene because "[m]y young friend is intelligent and clever, but she has never learned to observe" (167). The role of the instructor in this process suggests the similarity between Mitchell's Camp and Rest Cures: in both treatments, the expert separates the patient from the normal social connections and then orients her away from her individualistic emotional distortions and toward an accurate, communal perception of reality. F. G. Gosling notes that while the nineteenth-century physicians and therapists differed in their treatments of neurasthenia, they agreed on the centrality of suggestive education by a doctor who made "the patient feel that he knew exactly what to do and was confident of improvement if the patient was faithful in following all instructions" (112). In *Doctor and Patient*, Mitchell warns of Rest Cure patients who ruminate on their symptoms: "It then becomes the business of her physician to tell her what is real, what is unreal, what must be respected, what must be overcome or fought" (131). Of course, this is identical to Dr. Mandelet's disillusioning of Edna: after he explains "Nature" to her, she admits that "perhaps it is better to wake up after all, even to suffer, rather than to remain a dupe to illusions all one's life" (110).

Mitchell's word pictures and Dr. Mandelet's advice suggest the effort to attain the hegemonic consensus on reality central to progressivism. The conflict at the heart of *The Awakening* that makes it such a powerful novel is the tension between sympathy for a woman struggling against social conventions and a recognition of the impossibility of escaping those conventions. Reflecting the Progressive Era confidence in experts, the novel seems to suggest that the professional therapist can mediate between the therapeutic potential of the natural world and the conservative implications of its obduracy to human desire.

As William Deverell observes, after the Civil War, many Americans began to see nature as a source of psychological healing, a social construction of the natural that has continued to the present. In 2012 Cheryl Strayed published *Wild*, a best-selling memoir of her eleven-hundred-mile hike on the Pacific Crest Trail (PCT). On that hike, Strayed wrestled with many psychological issues, and her efforts to find healing suggest a continuity with turn-of-the-century nature therapy. As she nears the end of her hike, Strayed reflects on the history of the PCT, which was developed in 1926 as a cure for overcivilization. She understands that the experience "had only to do with how it felt to be in the wild. With what it was like to walk for miles for no reason other than to witness the accumulation of trees and meadows, mountains and deserts, streams and rocks, rivers and grasses, sunrises and sunsets. The experience was powerful and fundamental" (207). Although she is separated from professional psychologists while she is hiking the PCT, she does recall two earlier sessions she had with a therapist, and those memories help her come to terms with her memories of her father (131–34). When Strayed completes the hike, she has a vision of the future, of "everything I couldn't yet know, though I felt it somehow already contained within me" (310). Significantly, the most developed part of that future is the traditional construction of women's nature: marriage and two children.

A similar integration of psychology and outdoor recreation is evident in advertising for *Talkspace*, an online therapy website: a 2017 commercial narrates the story of Sharon, a woman who decided to walk the Appalachian Trail after breaking up with her boyfriend. *Talkspace* makes it possible for Sharon to access professional help since her "therapist is now able to go with her wherever she goes." In the twenty-first century, technology has enabled women to pursue nature therapy without any danger of escaping the therapeutic gaze of experts.

Chapter 4

Disciplining Nature in Sinclair's *The Jungle*

In the late nineteenth century, Massachusetts declared war on an invasive species even more troublesome than the Shakespearian starlings that had been released in Central Park. The gypsy moth (*Lymantria dispar*) was introduced to the state in the 1860s by Etienne Leopold Trouvelot, a French immigrant who had been trying to improve on nature by developing a hardier species of silk worm. Some of Trouvelot's moths escaped, and by 1890 they had become such a problem that Massachusetts funded a commission to exterminate them. Over the next ten years, this team attacked the insects with tremendous energy but little effect. Robert J. Spear, in *The Great Gypsy Moth War*, argues that the effort was misguided from the first. He critiques the commission's commitment to extermination rather than suppression (as was done in Europe), and he notes that their use of arsenic sprays killed many of the natural predators of the moth. By 1900, Massachusetts had spent more than 1 million dollars, and the moths were continuing to spread; accordingly, funding for the campaign was discontinued. The legislative joint committee concluded that, in the future, the pests could be controlled through such "natural laws" as "climatic influences, diseases, the preying of the higher upon the lower forms of life, the untranslated but ever-working law of migration and distribution" (qtd. in Spear 234).[1]

The committee's confidence in nature's ability to manage itself reflects the growing influence of the new science of ecology. In 1896, Stephen Forbes, president of the Association of Economic Entomologists, contrasted earlier reliance on insecticides and "mechanical means of destruction" with the new entomology, which "seeks diligently, first, to avoid all unnecessary disturbances of the normal play of life" (qtd. in Croker 112). However, Forbes recognized that, occasionally, entomologists needed to intervene and "direct the powers of nature herself, so far as possible, to the correction of such disorders as are nevertheless likely to arise" (qtd. in Croker 112). An ecocritical reading of Upton Sinclair's *The Jungle* (1906) illustrates the turn-of-the-century confidence in human ability to manipulate the nature of both the humans and the animals of the Chicago meat-packing industry.

⁓

The common name of the *Lymantria dispar*, "gypsy moth," suggests a linkage between nonnative species and concerns about human immigration. Indeed, in *American Perceptions of Immigrant and Invasive Species*, Peter Coates argues that early twentieth-century restrictions on imported plants and animals were "paralleled by growing support for tighter controls over human immigration" (9). By the late nineteenth century, prejudice against immigrants from southern and eastern Europe had undermined American confidence in the power of assimilation, especially since immigrants from these areas were associated with the growing labor unrest. For many Americans, the nonnative had become a threat.[2]

Fears about immigration were encouraged by growing popular acceptance of evolutionary theory. If natural selection is driven by a Malthusian struggle for limited resources, massive immigration could overwhelm older-stock Americans. Indeed, Darwin's *On the Origin of the Species* (1859) illustrates natural selection by positing a hypothetical country in the midst of a climactic change; he notes, "If the country were open on its borders, new forms would certainly immigrate, and this also would seriously disturb the relations of some of the former inhabitants" (81). Francis Walker's 1896 analysis of population trends warned that the new immigration brought "beaten men from beaten races; representing the worst failures in the struggle for existence" (828). As John Higham points out, Walker's theory enabled scientific racists to develop the pessimistic implications of evolutionary theory, namely, that "unobstructed natural selection might insure the survival of the worst people rather than the best" (144).

Many Americans turned to eugenics as a solution to the threat of race suicide. Theodore Roosevelt wrote a series of articles between 1913 and 1914 that both encouraged the fit to have more children and discouraged the unfit from breeding. Noting that he was affirming "a law of nature which can no more be ignored, defied, or evaded than any other law of nature," Roosevelt argued that unless parents have four children, the race was doomed, and he denounced "the cold, calculating, and most unmanly and unwomanly selfishness which makes so many men and women shirk

Figure 4.1. Immigrants arriving at Ellis Island, 1904 (Wikimedia Commons)

the most important of all their duties to the State" ("Premium" 164). He also insisted, "I wish very much that the wrong people could be prevented entirely from breeding. . . . Criminals should be sterilized, and feeble-minded persons forbidden to leave offspring behind them" ("Twisted Eugenics" 32).

Turn-of-the-century immigration simultaneously created a demand for increased food production and provided the workers for the meat industry that developed in Chicago to help fulfill that demand. In 1898, Robert Herrick insisted that the city could be seen as "an instance of a successful, contemptuous disregard of nature by man" (101). But rather than disregard, Chicago's meat industry represents a deliberate effort to reshape the natural world to meet human needs. By the 1890s, 13 million animals were received at the city's Union Stockyards each year, and the industry employed more than twenty-five thousand workers. To manage these large populations and to increase production, the packing houses rationalized both space and time through such strategies as the overhead assembly line (more accurately, the "disassembly line") and hierarchical management of the labor force. In *Nature's Metropolis*, William Cronon notes that artificial lighting and refrigeration meant that the process could operate continuously, free from the limitations of nature. The packers employed teams of chemists to develop artificial byproducts such as oleomargarine, thereby increasing profits while reducing waste. As Dominic Pacyga points out, these innovations made the meat industry a spectacle of the modern that attracted a half million tourists annually; the industry accommodated these visitors by providing viewing platforms, informational booklets, and professional guides (9–23).

But this marvel of modern efficiency did not operate without friction. The meat packers worked ten-hour days in difficult conditions, earning between twenty and fifty cents per hour. Frequent labor disputes such as the 1886 Haymarket Square riot were met with increased police and military presence. Smoke and waste products polluted the air and waters of Chicago, and fears of tainted meat led to legislation mandating federal inspections. After World War II, Chicago's domination of the industry declined as trucking shifted meat processing to other places. By the early 1960s, the big packers had left Chicago, and in 1971 the Union Stockyards closed.[3]

Today, the former stockyards are the site of an industrial park that includes several green companies, but when *The Jungle* was published, Packingtown was at the peak of its production. In 1904, Sinclair, who had recently become a socialist, published a stirring appeal to the stockyard workers who had been defeated in a recent strike. The editor of the social-

Figure 4.2. Chicago Stockyards, 1909 (Wikimedia Commons)

ist newspaper *Appeal to Reason* was impressed and gave him an advance to write a novel. After the novel was serialized in the *Appeal*, it was published by Doubleday, Page in early 1906, immediately becoming a controversial best-seller. Much like the chemical industry's attacks against Rachel Carson's *Silent Spring*, the meat packers accused Sinclair of misrepresentation, and he was forced to defend the accuracy of his charges. President Roosevelt's experiences with tainted meat in the Spanish-American War made him a sympathetic ally, and after investigating the truth of the novel, he pushed for legislation addressing the problems that Sinclair had exposed. In 1906, the Pure Food and Drug Act and the Federal Meat Inspection Act were signed into law, prompting Sinclair's oft-repeated *bon mot*, "I aimed at the public's heart, and by accident I hit it in the stomach" (*Autobiography* 135). Michael McGerr points out that the major meat producers welcomed federal regulation because the increased expense eliminated competition from smaller firms (162).[4]

Despite his support for a muckraking exposé of the meat industry, Roosevelt was disturbed by Sinclair's socialism and encouraged him to abandon "the pathetic belief" in the ability of weak individuals to raise themselves through cooperation (*Letters* 179). But Sinclair remained committed to socialism, and with the profits from *The Jungle*, he purchased Helicon Hall, a large building in Edgewater, New Jersey, where he conducted an experiment with communal living until it burned to the ground in March 1907. In *The Jungle*, Sinclair's commitment to communalism leads to a reinterpretation of evolution from a socialist perspective that emphasizes cooperation and efficiency over the waste of capitalist competitive struggle.

In *The Book of Life* (1921), Sinclair insists that evolutionary theory is "the basis of all modern thinking, and as generally accepted as the rotation of the earth" (1:17). As George Levine has observed, it is difficult to discuss the influence of Darwin on his contemporaries since he often expressed seemingly contradictory ideas in his works, and those ideas were interpreted in various ways; thus, there are "many possible Darwins" (11). By the turn of the century, conservative social Darwinists such as Herbert Spencer argued that evolution advanced through the Malthusian struggle for limited resources; accordingly, they believed that government should take a *laissez-faire* approach to allow the fittest to triumph. A more optimistic alternative was to focus on the principle of sexual selection that Darwin developed in *The Descent of Man*. For reform Darwinists such as Lester Ward (a major influence on Charlotte Perkins Gilman), human intelligence enables the species to direct evolution; thus, a scientifically informed government could control nature to benefit mankind. Kimberly Hamlin points out that feminist and socialist reformers preferred reformist Darwinism because it allowed for human control of the evolutionary process and thus "could lead to vast social change" (152). The tension between pessimistic and optimistic interpretations of Darwin can be seen in *The Jungle*: the novel begins naturalistically, with an emphasis on the deterministic struggle for existence, but it ends with a more hopeful vision of a socialistic future based on cooperation.[5]

With the exception of an excellent study by Steven Rosendale in 2002, *The Jungle* has received little attention from ecocritics. Rosendale attributes this neglect to Sinclair's focus on human rather than natural concerns, as well as a lack of interest in class issues by ecocritics. He reads the novel as a resistance narrative that depicts "the environmental consequences of capitalist industry not simply as the result of bad management or accumulation but as an integral feature of the productive process itself," and he sees hope in an uncorrupted nature "as a liberatory idea in a class society" (73, 65). In contrast, I argue that the novel reveals the strategies by which both capitalism and socialism manipulate the natural world to discipline the workers and the animals of the Chicago meat industry.

✦

Sinclair's title suggests that the immigrants in *The Jungle* are involved in a desperate struggle for survival. Jurgis's first impression of Chicago is "a vision of power," and the novel illustrates the pervasiveness of the forces that determine the lives of the immigrants (31). To survive, they must adapt to the baffling culture of America, "the mercilessness of the city, of the country in which they lived, of its laws and customs that they did not understand" (171). The workers are disciplined by the hierarchical management of the packing house that enforces the pace of production: "[R]anged in ranks and grades like an army, were managers and superintendents and foreman, each one driving the man next below him and trying to squeeze out of him as much work as possible" (59). Social order is maintained by a vigilant police and the threat of imprisonment, and disciplinary surveillance is extended through company spies and a blacklist that bars troublemakers. Ultimately, Jurgis learns that the culture of Chicago is "a world in which nothing counted but brutal might, an order devised by those who possessed it for the subjugation of those who did not" (221).

A central strategy of that subjugation involves converting the natural bodies of the workers into machines, so that the process becomes "pork-making by machinery, pork-making by applied mathematics" (36). To accomplish this mechanization, all unnecessary nature is repressed. At her sausage machine, Elzbieta becomes an automaton: "She was part of the machine she tended, and every faculty that was not needed for the machine was doomed to be crushed out of existence" (133). The repression of the natural extends to the workers' experience of the outdoors. The narrator notes that in the summer the middle-class reader might have "thoughts of the country, visions of green fields and mountains and sparkling lakes," but he points out that no such pastoral escapes were available for the workers: "The great packing-machine ground on remorselessly, without thinking of green fields; and the men and women and children who were part of it never saw any green thing, not even a flower" (100). As Rosendale points out, Packingtown is a "simulacrum of nature" where there is "no trace of unaltered, nonhuman nature" (60–61).

What nature does remain reinforces the disciplining of the workers. The brutal Chicago winter, which is described as "a power primeval, cosmic," forces the immigrants to work to avoid starvation and hypothermia (82). In these conditions, the immigrants must struggle for survival just as the branches of trees struggle for light, but as in nature, "some of them lose and die; and then comes the raging blasts" (78). Nature kills off the weak through a variety of means: one child is devoured by rats; another drowns in the mud of the streets (275, 201). Jurgis is puzzled that in such a highly civilized society "human creatures might be hunted down and destroyed by the wild-beast powers of nature, just as truly as ever they were in the days of the cave-men!" (113).

The countryside surrounding the city seems to represent a pastoral escape from the naturalistic conditions of the city. When Uncle Jonas disappears, the family assumes that he has become a hobo since they believe that "with a day's walk a man might put the smoke of Packingtown behind him forever, and be where the grass was green and the flowers all the colors of the rainbow!" (118). After the death of his wife and son, Jurgis himself becomes a hobo, and indeed, life in the country has restorative effects: his body is cleansed, he relishes simple food, and his health returns. Rosendale argues that "in addition to restoring Jurgis's humanity, the countryside affords him enough respite that he can evaluate his Packingtown experience with some clarity and begin to imagine a better life" (71). But, as Cronon points out, any belief that "city and country are separate and opposing worlds" is illusory (*Nature's Metropolis* 17). Like Twain and Chopin, Sinclair recognizes that excursions into nature are compromised by industrial civilization;

accordingly, Jurgis's flight is temporary, and fear of winter, "the stern system of nature," drives him back to the city to find work (208).

The goal of this manipulation of and by nature was the assimilation of the immigrants into American culture as useful workers. Matthew J. Morris argues that the novel shows how industrial capitalism "could strip away the uniqueness of folkways as it transformed immigrant farmers into industrial workers" (147). The young Lithuanians at the wedding speak English and reject the fashions of the old country to the point that "some of the young men you would take to be Americans" (13). The meat-packing industry even shapes the physiology of the workers, so those at the sausage machine become the color of the sausage, following "the ancient custom of nature, whereby the ptarmigan is the color of dead leaves in the fall and of snow in the winter" (129). Likewise, after a few years of stooping, the hoisters walk "like chimpanzees" (97).

However, these animal metaphors suggest the limits of capitalist discipline. Instead of assimilating the immigrants, the brutal conditions have led to evolutionary degeneration. Marija is "a human horse"; Ona is a "hunted animal"; Jurgis is "a dumb beast of burden" (103, 138). Elzbieta endures after the death of her daughter since she "was one of the primitive creatures: like the angle-worm, which goes on living though cut in half" (185). While these metaphors suggest passivity and even usefulness, other manifestations of animality are more threatening. When Jurgis encounters a prostitute, "the wild beast rose up within him and screamed, as it has screamed in the jungle from the dawn of time" (209). Trying to get into the station house to escape the cold, "men fought and tore each other like savage beasts" (218). In the detention hospital, the prostitutes lose all humanity, "barking like dogs, gibbering like apes, raving and tearing themselves in delirium" (220).

The much-maligned ending of the novel presents socialism as an alternative to the inefficient discipline of capitalism. At first, Jurgis rejects the union because he is certain that he is strong enough to survive in the Hobbesian "war of each against all" (74). However, his subjugation by industry undermines his confidence in individualism, and he joins the union with the hope that combination will improve his life. Eventually, when he is completely defeated, he stumbles into a socialist meeting, where he is exposed to a deeper vision of the possibility of cooperation. He sees socialism as a liberation that paradoxically would give him individuality through unity: "He would no longer be the sport of circumstances, he would be a man, with a will and a purpose" (293). At a subsequent meeting, a socialist speaker explains that "economic evolution" offered the only hope: "Life was a struggle for existence, and the strong overcame the weak, and in turn were overcome by the strongest. Those who lost in the struggle were generally exterminated; but now and then they had been known to save themselves by combination—which was a new and higher kind of strength" (309).

Jurgis's introduction to socialism reflects the revisionist Darwinism of Prince Peter Kropotkin, who is praised by Sinclair in *The Book of Life* for his "complete refutation of the old bourgeois biology" (1:18–19). Kropotkin was a Russian anarchist and scientist whose observations of nature in the underpopulated ecosystems of Siberia led him to challenge the social Darwinist emphasis on intraspecies competition. In *Mutual Aid as a Factor in Evolution* (1902), he discussed examples of cooperation among both animals and humans. Arguing that the real threat to survival is the "hard struggle against a hostile nature," he underscored the efficiency of mutual aid, noting that it produces "the greatest amount of welfare and enjoyment of life for the individual, with the least waste of energy" (130, 6). Accordingly, cooperation is essential "for industrial progress, as for each other conquest of nature" (298). Kropotkin's emphasis on efficiency suggests the progressive reconciliation of capitalism and socialism: by avoiding individualistic competition, a more efficient system would increase production while minimizing the waste of human and nonhuman resources.

In *The Jungle*, many of Kropotkin's ideas are articulated by Nicholas Schliemann. A "philosophic anarchist," Schliemann denounces "the negative wastes of competition" and celebrates the "positive economies of cooperation" (319, 323). Obsessed with efficiency, Schliemann insists that, through "scientific chewing," he "tripled the value of all he ate" (315). Like the progressive conservationists, Schliemann understands that "there was only one earth, and the quantity of material things was limited" (319). But he rejects Malthusian pessimism because he has confidence in technological innovation. He notes that we have no way of knowing "the productive capacity of society if the present resources of science were utilized," and he is confident that "the new science of agriculture" administered by "expert agricultural chemists" will solve the food supply problem (319, 324).[6]

Schliemann's vision of the socialist future also restores therapeutic recreational nature since land unfit for farming would become a timber reserve, "in which our children play, and our young men hunt, and our poets dwell!" (324). The socialist restoration of nature is also suggested through the language used to depict Jurgis's conversion. Like mid-nineteenth-century encounters with the natural sublime, Jurgis experiences socialism as an emotional disturbance: "It was like coming suddenly upon some wild sight of nature,—a mountain forest lashed by a tempest, a ship tossed about upon a stormy sea" (285). He compares his early individualist efforts to "wandering and blundering in the depths of a wilderness" in contrast to the vast perspective offered by socialism, equivalent to a mountaintop from which he "could see the paths from which he had wandered, the morasses into which he had stumbled, the hiding-places of the beasts of prey that had fallen upon him" (299).

Reviving the natural is problematic, however, since it entails the risk of degeneration into the bestial. As he continues to listen to the speaker, Jurgis becomes a dangerous animal: "[H]e stood there, with his clenched hands upraised, his eyes bloodshot, and the veins standing out purple in his face, roaring in the voice of a wild beast, frantic, incoherent, maniacal" (292). To control such atavism, careful management is necessary, so Jurgis is educated and trained as a socialist by a variety of mentors. After the success of the socialists in the election, the speaker insists that the party must "find these men who have voted for us, and bring them to our meetings, and organize them and bind them to us! . . . And we shall organize them, we shall drill them, we shall marshal them for the victory!" (328).[7]

But even after his education, Jurgis remains undisciplined. One of the most significant differences between the *Appeal to Reason* and the Doubleday, Page texts is the ending. In the book version, Jurgis gradually disappears: he is a silent observer of the discourses by Schliemann and the other socialists, and the book ends with him listening to the election-night orator. However, in the earlier *Appeal* version, he plays a much more active role. "Crazy with excitement," Jurgis confronts the Democrat senator at a meeting by describing his own corrupt work for the party, until he sees his enemy, Phil Connnor, the man whom he had impulsively beaten for seducing Ona (341). Jurgis tries to flee, but he is arrested and is sentenced to two years in the state prison. The ending of the *Appeal* text presents Jurgis as an undisciplined convert, and it suggests that the problem is his ethnicity. Before the meeting, he is "reckless and impatient" to become involved in party activities, despite having been warned by his mentor "of the harm it might do the party to have one of its workers arrested for a crime" (337). When Jurgis confronts the senator, the narrator condescendingly notes "his peculiarities of pronunciation, which have not been reproduced here" (341). His capture occurs because he "was slow of thought" and thus unable to respond to the danger (341).

The failed education of Jurgis suggests that socialist discipline might demand a more intrusive manipulation of immigrant nature. Nicole Mellow points out that since the progressives saw the ideal citizen as possessing such middle-class values as self-control and a willingness to place the interests of the community above those of the individual, the increasingly heterogeneous electorate of the late nineteenth century inspired concern over the "mental, moral, and physical capacities" of voters (198). Accordingly, the eugenics campaign "flourished as an effort to increase the proportion of citizens deemed fit to those identified as unfit" (205). In 1914, the progressive zoologist Robert H. Wolcott exulted that, through eugenics, "we have harnessed the forces of nature, and they answer to our bidding" (16).

But fascination with eugenics was not restricted to the progressives: many socialists believed that environmental reconstruction was useless without a corresponding scientific control of human heredity. In his defense of Marxism's ecological credentials, Paul Burkett notes that Marx and Engels saw human labor itself as a natural force that required control in order for production to be nonexploitative and sustainable (157). In *Dialectics of Nature* (1883), Engels observed that "at every step we are reminded that we by no means rule over nature like a conqueror over a foreign people, like someone standing outside nature—but that we, with flesh, blood, and brain, belong to nature, and exist in its midst, and that all our mastery of it consists in the fact that we have the advantage over all other beings of being able to know and correctly apply its laws" (292). For many socialists, the correct application of nature's laws meant eugenics. In 1917, the British socialist Eden Paul insisted that "racial degeneration" can only be averted by using our developing knowledge of eugenics "to control nature" (133). Likewise, at the 1912 Eugenics Congress in London, Kropotkin affirmed his shared interest in "the prevention of the deterioration and the improvement of the human race by maintaining in purity the common stock of inheritance of mankind" ("Sterilization" 121).[8]

From an evolutionary perspective, cooperation is most likely to occur in environments that are underpopulated, such as Kropotkin's Siberia; thus, management of populations is necessary to avoid intraspecies competition. In 1912, Sinclair novelized the popular proeugenics play *Damaged Goods*, and in the *Book of Life*, he expresses concern about the possibility of race suicide: "[W]hile all our Anglo-Saxon stock, those who founded our country and established its institutions, are gradually removing themselves from the face of the earth, our ignorant and helpless populations, whether in city slums or on tenant farms, are multiplying like rabbits" (2:62).

Eugenic concerns are certainly present in *The Jungle*. As Scott Derrick observes, nature is represented as a "threatening fecundity" with "an anxiety-inducing profusion of life" (86). The various groups who had been tenants of the Rudkus house all had too many children, "which was a common failing in Packingtown," and the birth of Elzbieta's handicapped son "had been intended by nature to let her know that she had had enough" (67, 123). Indeed, despite Sinclair's putative sympathy for the immigrants, the harshest ethnocentric judgments come from the narrator. The strikebreakers are "an assortment of the criminals and thugs of the city, besides negroes and the lowest foreigners—Greeks, Roumanians, Sicilians, and Slovaks" (255–56). The representation of African Americans is especially disturbing: the narrator notes their laziness and violence and is horrified that young white girls were mixed with the negroes, who were "free to gratify every passion, free to wreck themselves. . . . an army of fifteen or twenty thousand human beasts" (261). Schliemann includes "the scientific breeding of men and women" on his list of social changes that will result in a better world (323). Sinclair's novel makes it clear that, in the early twentieth century, the manipulation of nature, including the nature represented by the immigrant workers, was a project shared by both capitalist and socialist thinkers.

∽

Sinclair was not the only turn-of-the-century author who was influenced by Kropotkin. The Canadian nature writer Ernest Thompson Seton was also inspired by the Russian anarchist, whom he met in Toronto in 1897. Seton helped to found the Boy Scouts, but he was best known as the author of popular wildlife stories that showed animals engaged in cooperation rather than competition. In Seton's stories, crows communicate with each other to avoid danger, foxes attempt to help their young escape from traps, and rabbits and quail are carefully trained by their mothers.[9]

In 1903, Seton became entangled in controversy when John Burroughs attacked him and other nature writers in an article published in the *Atlantic Monthly*. In "Real and Sham Natural History," Burroughs charged that their stories indulged in the "sensational and improbable" by depicting such things as crows teaching their young in schools or foxes deliberately leading hounds onto railroad trestles to avoid capture (129). The subsequent "Nature Faker" debate lasted through 1907 and even involved President Roosevelt, who could not resist publicly denouncing those writers who violated his sense of realism. But, as Ralph H. Lutts points out, the controversy involved more than just questions of verisimilitude; instead it represented "a cultural transition regarding the relationship between people and nature" (*Nature*

Fakers 161). As Darwin effaced the difference between humans and animals, questions of animal rights became unavoidable. In *Wild Animals I Have Known* (1898), Seton argues, "Since, then, the animals are creatures with wants and feelings differing in degree only from our own, they surely have their rights" (12).[10]

As the nature faker controversy was coming to its climax, Sinclair published a novel about an industry that prided itself on its ability to "process" more than 13 million animals annually. Yet, oddly, there is little focus on the suffering of animals in the slaughterhouse. Schliemann predicts that meat-eating will diminish, citing vaguely anthropocentric reasons: "Meat is obviously more difficult to produce than vegetable food, less pleasant to prepare and handle, and more likely to be unclean" (325). The most sustained engagement with animal rights occurs when Jurgis tours the packing plant. After describing the shrieking of the hogs as they were attached to the disassembly line, the narrator suggests that even the most "matter-of-fact person" would feel sympathy: "[T]hey were so innocent, they came so very trustingly; and they were so very human in their protests" (36). He then becomes "philosophical" and speculates on whether the hogs will be compensated for their suffering in the afterlife: "Was one to believe that there was nowhere a god of hogs, to whom this hog-personality was precious, to whom these hog-squeals and agonies had a meaning?" (37). In his autobiography, Sinclair was defensive about the ridicule he received over this passage, insisting that he intended it as "hilarious farce" (175).[11]

Not everyone who toured the packing plants saw the humor of the disassembly line. John Harvey Kellogg called it "organized murder," and Rudyard Kipling grimly reflected, "They were so excessively alive, these pigs. And then they were so excessively dead" (Kellogg 148; Kipling 151). But, as Wilson Warren points out, "Sinclair apparently did not intend to espouse vegetarianism as a solution to the problems in the meat industry.... Nor did *The Jungle* prompt much concern over the treatment of animals" (127). Why would Sinclair, who would within a few years experiment with vegetarianism, seem so indifferent to the ethical implications of the slaughterhouse?

One possible answer is that the slaughtered animals are not real to him. Cronon points out that the meat industry reified the violence of the slaughterhouse by transforming the living nature of cows and pigs into a commodity: "Meat was a neatly wrapped package one bought at the market. Nature did not have much to do with it" (*Nature's Metropolis*, 257). For a novel about the meat industry, there is a curious lack of live animals in *The Jungle*. Other than the doomed hogs that Jurgis sees on his tour, the escaped steer that injures him, and the rats that devour young Stanislovas, animals appear only as already-dismembered parts.

But, despite their physical absence, animals perform important ideological work in *The Jungle*. Recent discussions of speciesist discourse have explored how humanism struggles to establish a clear boundary between the animal and the human in order to erect a barrier against the limitations of the natural. Noting the Greek distinction between *bios*, political life, and *zoē*, bare or natural life, Giorgio Agamben points out that Foucault, in *The History of Sexuality*, sees modernity as driven by biopolitics, or the politicization of *zoē*, the inclusion of natural life into the power of the state. However, Agamben insists that Foucault does not go far enough, arguing that in modern politics, "the realm of bare life—which is originally situated at the margins of the political order—gradually begins to coincide with the political realm, and exclusion and inclusion, outside and inside, *bios* and *zoē*, right and fact, enter into a zone of irreducible indistinction" (9). In *Before the Law*, Carey Wolfe critiques Agamben's "dismissal and disavowal of the embodied existence that we share with nonhuman animals" (24). For Wolfe, Agamben and other contemporary thinkers demonstrate an "almost hysterical condemnation and disavowal of embodied life as something constitutively deficient," perhaps because it "links us fatefully to mortality, and thus to a domain of contingency over which we finally have less than complete control" (30). In *Animal Rites*, Wolfe argues that such speciesism is central "to the formation of Western subjectivity and sociality" since "the full transcendence of the 'human' requires the sacrifice of the 'animal' and the animalistic" (6). Likewise, Neil Evernden insists, "For the humanist concept of 'Human' to exist, we must first invent Nature: our freedom rests on the bondage of nature to the 'Laws' which we prescribe" (60).

A disavowal of natural life can be traced in *The Jungle*. Sinclair complained that his subject matter left him at a disadvantage as compared to Harriet Beecher Stowe's *Uncle Tom's Cabin*: "Who can thrill the reader with the tale of a man-hunt in which the hunted is a lousy and ignorant foreigner, and the hunters are the germs of consumption, diphtheria and typhoid?" (qtd. in Arthur 44). Given this conception of the deficiency of his subject matter, Sinclair emphasized the insentience of his animals to affirm the significance of his Lithuanian immigrants. Thus, rather than embodied nature, animals appear primarily as metaphors to establish a baseline of humane treatment, and the horror of industrial capitalism is that humans are being forced to live at or below that level. On his tour of the packing house, Jurgis mutters, "I'm glad I'm not a hog!" but, after his conversion to socialism, he realizes that he has been forced to live under conditions that are only appropriate for animals: "[A] hog was just what he had been" (37, 299). The animal-human distinction is affirmed by the socialist speaker who notes that the workers "ask no more than the wages of a beast of burden, the food and shelter to keep you alive from day to day," thereby suggesting that the animal represents no more than the basic biological existence that humans and nonhumans share (287). When Jurgis is sentenced to prison, he is outraged because he has been treated "as if he had been a wild beast, a thing without sense or reason, without rights, without affections, without feelings" (155). Thus, animality means the absence of the characteristics assumed to be exclusively human—rationality, emotions, sentience. But most importantly, unlike humans, animals lack all rights.

Sinclair's lack of interest in the suffering imposed by the meat industry might also reflect antimodern anxiety about the enervation produced by modern civilization. Vegetarianism was hotly debated at the turn of the century, and a key issue was whether meat was necessary to produce the vigor that would be required of a race that had imperialist ambitions. In 1899, Kellogg demonstrated the negative effects of meat-eating on moral character by quoting a former carnivore, who reflected, "Before, when I ate great bloody beefsteaks, I would rise from the table feeling just as if I must strike somebody or bite something. I felt savage. . . . Now it is easy to be calm, to be kind. I have self-control" (161). In 1911, Alfred Daniel Hall, director of a British agricultural research institution, conceded the pacifying effects of vegetarianism, noting that it leads to "quieter and more law-abiding citizens" that can "better adjust their lives to the requirements of a modern city civilization" (211). However, Hall argued that such a diet would be dangerous because it would eliminate from society "the full-blooded and the adventurous; the big men, the men who make things" (211). More ominously, he predicted that in the Darwinian struggle for the world's resources between the West and the vegetarian East, victory will go to the "flesh-eating races" because of their superior vigor, initiative, and masterfulness (213).

But, perhaps most centrally, the repression of the animals and the disciplining of the workers in *The Jungle* registers the rise of biopolitics. In *The History of Sexuality, Volume I*, Foucault discusses biopower as the modern state's efforts to control the body of the species, addressing such issues as "propagation, births and mortality, the level of health, life expectancy and longevity" (139). Foucault notes that while biopolitics was an essential part of the development of capitalism, socialists and other reformers drew upon the same assumptions about the role of the state in furthering life, "understood as the basic needs, man's concrete essence, the realization of his potential, a plenitude of the possible" (145). In *Mammonart* (1924), Sinclair insisted, "I am a Socialist who believes in machinery, and has no interest in any world that does not develop machine power to the greatest possible extent" (238). When they first arrive in Packingtown, the immigrants see it as "a dream of wonder, with its tale of human energy, of things being done, of employment for thousands upon thousands of men, of opportunity and freedom, of life and love and joy" (31). The novel does not reject this dream of industrial plenitude; instead, it critiques capitalism's perversion of it.

Rejecting capitalist repression of nature as inefficient, *The Jungle* suggests instead that a carefully managed nature would increase industrial production and the happiness of human society—the workers would be disciplined, and the animals would be processed to employ and to feed an expanding America. Foucault's description of "a power that exerts a positive influence on life, that endeavors to administer, optimize, and multiply it, subjecting it to precise controls and comprehensive regulations" neatly captures the goals of progressivism, which is a reconciliation of capitalism and socialism (*History* 137). Indeed, biopower is exemplified in the government's response to Sinclair's critique of American capitalism: the passage of the Pure Food and Drug Act and the Federal Meat Inspection Act.

Sinclair compared his discovery of socialism to "the falling down of prison walls about my mind" (*American Outpost* 143). Walls have always had the function of maintaining distinctions. One of the innovations of the Union Stockyards was its use of moveable fences, chutes, and elevated passages to enable efficient processing of the livestock. These barriers enabled the classification of animals, and they also made them easier to control. The novel makes it clear that barriers are also used to control human populations. When Jurgis feels most alienated, he sees his placelessness symbolized by "the residences, with their heavy walls and bolted doors, and basement-windows barred with iron; the great warehouses filled with the products of the whole world, and guarded by iron shutters and heavy gates; the banks with their unthinkable billions of wealth, all buried in safes and vaults of steel" (221). At this moment, even nature, "all outdoors," seemed a "colossal prison" to Jurgis, the psychological walls as controlling as the physical walls of his earlier experience in the prison (221).

During the 2016 Republican presidential campaign, Donald Trump promised that he would build a fifty-foot-high wall the length of the two-thousand-mile Mexican border to prevent illegal immigration. Shortly thereafter, Trump scaled back the scope of his proposed wall, insisting that it would only need to be one thousand miles long because of "natural barriers" (qtd. in "Third Republican"). After being elected, he explained this concept further, noting that "we don't need a wall where you have rivers and mountains and everything else protecting it" (qtd. in Tatum). Thus, as with the gypsy moths and the working-class immigrants in Chicago, nature itself could be employed to manage a troublesome population.

Of course, Trump's proposed wall is only an expansion of the current system of physical barriers and surveillance that marks the border. Rachel St. John points out that the first governmental border fence was constructed in 1909 to prevent the migration of Mexican cows infected with Texas Cattle Fever (103). By the 1930s, some Americans had also become concerned about human migration across the Mexican border. Sacramento businessman Charles M. Goethe was a member of the Sierra Club, a pioneer in the effort to save the California redwoods, and a driving force for nature interpretation programs in the national parks. He also was one of America's leading eugenicists, an enthusiastic supporter of Hitler's sterilization programs, and a strong opponent of Mexican immigration, which he compared to the infestation of the nonnative English Sparrow. Clearly, sensitivity to environmental issues is not incompatible with a commitment to the social control of populations deemed to be problematic.[12]

Chapter 5

Progressive Conservation in Austin's *The Ford*

In 1910, geologist W. J. McGee, whom Gifford Pinchot called the scientific brains of progressive conservation, insisted that "the Conquest of Water" was the sole remaining barrier to be overcome "before Man becomes master over Nature" (363). At the time, the indisputable leader of that struggle was William E. Smythe. Editor of the Omaha *Bee* during the drought of 1890, Smythe became chair of the National Irrigation Congress, founder and editor of the magazine *Irrigation Age*, and author of a series of articles and books on irrigation. In *The Conquest of Arid America* (1900), Smythe insisted that the western United States promised a noble future for the republic because, unlike the East, where farmers have a "crude, uncalculating, and unscientific" dependence on rainfall, the arid West demands irrigation, which creates scientific agriculture and democratic clusters of small farms that depend upon cooperation (21, 30). The result would be a pastoral utopia where "farms that blend into beautiful towns" replace "crowded cities festering with vice and poverty" (309). For Smythe, the war on aridity represents "the powerful dominance of the ancient Saxon spirit, engaged in the conquest of its waste-places and the making of new forms of civilization worthy of the race, the place, and the age" (309).

A similar emphasis on the potential for science and cooperation to solve the problems created by urbanization is evident in the work of Smythe's contemporary, Mary Austin, who engaged with irrigation issues most directly in her 1917 novel, *The Ford*. Previous ecocritics have typically seen Austin as a voice of resistance against those who would dominate the natural world. Anne Raine sees *The Ford* as a "feminist, conservationist novel" and argues that it shows that "both sensibility and power are necessary for effective resistance to male dominance and capitalist instrumentality" (247, 262). Stacy Alaimo insists that Austin rejected the progressive view of conservation as she sought to "release nature from the grip of utilitarianism"

(72). She argues that in *The Ford*, Austin "represents nature as a force that resists man's mastery" and that she "understands nature as an actor, not as a passive, malleable resource, as an influence on culture, not as culture's raw material" (76–77). Lawrence Buell reads *The Ford* as an anticipation of "modern watershed consciousness" (*Writing* 252). While Austin does indeed value the nonhuman world in a way that is unique among her contemporaries, I argue that her representation of nature in *The Ford* is more closely embedded in the Progressive Era manipulation of nature than these critics have suggested. Austin's novel reconciles the environmental and human tensions of the emerging industrial state by integrating ideologies of nature with progressive technologies of social control.[1]

∽

In the film classic *Chinatown* (1974), Noah Cross (John Huston) explains to J. J. Gittes (Jack Nicholson), "Either you bring the water to L.A.—or you bring L.A. to the water" (Towne 122). The film is loosely based on the California water wars of the early twentieth century, and since water, or the lack thereof, is a central theme in Austin's best work, it is not surprising that she was drawn to the conflict as a subject for a novel. The topic was especially inviting since Mary and her husband, Wallace, were key players in the water wars.

The Austins came to the Owens Valley of the eastern Sierras in 1892, when Wallace began an irrigation colony at Lone Pine. Like most of these private ventures, the colony failed, and in 1899 the couple moved fifteen miles north to Independence, where Wallace became register of the local federal land office. In 1903 Mary published *The Land of Little Rain*, which was critically acclaimed for its depiction of the beauty of this harsh environment. That same year the Reclamation Service initiated the process of making the Owens Valley one of its first major projects. More than 100,000 acres of federal land were withdrawn from settlement, and preliminary mapping was begun. However, in 1905, Joseph Lippincott, the Reclamation Service's chief of operations in California, began working secretly with William Mulholland of the Los Angeles Water Department in a scheme to bring the water of the Owens Valley to the city through a 233-mile-long aqueduct. While Lippincott was scuttling the government's project, the city's agents were purchasing the necessary private land from sellers who assumed that they were dealing with representatives of the federal irrigation project.

In the summer of 1905, Wallace Austin wrote to the Department of the Interior and President Theodore Roosevelt, charging that the Reclamation Service had misled the ranchers and that the city's plans would devastate the valley. In September, Mary published an article in the *San Francisco Chronicle*, criticizing Los Angeles's scheme. During the subsequent year-long political struggle between the city and the valley, Governor George C. Pardee and Senator Frank P. Flint both supported Los Angeles, and Flint was able to use his friendship with Gifford Pinchot to gain an audience with the President. Roosevelt ultimately agreed that sending the water to Los Angeles represented the greatest good for the greatest number of people, and on June 28, 1906, he signed the bill that sealed the valley's fate. The aqueduct was completed in 1913, and the city and the valley have been fighting over the city's management of this water resource ever since. Wallace Austin's

Figure 5.1. LA Aqueduct construction, 1912 (Wikimedia Commons)

reputation and spirit were destroyed by the defeat. He resigned his position and retreated to Death Valley; shortly thereafter, Mary left him and moved to the artists' colony at Carmel-by-the-Sea. Eleven years later, in 1917, *The Ford* was published, which Mary had written while living in New York City.[2]

The Owens Valley conflict reflects a larger pattern of Progressive Era water development. Donald Worster, in *Rivers of Empire*, argues that the western United States is a hydraulic society where the manipulation of water in an arid environment has led to a "coercive, monolithic, and hierarchical system, ruled by a power elite based on the ownership of capital and expertise" (7). He notes that by the late nineteenth century, the movement for reclamation of the West had become "a veritable crusade" with a variety of ideological rationalizations (114). Proponents such as Smythe believed that irrigation would lead to more rational, scientific agriculture; it would provide a safe outlet for the overflowing eastern cities; and it would restore manliness to overcivilized Americans, who would develop the characteristics required for imperialistic ventures as they conquered the wasted lands of the desert. Worster points out that to develop its water resources, the West relied upon an army of hydraulic engineers who pushed for increased centralization to avoid the inefficiency of irrigation systems run by individual farmers and ranchers (147). Despite their putative frontier individualism, Westerners increasingly turned to the federal government for capital and technical expertise, and in 1902 the Reclamation Service was created to develop irrigation projects. From the beginning, there was tension between Reclamation's goal of encouraging democracy by providing water to small farms and the actual results of their projects, which mostly increased the wealth of established owners and agribusinesses, what Worster calls "the modern technician-capitalist alliance" (203).

The Ford explores the tensions embedded in progressive water conservation. At the end of the novel, Kenneth Brent attempts to explain to Timothy Rickart his belief "that the earth was the right and property of those who worked it, and that its values should accrue to them if to anybody. Incidentally he said something of his newfound appreciation of the need and power of working together" (436). Rickart immediately links Kenneth's convictions to the larger social movement, asking, "This 'Progressive' business,—I suppose that's something in the same line?" (436). In her autobiography *Earth Horizon* (1932), Austin notes that she was introduced to progressive issues through the Women's Christian Temperance Union, which became a forum "for almost anything you might mention which has since worked to the surface of our national interest among the liberal-minded" (149). In her 1912 essay "Why I Am a Progressive," Austin mentions three issues: women's suffrage, the elimination of child labor, and the conservation of natural resources (4). From 1910 to 1920, Austin lived in New York City, where she became friends with many of the era's most prominent radicals: Lincoln Steffens, John Reed, Margaret Sanger, Emma Goldman, Alice Paul, John Sloan, and Ida Tarbell. Austin immersed herself in the city, wandering through its seamiest neighborhoods and taking lower-class jobs so that she could understand the life of the poor, which she wrote about in articles published in such journals as *The Nation*.[3]

However, Austin remained deeply ambivalent about radical social reform. In 1919, she criticized reformers for not being grounded in the sorrows of life, and in 1925, she complained of their "stale ideas" (qtd. in Goodman and Dawson 154). Even more troubling, in 1913, she seems to have engaged a private detective to gather information about her radical friends, perhaps as material for her novel *No. 26 Jayne Street* (1920), which she described as an attempt to expose "the sleazy quality of current radicalism" (*Earth Horizon* 337). Her detective work might also have been at the behest of her long-term friend Herbert Hoover. During World War I, when Hoover directed the Food Administration, the man Austin called "My dear Chief" relied on her as an advisor on "constructive propaganda" (Goodman and Dawson 146, 157). Austin's distaste for radical reform surfaces in *The Ford* as a linkage between progressive management of a threatening nature and control of social dissidents.

⁂

The water fight depicted in the novel is as complicated as the historical events on which it is based. The main characters are Kenneth and Anne Brent, the children of Steven Brent, a rancher who idealistically dreams of irrigating the Tierra Longa valley. Brent's ranch is destroyed by drought, and his attempt at drilling for oil is equally unsuccessful; ultimately, his failures result in the death of his wife, Molly, who has desired a more urbane life. After the death of their mother, Anne becomes a successful real estate agent, and Kenneth goes to work as a paralegal for the wealthy businessman Timothy Rickart. Anne buys back the family ranch with the help of Rickart, who warns her to abandon her father's dream of building a storage dam. His admonition makes her think that he has his own irrigation plans, but she also suspects that the government is interested in developing a water project. Meanwhile, the shifty Ellwood, who seems to be acting as Rickart's agent, is buying options on land that has water rights. To force the issue, Anne directs Kenneth to file an appropriation on the river surplus that Rickart would need to complete his project. Furthermore, she initiates a newspaper investigation that eventually reveals that Rickart is conspiring with San Francisco to divert Tierra Longa's water to the city. Kenneth tries to organize the ranchers into an association that will force Rickart to pay a high price for the remaining land, thereby making the water grab cost-prohibitive. But his plan is undercut by the inability of the ranchers to unite, and Rickart threatens a lawsuit to gain the appropriation that Kenneth made while he was his employee. Unlike the historical incident, there is a happy ending for the valley: the exposure of the plan leads San Francisco to turn to the Hetch Hetchy valley for its water supply; Anne is able to persuade Rickart to drop the lawsuit; and, with the help of the local ranchers, Kenneth develops a successful irrigation canal and a real estate development.

As Anne Raine has noted, a central conflict in the novel is Kenneth's search for purpose in life. Like his father, Kenneth is driven by the impulse to shape "the purposeful earth," and he hears "the clear call of the empty land to be put to human use" (92, 294). On a trip to Tierra Longa, he feels the fecundity and invitation of the land: "It came and offered itself to the hand, and yet no man had tamed it" (225). But while Kenneth is attracted to pastoralism, he is also driven to succeed in the business world. He realizes that the two influences that have shaped his life are the Torr mountain that overlooks Tierra Longa, which sustains his feeling "of being born to live upon the earth and work it," and his mother's dissatisfaction with rural life, which leads him into business (431). Ultimately, he decides to be a producer of food, affirming, "Land was to be cherished, to be made productive" (403).

As in *Land of Little Rain*, where Austin describes drought as a "squalid tragedy," *The Ford* represents sustained aridity as a threat to the land's productivity (18). Kenneth is haunted by "the famished eyes" of the starving cows, and Steven Brent is dismayed that "the land turns against us" (58, 61). He expresses his outrage that "the beasts die—starve—on our hands. We that took them out of their native state and taught them to depend on our care!" (61). Of course, a possible response to this situation is to reconsider the wisdom of attempting ranching in such an arid region. However, *The Ford* searches instead for a way to manage a threatening nature so as to develop its resources efficiently. The omniscient narrator describes the valley's river anthropomorphically as "swift and full, beginning with the best intentions of turning mills or whirring dynamos, with the happiest possibilities of watering fields and nursing orchards, but, discouraged at last by the long neglect of man, becoming like all wasted things, a mere pest of mud and malaria" (34). As David N. Cassuto points out, "The narrator's claim that rivers (and all other things as well) require human intervention to avoid a sordid and ugly uselessness goes unchallenged despite its apparent incongruity with Austin's oft-stated reverence for nature" (42).

Indeed, the view of reclamation presented in *The Ford* is not very different from that in Hamilton Bell Wright's bestseller *The Winning of Barbara Worth* (1911). Set during the development of California's Imperial Valley, the novel celebrates those who defeat the "sinister" desert and attain "the victory over barrenness and desolation" (218, 236). Concomitant with the reclamation of the desert, the engineer Willard Holmes is transformed from an effete, urban Easterner into a rugged Westerner, fit to claim Barbara Worth, the wholesome daughter of the West, as his bride.[4]

Wright's linkage of his romantic plot with the reclamation of the desert anticipates a similar theme in *The Ford* and raises questions about the ecofeminism that is often attributed to Austin. Many of the male characters represent nature as a feminine entity that requires domination by humans. Steven Brent sees the unirrigated valley like a virgin wife imagined in "full matronly perfection" (35). Perhaps reflecting his own marital difficulties, he insists that the land laughs at us, but "we've got to master her—we've got to compel her" (62). Kenneth's attitude toward the land is subtler and is closely connected to his struggle to understand women in an era when social roles were changing. He puzzles over the success of men like Rickart who were able to establish a "proper relation" to "women and land and things," and he regrets the "waste" of women like his sister, who are too intelligent for most men to accept (172, 372). When his childhood friend Virginia Burke becomes involved in a morally compromised situation, he is tempted to "re-create and reëstablish" her through "a public and exclusive possession" (326), a gesture that exactly parallels his attempt to transform the desert through his water appropriation. Similarly, at the end of the novel, Kenneth professes his love for Ellis Trudeau while standing near the river that provides water to his canal; he takes "a firm proprietary hold" upon her, thus uniting his strategies for taming and making productive both land and women (440).

Of course, this masculine desire for dominance might be contested in the novel, which is how critics such as Anne Raine read these passages. But the evidence for this reading seems scant, especially given the lack of clearly developed ecofeminist alternatives. In *Earth Horizon*, Austin uses the same gendered language, comparing the "spell of the land" that seduced the settlers in the Owens Valley to the power of a beautiful woman: "It is the way Beauty works to set up in men the desire to master and make it fruitful" (270). But she insists that in desert conditions, that impulse to master is threatened by almost-insurmountable obstacles: "To bring such a land to fruitage requires an available water supply, organizing capacity, and that commodity known as capital" (271). In *The Ford*, Austin seems less troubled by the desire to dominate nature than she is by the failure of the capitalist state to effectively organize that domination.[5]

Kenneth is briefly interested in the radical critique of such capitalism when he is drawn into the world of Virginia Burke. But he becomes disillusioned when he recognizes the limitations of the radicals. Initially, he reacts with distaste to the racial otherness of the working men: "Kenneth could feel his soul, sniffing the wind tainted by ineradicable difference of type, answer to the old savage instinct to protect his own by discrediting the unknown, the unconformable" (191). He is then filled with "terror" as the one-eyed labor organizer turns the audience into "a perfectly contrived machine" and wonders, "[D]id anybody know what was to come out of all this?" (192–93). Attracted to Virginia, he reads Kropotkin and Henry George, but he ultimately sees the radical movement as inferior to the acquisitive capitalism of his boss, Rickart.

In contrast to the mechanical metaphors used to depict the socialists, Kenneth sees Rickart's capitalism as "a work of nature, gigantic, inevitable" (245). Austin's depiction of Rickart is certainly based on T. B. Rickey, the major landowner of Inyo County, whose sale of land to Los Angeles insured the success of the city's water grab. But, as Donald Ringler points out, she also drew upon her acquaintance with Henry Miller, the largest cattleman in California, who in the 1880s became involved in a protracted legal struggle that would help to define western water rights (46–49). In *Earth Horizon*, Austin presents Miller sympathetically as driven by "the wisdom of the subjection of the land to the possessorship of man" (204). She praises him for building a canal that prevented the waste of the waters of the Sierras and thus reclaiming land from "desertness" (211). Like Miller, Rickart has made his empire through superior vision: he explains that in contrast to the smaller ranchers, "we look out *better*" (*Ford* 117). Kenneth understands that Rickart's success is based on "knowledge, knowledge of land and minerals, knowledge of law, and, more than everything else, knowledge of men" (437). But Rickart's blind spot is "the human element," the psychological and moral consequences of his business dealings on the people he exploits (385).

Indeed, he seems incapable of acknowledging morality, "the thing which he couldn't always calculate in others or get the better of in himself" (437).

An alternative to Rickart's ruthless individualism is represented by Anne Brent, who seems to be the moral center of the novel. More practical than her brother, she restores the family's finances and rescues Kenneth's reputation. Buell notes that Anne is "every bit as landwise as her father and brother but endowed as well with a keen business sense" (*Writing*, 255). But Buell's celebration of her "pragmatically nuanced ecofeminist ethic of care-based land stewardship" is problematic and ignores the traits she shares with Rickart (255). Both become successful through scientific detachment. When the Brents are constructing an irrigation canal, Anne focuses on only those factors that affect the construction, and she has little interest in the desert environment, "the intimate properties of earth, the burrow folk dispossessed, the shrubs uprooted" (414). Likewise, both Anne and Rickart take delight in "the stalking of a man's secret thought in his mind," and she shares his sense of the interrelatedness of things, "the way in which inconsiderable items jumped together in his mind" (274).[6]

Unlike Rickart, however, Anne does not ignore the human element. Instead, she seeks to integrate psychology with her practice of real estate as a "liberal profession," which she defines as matching the different parcels of land with specific types of farmers (200). She observes, "Many a man fancied himself a vine grower, whereas he had been equipped by nature for general cropping" (200). Every property that Anne sells is accompanied with a report on the soil and the crops that are best suited to it, and she is frustrated that she cannot have a similar analysis of her clients. The university analyzes the soil of the property she sells, but she complains that "there's nobody can analyze the man that wants to buy it from me" (234).

Anne's dream of a science that would fit people to their natural place in society was very quickly becoming a reality in the early twentieth century. Indeed, rather than a protoecofeminism, Anne seems to be influenced by the new discipline of industrial psychology, which attempted to use scientific methods to help managers select the best employees and then to maximize the efficiency of their work. A key technology of industrial psychology was standardized intelligence testing. Originally designed to distinguish among different levels of mental disability, intelligence tests took on a new role during World War I, when the army used them to place recruits. After the war, they were widely adopted by businesses and reflect the ecological assumption that if society is an interconnected organism, it is crucial that each individual be fitted to his or her proper niche.[7]

From the beginning, industrial psychology linked the elimination of wasted time and effort in industry to progressive efficient use of natural resources. Frederick Winslow Taylor, in *The Principles of Scientific Management* (1911) noted, "We can see our forests vanishing, our water-powers going to waste, our soil being carried by floods into the sea; and the end of our coal and our iron is in sight. But our larger wastes of human effort . . . are less visible, less tangible, and are but vaguely appreciated" (5). Likewise, James Hartness, in *The Human Factor* (1912), stressed the importance of discovering men's "natural work—the work in which they most efficiently use their energies and in which they get the best development of mind and body" (33). Worster notes that in the 1920s the failures of the Reclamation Service to live up to its agrarian mission led to social engineering experiments to train farmers to work the land appropriately; governmental experts began "fitting people to the apparatus" (*Rivers* 180).

A similar integration of the control of nature and the control of people is evident in *The Ford*. Rickart replaces his ranch superintendent because he needs "more scientific management," and after Stephen Brent is ruined by the oil business, he is offered a job at the mill, where they were looking for "some man who could be trusted to get out of the boys the work that you know in reason is in them" (65, 141). Significantly, Anne identifies mismatches between farmers and their land as the primary cause of radicalism: she insists, "I can make a Socialist out of a prune man . . . by keeping him six years on a piece of ground that was only meant to grow potatoes" (234). In contrast to her hypothetical socialists, the Mexicans in the novel know their place and humbly submit to their natural role. When the white children discuss potential future careers, Ignacio Stanislauo remains silent: "[P]erhaps he knew as well as they what was foredoomed in his blood" (46).

On the other hand, the white rural folk of Tierra Longa are depicted rather unsympathetically as individualistic rubes who are desperately in need of scientific management. When the oil well in which Steven Brent and Pop Scudder invests gushers, signaling disaster for their hopes and the waste of a natural resource, Scudder reacts with childish wonder at the height of the gusher (107–08). The ranchers' fundamental problem is that the solitary nature of their life makes them incapable of working together towards a common goal. Their irrigation projects are compromised by their "invincible rurality," and Kenneth becomes frustrated because they "plotted without knowledge and imagined childishly" (221, 289). But when he fails to organize the valley to resist the scheme to divert their water, Anne lectures him that he does not understand the psychology of the locals: "It's true they weren't with you, but then you weren't within a mile of them. Maybe if you'd been a little closer, they could have come the rest of the way" (431). He gradually begins to comprehend the people of Tierra Longa, and at the end of the novel, he is able to secure their cooperation in his canal project.[8]

⁓

There has been little critical discussion of the role of oil production in *The Ford*, despite the fact that it dominates the first third of the novel.[9] Paul Sabin, in *Crude Politics*, points out that the early twentieth-century California oil industry was driven by rapid development and an inefficient waste of natural resources. The federal government essentially gave away the mineral rights of public lands to speed economic development, and the rule of capture encouraged oil companies to extract oil rapidly because they were in competition with those drilling on neighboring properties who might be tapping the same subsurface pools. The resulting overproduction led to fears among progressive conservationists that the nation's oil resources would soon be depleted. Accordingly, in 1912, President William Taft set aside land in the San Joaquin valley of California as a petroleum reserve for the navy, and over the next several decades the oil industry and the government struggled to establish rational production and stable prices. Ultimately, however, Sabin argues that neither voluntary nor governmental efforts were effective, and the wasteful overproduction in California became "part of a recurrent pattern in the American oil industry" (112). In addition to squandering a natural resource, the California oil industry was dangerous and environmentally destructive. Nancy Quam-Wickham discusses the frequent blow-outs, gushers, and well fires, as well as the pervasive pollution caused by oil spills (191–94).

In *The Ford*, Austin depicts the oil industry negatively, comparing the wells to "great ticks sucking the black juices of the land" (145). The owners are driven to produce inefficiently, regardless of demand: one of Stephen Brent's associates insists, "Once you know where the stuff is, you're losing money every day it's in the ground" (98). The Brent well gushes, and when it finally ceases, "nothing was left of it but the shimmering, stinking pool that spread far over the adjacent land and fouled the ancient bed of the river" (130). The oil is wasted, the environment is degraded, and the locals are ruined by the machinations of the capitalists who control the pipeline that brings the oil to market; eventually, the spilled oil catches on fire. To the young Kenneth, the derricks seem to represent an ungovernable natural power: he fears that the thing "which men had made had grown suddenly too big for them and was stirring in its own control" (145).[10]

But the novel suggests that control of this resource is still possible. While recognizing the threat posed by oil development, Kenneth also feels the "purposeful earth" even in the oil boom town, and he insists that the constructed derricks are as natural as trees, "for does not iron come up out of the earth even as oak and pine?" (92). He realizes that the wells talk of "the absurdities and limitations of men," the lack of vision that results in the waste of a precious natural resource (92). Thus, the threat is not the oil extraction itself, but rather "power ungoverned by sensibility" (145). Indeed, at the end of the novel, Rickart reveals that his experts have discovered oil on the Brent ranch, and he promises to help Anne extract it. Thus, whether it is an oil field or a water ditch, Austin reconciles the threat and the promise of nature through the concept of "sensibility," which seems similar to Gifford Pinchot's definition of progressive conservation as "the wise use of the earth and its resources for the lasting good of men" (*Breaking* 505).

This progressive conservationist view of nature is evident in Austin's other works, where she celebrates the human effort to control and develop nature. In *Earth Horizon*, she describes the insect plague that attacked the farms in Illinois as the "epic struggle of man with the creeping, flying things for the fruits of the earth" (48). When she moved to California and first saw the desert, she was drawn to it as "beauty-in-the-wild, yearning to be made human" (187). As a teacher near Bakersfield, she enjoyed watching "the confused activities of subduing the land to human use and occupancy" (227–28). In *California: The Land of the Sun*, a promotional book that she wrote in 1914, she describes the Central Valley's irrigation pumps as "strenuous little Davids contending against the Goliaths of drouth" (136). Even *The Land of Little Rain*, her putative tribute to untamed nature, devotes a chapter to irrigation canals, in which she insists, "It is the proper destiny of every considerable stream in the west to become an irrigating ditch. It would seem the streams are willing" (85).

☙

The question of whom or what Austin blames for the water grab has preoccupied critics. For Susan Goodman and Carl Dawson, her target is big business, especially the corruption of politics by capitalism (161). Similarly, John Walton sees the novel as a class struggle between "the rich, urban, and powerful bent upon dispossessing the humble poor" (*Western Times* 225).

William L. Kahrl argues that Austin does not represent Los Angeles as the villain, perhaps because the novel was written "at a time when relations between the city and the valley were at their best, and it still seemed possible to imagine a future of prosperity for the valley" (325).

In *Earth Horizon*, Austin narrates the water grab from an oddly passive perspective. She notes, "The Reclamation Service had been won over. The field papers had changed hands. Transfers had been made. Sales had been effected" (307). She accuses Fred Eaton (the source for Elwood) of "spying and buying" and notes that "there were lies and misrepresentations," but, on the whole, Austin describes it as an act of an impersonal fate (307). When it had become clear that the city would win, Austin takes a walk in the fields and seeks spiritual guidance, asking what she can do: "She called upon the Voice, and the Voice answered her—Nothing. She was told to go away" (308). The passivity of this experience is curiously inconsistent with the activist spirituality depicted elsewhere in *Earth Horizon*, a spirituality that gives her confidence that "there is always something to be done about everything. Man is not alone nor helpless in the universe" (276).

But if the novel does not specifically critique the city of Los Angeles, it does seem to identify the rapid growth of cities as a threat to rural integrity. When Rickart's plan is first revealed, Steven Brent sadly reflects on his lost dream of "water and power . . . and farms . . . farms, not cities" (361). Rickart's somewhat decadent son Frank has "an air of cities about all he did," and the conniving Elwood is able to trick the valley people because he diffuses "the bright air of cities" (104, 410). When Elwood drunkenly boasts that "he had looted the wilderness; he had led a river captive," the narrator explains his motivation as urban boosterism, his vision of "the river dammed and stored, not to unending fruitfulness, as Steven Brent had seen it, but of an arched, concreted aqueduct leading from the Gate to the city's faucets; a vision worthy of the most exalted cult of Locality" (365–67).

In a 1931 letter to Sinclair Lewis, Austin outlined her plan for a three-part history of Western water development; she described the phase covered by *The Ford* as "how the cities 'framed' the farmers and stole the river for the use of the realtors" (qtd. in Goodman and Dawson, 216). Throughout *Earth Horizon*, Austin reacts against the modernizing tendency of cities. Her first impression of Los Angeles was a place where "natural beauty" was "slavered over with the impudicity of a purely material culture" (188–89). She notes that she lived in Carmel-by-the-Sea before it was destroyed by "the metamorphosis of asphalt, concrete, and carbon monoxide, which go in the world of realtors by the name of improvements" (301). Likewise, she nostalgically eulogizes the Owens Valley as a place where "modern America has laid a greedy, vulgarizing hand" (234).

In any case, the villain is clearly not irrigation culture. In addition to providing him with meaningful work, Kenneth's experiences working outdoors developing his canal keep him from becoming an overcivilized, effete city boy: "He grew brown and leaner and at ease with himself" (414). Despite her ecological sensitivity and an awareness of the problems with irrigation that she might have developed through Wallace's failed colony, Mary Austin remained thoroughly committed to progressive reclamation throughout her life. In 1905, in the midst of the campaign by Los Angles to divert the valley's water, Austin represented the fundamental problem as "how far it is well to destroy the agriculture interests of the commonwealth to the advantage of the vast aggregations of the cities" ("Owens River" 19). Similarly, in 1927, when she was representing Arizona at the Boulder Dam conference, she objected that in the proposed plan "irrigation demands are sacrificed to power prospects" ("Colorado" 511). Rather than rejecting the construction of any dam, Austin supported Arizona governor George Wiley Hunt's proposal to build a state-controlled dam at Glen Canyon rather than a federal dam at Boulder Canyon. Caught up in the Western enthusiasm for water projects, Austin did not seem to be concerned with the environmental implications of efforts to move water in order to make arid lands habitable.[11]

When "the Voice" told Austin that nothing further could be done to stop the aqueduct, she left the Owens Valley, knowing "that the land of Inyo would be desolated" (*Earth Horizon* 308). After the completion of the aqueduct in 1913, the relationship between Los Angeles and the valley varied. Before 1920, there was little change since the city's withdrawals from the river were negligible, and the ranchers in the valley hoped that the relationship to the city would prove profitable. But a series of droughts in the 1920s led Los Angeles to divert more water, destroying the agriculture of the valley and returning it to desert conditions. Failed attempts at negotiation with the city led to protests and violence: between 1924 and 1927, valley residents seized control of the water gates and repeatedly dynamited the aqueduct. But Los Angeles refused to back down and kept acquiring additional water rights that would guarantee its dominance in the valley; accordingly, after 1930, the valley was little more than a colony of the city. Limited ranching was permitted on leased lands, and Los Angeles promoted the valley's potential for recreational tourism. In 1936, geographer Ruth E. Baugh described the Owens Valley as a wasteland that was slowly reverting to nature: "Land formerly productive has turned to sage brush, and commodious farm buildings are now in ruins. Weed-choked irrigation ditches, abandoned farm machinery, and rows of stark, bleached tree trunks identify the sites of former ranches" (qtd. in Ewan 134).

During World War II, the government erected the Manzanar Japanese internment camp in the valley, and, after the war, Hollywood found its stark conditions to be an ideal setting for westerns and science-fiction movies. In 1970, when Los Angeles completed a second aqueduct, hostilities between the city and the valley erupted again since the groundwater pumping that was necessary to fill it destroyed vegetation, negatively affected wildlife, and created massive dust storms. Accordingly, the residents of the valley used the new legal weapons made possible by the environmental movement to sue the city. The subsequent legal battles were not settled until 2006, when Los Angeles was forced to limit their groundwater pumping and to rewater sixty miles of the lower Owens River.[12]

The valley's environmental struggles are part of the larger war on drought that has been central to the development of the American West. In *Cadillac Desert*, Marc Reisner describes the period of the 1930s to the 1970s as the "Go-Go Years," when the Bureau of Reclamation and the Army Corps of Engineers built thousands of dams and other projects in the West to provide flood control, irrigation, and cheap hydroelectric power. He points out that the environmental consequences of those efforts have been dam collapses, over-pumping of groundwater, salt poisoning of soil from irrigation runoff, and silt buildup that will soon render the dams obsolete (379–476). Likewise, Worster predicts that the post–World War II hydraulic society will face three problems: an ever-increasing demand for water that exceeds the quantity available; a steady deterioration of water quality from fertilizers, pesticides, and salinization; and a growing movement among the public to prevent further degradation of pristine ecological communities (*Rivers* 310).

One contemporary of Austin who foresaw the potential environmental consequences of reclamation was John C. Van Dyke, who published *The Desert* two years before *The Land of Little Rain*. Like Austin, Van Dyke sees the desert as a site of savage beauty, an antimodern alternative to the city that simplifies the complexity of modern life: "The joy of mere animal existence, the feeling that it is good to be alive and face to face with Nature's self, drives everything else into the background" (200). But, unlike Austin, Van Dyke emphatically rejects all efforts to irrigate the desert, insisting,

"The deserts should never be reclaimed. They are the breathing-spaces of the west and should be preserved forever" (59). He expresses contempt for the practical men of mining, lumbering, and agriculture, who have destroyed the beauty of nature and replaced it with "weeds, wire fences, oil-derricks, board shanties and board towns" (61). He warns that ultimately nature will send sustained drought to subvert man's reclamation efforts and restore the desert (228). In contrast to Van Dyke, Austin had a progressive, instrumental view of nature: like Chopin and Sinclair, Austin suggests that, left unmanaged, nature is a threat, but with expert control, the natural world can ease tensions among women, immigrants, and social radicals.[13]

Focusing primarily on *The Land of Little Rain*, ecocritics have insisted upon Austin's ecological credentials in ways that diminish her complexity. Anna Carew-Miller argues that Austin's men try to master the land: "[T]his is not only the 'mastery' of dams and fences, but also the scientific approach to the natural world that tries to diminish its power by dissecting it intellectually. For men, the desire that the land stirs is for possession and control; the result, according to Austin, is eternal damnation" (90). Vera Norwood insists that Austin "espouses a humility before nature that entails rejecting the burgeoning scientific and technological approaches to the wilderness" ("Heroines" 334). Likewise, Benay Blend notes that unlike Mary Hallock Foote, who "falls quite squarely into the irrigationist camp," Austin "opposed any ideology that ignored the repercussions of unlimited mastery over the environment" ("Victorian Gentlewoman," 97–98).

Perhaps ecocritics have insisted so vigorously upon Austin's ecofeminist awareness because *The Land of Little Rain* is a significant work of nature writing in a field that is far too top-heavy with male writers. And it is equally possible that John C. Van Dyke's relative obscurity can be attributed at least in part to his status as a minor white male author, rather than to any superior ecological awareness in Austin's work. In any case, the ecocritical canonization of Austin should take into account the ambivalence of her environmental ideology. Writing at a time when nature could be seen as threatened, threatening, and useful, Austin negotiated between a sensitivity towards nonhuman nature and a confidence in progressive manipulation of both the natural and the human.

Chapter 6

Surveilling Wilderness in Dreiser's *An American Tragedy*

On July 11, 1906, Chester Gillette and Grace Brown rented a small boat from the Glennmore Hotel at Big Moose Lake in the Adirondacks. When they had not returned by the next morning, a search was initiated, and within a few hours, the overturned boat and Grace's body were found in a small bay of the lake. The subsequent police investigation revealed that Grace was pregnant and that she had been having a sexual relationship with Chester, her supervisor at the Cortland, New York, skirt factory at which they worked. Chester was arrested, and his trial and conviction for murder drew widespread attention.[1] One avid reader of the newspaper accounts of the trial was Theodore Dreiser, who saw the case as the consummate example of the American-Dream-gone-wrong story that he had long contemplated writing. Dreiser studied court records and newspaper accounts of the Gillette trial, and, in July of 1923, he and his then mistress Helen Richardson (later Dreiser) toured the sites associated with the murder. His 1925 novel, *An American Tragedy*, is an imaginative retelling of the incident at Big Moose Lake.[2]

Unlike Mary Austin, there has been little ecocritical discussion of Dreiser. Cara Elana Erdheim focuses on the role of water in *An American Tragedy*, arguing that "the novel's hierarchy of lakes shows readers how waters function differently depending upon the status of those using them" (3). Consistent with the resistance narrative of recent ecocriticism, she discusses his "environmental advocacy" and suggests that *An American Tragedy* anticipates the environmental justice movement by exposing "the inseparability of class-based and environmental injustices" (5, 3). In contrast, I see the novel's environmental themes paralleling early twentieth-century fears about the potential lawlessness of unsupervised spaces. *An American Tragedy* suggests that as progressive conservation produced recreational wilderness areas to relieve the stress of industrial civilization, new technologies of surveillance were implemented to ensure that these areas did not turn into sites of resistance to social order.

∽

The time between the Gillette case and the publication of Dreiser's novel was a period of profound change in the history of the Adirondacks. While recreational tourism in the area began in the 1840s, it was not until the turn of the century that the railroads had opened up areas such as the Fulton Chain of Lakes (the setting for the murder). Subsequently, a summer trip to the Adirondacks became fashionable, and by the mid-1920s, this tourism was peaking, as the wealthy flocked to the region's resort hotels and great camps.[3] In 1915, the legal struggle to protect the Adirondack wilderness that had begun in the 1870s culminated in a revision to the New York State Constitution guaranteeing that the publicly owned parts of the Adirondacks would become a forest preserve, permanently protected from lumbering. As Philip Terrie argues, the impetus for this legislation was primarily a desire to protect the state's watersheds; indeed, the conservation agencies created to administer the Forest Preserve resented the "forever wild" clause and hoped to revoke it and institute scientific forestry in its place. However, Terrie notes that after World War I, there was a growing recognition of the value of the aesthetic and recreational potential of the Adirondack wilderness (92–135).

The protection of the Adirondacks was not achieved without significant tensions between the Forest Commission and the approximately sixteen thousand people who were living in the area. Karl Jacoby argues that the creation of the Adirondack Forest Preserve "established a viable new role for the state: active supervisor of the environment" (17). The first step was surveying and mapping the park so that standardized practices could replace local laws and customs. To enforce the new game and timber laws, the state created a forest police, whose numbers grew steadily throughout the early twentieth century. One challenge faced by the Forest Commission was the presence of squatters on what was now state land. Jacoby points out that the fear of violence from squatters resulted in a policy of "benign neglect" until 1900, when the Forest Commission began forcibly evicting them (33). Other tensions were created by attempts to enforce the new timber and game laws. The locals also resented the rapid growth of private parks owned by the wealthy: by 1893 nearly a million acres of the best hunting

Figure 6.1. Big Moose Lake postcard, ca. 1929. South Bay, where Grace Brown drowned, is on the far side of the lake, directly opposite the figures.

and fishing land in the Adirondacks had been surveyed and marked with barbed-wire fences and "No Trespassing" signs.

Adirondack natives responded to the changed circumstances in various ways. Jacoby notes that there was an outbreak of vandalism and violence in the early years of the twentieth century as residents destroyed signs, cut fences surrounding private parks, and shot at security guards. Between 1899 and 1913, arsonists started a series of forest fires that resulted in the burning of over a million acres. Locals ignored timber laws, and they poached game, including animals such as moose and elk that were being reintroduced by the Forest Commission. This resistance was met with increased methods of control and surveillance. Jacoby notes that additional foresters and private security guards were hired, "turning the Adirondacks of the early 1900s into a tense, armed camp" (42) William Rockefeller installed floodlights around the perimeter of his private estate, and to fight arson the Forest Commission built a series of fire towers: by 1914, fifty-one of these "observation stations" had been erected.

Tensions exploded in 1903, when Orrando Dexter, a millionaire owner of a private park, who had angered locals by suing trespassers, was fatally shot while driving on his estate. Pinkerton detectives were hired, and Dexter's father offered a $10,000 reward, but the murderer was never found.[4] The response to the Dexter murder and other similar incidents illustrates turn-of-the-century fears that the Adirondack wilderness might become a place where crimes could be committed outside the gaze of law. The *New York City Sun* described the area where Dexter was murdered as "a lonely spot, and a place where a murderer could be secreted in the woods and not be seen by anyone passing" ("O. P. Dexter's" 1). The solidarity of the locals increased the potential for concealment. The Forest Commission complained that locals "often profess to be unable to recognize their nearest neighbors while cutting State timber a few rods away. . . . Every conceivable evasion is resorted to" (qtd. in Jacoby 51). In 1904, a *New York Times* article noted the dangers faced by guards on William Rockefeller's private estate: "Several of these guards have been fired at recently while patrolling their lonely beats in the dense forest. . . . As smokeless powder has been used in every case, all efforts to locate and capture these 'snipers' have proved futile" (qtd. in Jacoby 42). The *Plattsburgh Sentinel* warned that "if the murderer of Dexter went undiscovered and unpunished it would tend to breed crimes of a similar nature against others of his class and a reign of terror throughout a wide territory" ("Hunt" 5).

Despite these clashes, the 1915 protection of the Adirondacks inspired a broader twentieth-century movement to set aside recreational wilderness areas. In the 1920s, Aldo Leopold, a US forester in New Mexico, published a series of articles calling for the protection of remnant wild areas within the national park and forest system. In "Wilderness as a Form of Land Use" (1925), he defined wilderness recreationally, as "a wild, roadless area where those who are so inclined may enjoy primitive modes of travel and subsistence" (*River* 135). In 1924, as Dreiser was completing *An American Tragedy*, Leopold's efforts resulted in the establishment of the Gila Wilderness as the first officially designated wilderness area. In 1935 Leopold, Robert Marshall, Benton MacKaye, and five others formed the Wilderness Society to lobby for permanent protection of these areas, similar to the "forever wild" status of the Adirondacks. Their work culminated in the 1964 Wilderness Act, which preserved 9 million acres of wild land.[5] But, as the conflicts in the Adirondacks suggest, the production of such areas can create lawless zones outside the gaze of the state. In *An American Tragedy*, surveillance reconciles the recreational potential of wilderness areas with the need for social control.

As Ellen Moers has discussed, Dreiser's view of human nature was shaped by both psychological and environmental determinism, but Sigmund Freud's theories had an especially powerful influence on him. In 1931 Dreiser recalled that Freud's work was "a strong, revealing light thrown on some of the darkest problems that haunted and troubled me and my work" ("Remarks," 250). In particular, Dreiser was influenced by Freud's analysis of the antagonism between the desires of the individual and the repressions of civilized society. Freud's most sustained discussion of this opposition is in *Civilization and Its Discontents* (1930), but the concept is suggested in earlier works, especially, "'Civilized' Sexual Morality and Modern Nervous Illness" (1908), where he discusses "the harmful suppression of the sexual life of civilized peoples (or classes) through the 'civilized' sexual morality prevalent in them" (185). In *An American Tragedy*, Clyde Griffiths's search for places where his desires can be fulfilled without social consequences leads him to the Adirondack wilderness.[6]

From the beginning of the novel, Clyde is depicted as being in conflict with society's codes, especially in regards to human sexuality. He grows up in a deeply religious family, and through their street ministry, he is constantly exposed to the humiliating gaze of strangers. Clyde's nature is "innately sensual and romantic," and, like a Horatio Alger Jr. character, he is driven by desire: he was "constantly thinking of how he might better himself, if he had a chance; places to which he might go, things he might see, and how differently he might live, if only this, that and the other thing were true" (72, 11). Clyde's early experiences with sexuality create tension with the strict social code he has learned from his parents. He is fascinated by the world of prostitution, but his budding libertinism is challenged when his sister Esta is abandoned after becoming pregnant. Ultimately, Clyde concludes that rather than sex itself, the problem was "the consequences which followed upon not thinking or not knowing" (112). In other words, with shrewdness, one could enjoy pleasures without consequences. However, Clyde's frustrating pursuit of a sexual relationship with Hortense Briggs leads to the accident that forces him to flee Kansas City, and, as a result, he resolves to imitate "the soberer people of the world" and remain "indifferent" to sex, which he now sees as "a disgraceful passion" (192–93).

In Lycurgus, Clyde meets his wealthy uncle, Samuel Griffiths, who becomes a surrogate father and offers him a chance to attain his dreams of success. Griffiths adheres to a code of psychological scarcity, whereby those aspiring to improve their social standing must "become inured to a narrow and abstemious life" (201). Clyde's cousin Gil, who resents him as a rival for his father's affection, delivers an injunction against relationships with women under his supervision. He emphasizes that since Clyde is a member of the Griffiths family, he must become his own observer; he tells him to "be on your guard and watch your step" (267). Accordingly, Clyde is placed in a dilemma: strongly driven by sexual desire, he is banned from relationships with factory women; his social aspirations prevent him from considering marriage to a woman of a lower class; and he is blocked by a lack of opportunity and means to develop relationships with upper-class women. Since Clyde is subject to constant surveillance in both the factory and the city, he tries to internalize the Griffith code and "to conduct himself always as his cousin wished" (266).

Soon, the constant contact with the women of the factory under working conditions designed to promote escapist fantasy leads Clyde to consider the possibility of enjoying a relationship "without detection on the part of any one" (273). As he becomes involved with Roberta Alden, Clyde imagines a privacy that proves to be illusory. Clyde and Roberta assume that they are outside of society's gaze: "Not having been detected to date, they were of the notion that it was possible they might not be" (349). Although they are certain that their trip to a local resort is "quite unobserved," they are seen by Roberta's roommates (324). Likewise, Roberta's new room seems private, but witnesses will later testify at the trial that they were aware of Clyde's visits (749).

Because of his physical similarity to Gil Griffiths, Clyde draws the attention of Sondra Finchley, who represents "wealth, beauty, the peculiar social state to which he most aspired" (356). From the beginning, their relationship is based on spectacle. Clyde observes Sondra, who observes Clyde watching her; indeed, Clyde's scopophilia is what makes him attractive to her (368). In Lycurgus, sexuality is carefully structured according to class lines, and Sondra explains that their relationship must remain a secret from her parents. At first, this is possible because Clyde confounds the social structure: although he is one of the Griffiths, he has little money. Thus, Sondra's mother, although of "an especially shrewd and discerning turn socially," assumes that Clyde is "more solidly placed in this world than she had heard" and fails to see the significance of the developing relationship (484–85).

As he becomes more deeply involved with Sondra, Clyde briefly wonders about the effect that knowledge of his infidelity would have on Roberta, but once again his ability to deny reality through his fantasies of privacy enables him to dismiss these concerns: "She could not see into his mind, could she—become aware of any such extra experiences as this unless he told her" (361). Clyde's libido leads to further involvement with Roberta, and, given their lack of knowledge of birth control, the inevitable result is pregnancy. Clyde's efforts to obtain help are frustrated by his resemblance to Gil and by the suspicious gaze of the town. Consequently, as Roberta becomes more visibly pregnant and threatens to go to his family, he faces "exposure and destruction" (470).

Since he insisted on his innocence to the end, we do not know why Chester Gillette selected Big Moose Lake as the place to murder Grace. One of Dreiser's changes to the original story is to provide an explanation for this choice: Clyde's desire to evade the surveilling gaze of civilization. A few weeks before the murder, Clyde travels to Big Bittern Lake (the fictional Big Moose Lake) with Sondra's friends, and the solitude and remoteness of the Adirondacks suggest an escape from his dilemma. Clyde is impressed with "the desolate and for the most part lonely character of the region" and thinks of it as "almost tenantless" (525–26). The narrator notes, "He did not realize it, but at the moment his own subconscious need was contemplating the loneliness and the usefulness at times of such a lone spot as this" (526).

When Clyde returns to Lycurgus and faces more demands from Roberta, he is torn between his desire to escape the threat of public exposure and his fear of violating the social code. He walks into the countryside surrounding Lycurgus, seeking solitude, so as "not to be heard in his thinking" (530). Later, he is reminded of the loneliness of Big Bittern by a genii or efrit, who represents "some leering and diabolic wish or wisdom concealed in his own nature" (532). The narrator points out that in certain situations, a weak individual can become a victim of "temporary unreason," so that "mistaken or erroneous counsel would appear to hold against all else" (532). In Freudian terms, Clyde is in a state of denial, and his rational ego is dominated by his unconscious desires.

Each time Clyde acknowledges the possibility of being observed by others, the efrit reassures him that he will be safe by emphasizing the deserted nature of the Adirondacks. Thus, as he drifts towards the murder, Clyde continually represses opportunities to comprehend reality accurately. At Grass Lake, he recognizes that there are too many people and thinks that he is "probably continually observed," a surveillance that is symbolized by the pines, which seem like "armed and watchful giants" (550). On the trip to Big Bittern, he suddenly realizes that the guide might remember him and that there could be witnesses at the lake; he reflects, "[H]ow strange he had not thought of that. This lake was probably not nearly as deserted as he had imagined" (553). But the defense mechanism of denial enables him to suppress these problematic thoughts.

At Big Bittern, Clyde continues to replace external reality with his desire for freedom. Climbing into the boat, he feels disconnected from reality. Roberta seems "an almost nebulous figure" as she steps into "an insubstantial rowboat upon a purely ideational lake" (556). Clyde briefly worries that someone might be observing him, but he reassures himself of the complete absence of people. The changes that Dreiser makes to the geography of the lake help to enable Clyde's distortion of reality. The Glennmore Hotel was located at the southern end of Big Moose Lake, 1.75 miles directly west of South Bay, where the drowning took place. Sitting on the veranda of the hotel, one could see the bay, but not with any clarity. Dreiser shifts the orientation of the lake from east-west to north-south and almost doubles its length from four miles to seven. He places the hotel at the far north end of Big Bittern, at least five miles from the bay, and shifts the position of a large island so that it further blocks the view. Finally, he makes Big Bittern less heavily tenanted than Big Moose. Big Bittern has only one hotel and no permanent camps, but at the time of the Gillette murder, Big Moose had seven hotels or camps, and there were nine in 1923, when Dreiser visited the lake. The net effect of these changes is to reinforce Clyde's confidence that he is hidden from any potential observers.

Once he enters the fatal bay, Clyde rapidly moves through a series of psychological states that distorts his perception of external reality. At first, he feels a strange comfort from the scenery, which suggests a place of refuge for "one who was weary of life and cares" (560). He then realizes that the comfort comes from the suggestion of death, but a death that represents an escape from his problems. This comforting nature becomes personified as Clyde feels "the grip of some seemingly strong, and yet friendly sympathetic, hands," as he slips "away from the reality of all things" (560–61). But then the comforting presence is replaced by a vision of an unsympathetic nature: he feels cold as he gazes into "the fascinating and yet treacherous depths" of the lake (561). The cry of a bird reminds him of his problems, but he cannot determine whether the cry is a warning, a protest, or a condemnation. In a daze, Clyde continues to drift toward the planned murder. At the critical moment, he is torn between "a powerful compulsion to do and yet not to do," as he is driven to attain his desire, while fearing the censure of society (563). Paralyzed by a sense of his own cowardice, Clyde is unable to act until Roberta moves to comfort him.

Impulsively striking out at her, he accidentally knocks her into the water and then passively watches her drown.

Clyde's subsequent flight to Sondra and her friends at the Indian Chain (the fictional equivalent of the Fulton Chain) suggests that he is not alone in his denial of external reality. For the wealthy, the Adirondacks represent an escapist world of natural beauty and outdoor recreation. The younger generation sees the wilderness as a private place where intimacies between lovers can take place unobserved by parents. Sondra promises Clyde that the proposed camping trip to Bear Lake will provide "opportunities for love—canoe trips on the lake—hours of uninterrupted love-making" (617). Just as Clyde effaces the locals who would later testify against him, the wealthy residents of the great camps and resort hotels of the Indian Chain ignore the presence of the Adirondack natives who are necessary to make their recreation possible. Like Clyde, Stuart Finchley sees Big Bittern as devoid of people: "[I]t's so different, scarcely any one living up here at all, it seems" (528).

But the novel insists upon the presence of the Adirondack natives. As Cara Erdheim notes, the wealthy "cannot detach themselves from the workforce that has helped to maintain these spaces of lakeside recreation" (9). On the camping trip to Bear Lake, the hard work is performed by the cooks and servants who accompany the rich tourists. When Sondra's friends go on a car tour, an unnamed guide at Big Bittern reveals the ambivalence that locals felt over the rapid development of outdoor recreation in the area. Harley Baggot asks about the fishing opportunities, and the guide promotes Big Bittern as a potential destination but then cautions against excess: "I've seen a coupla men bring back as many as seventy-five fish in two hours. That oughta satisfy anybody that ain't tryin' to ruin the place for the rest of us" (527).

Most crucially, the repressed locals emerge as observers of criminality. Once Clyde actually commits the murder, he discovers that the Adirondacks are far from tenantless; instead, recreational development has turned the wilderness into a panopticon. As he makes his way through "a dark, uninhabited wood," he is discovered by three hunters, who later testify at his trial (566). The prosecution establishes his movements on the day of the crime through 127 witnesses—train conductors, hotel employees, guides, boat keepers—mostly connected with the outdoor recreation industry (754–59). The most damaging witness is a tourist who had been camping on Big Bittern: she testifies that while fishing on the lake, she heard a cry that came from the direction of the bay. As the prosecution develops its case, Clyde is entranced by "the unbreakable chain of facts that could thus be built up by witnesses from such varying and unconnected and unexpected places" (756).

Clyde's illusory sense of the Adirondacks as a lawless, deserted wilderness is destroyed, and he is arrested, tried, and convicted. His experience in the criminal justice system reveals the intersection of a culture of surveillance with a new awareness of a subconscious realm that requires observation. Although he is caught and convicted, the state's disciplinary machinery remains unable to understand Clyde's crime because its agents are destabilized by the intrusion of the psychological. Prosecutor Orville Mason was unattractive as an adolescent, so he suffers from "what the Freudians are accustomed to describe as a psychic sex scar," and he cannot see Clyde as anything other than a monster (578). Mr. Catchuman, a trained cross-examiner sent by the Griffiths' lawyer, is equally unsuccessful in his attempt to extract the truth because he is "too legal, chilling,—unemotional" (677). Clyde's lawyer, Alvin Belknap, impregnated a woman before he was married, and thus he is in a better position to understand his client. Before he introduces himself, he secretly observes Clyde crying in his cell, and then, his sympathy aroused, he listens carefully as Clyde tries to tell him the truth. But the confession leaves Belknap "wearied and confused," and he agrees with his partner, Reuben Jephson, that no jury would believe the truth, so they develop the defense that Clyde was a "moral coward" (684, 698). And Clyde withholds the most significant details of the truth even from his sympathetic lawyers: he realizes that "never, even to Jephson and Belknap, had he admitted that when Roberta was in the water he had not wished to save her" (817).

During the trial, Clyde is subject to the "persistent gaze" of everyone in the courtroom (765). Accordingly, he is carefully coached by Jephson on the theatrics of innocence: "Now you're not going to get frightened or show any evidence of nervousness at anything that may be said or done at any time, are you, Clyde?" (724). Even Clyde's mother is part of the scrutiny: in a humiliating return to the spectacle of Clyde's childhood, she becomes a newspaper correspondent, whose duty is to interview her son. After Clyde's conviction, everyone in the courtroom wants to "see how he was taking it" (849).

The close observation of Clyde continues as he awaits execution, suggesting that his interior self must be conformed to the judgment of society. Some of that reshaping is accomplished by the physical space of the prison. The narrator details the recent structural changes to the death house, noting that although it was ostensibly modified by a humane desire to avoid solitary confinement, the real effect was to create a site for psychological reformation. The layout of the new death house eliminates "true privacy" and exposes the prisoners to the constant watchful gaze of both the guards and the other prisoners (872). Although curtains keep the convicts from seeing the procession to the electric chair, the design of the prison makes them even more intensely aware of each execution. Thus, the effect of the new architecture is to lead the convicted to self-examination and confession of their sins.

Society's final effort to imprint its sentence onto Clyde's consciousness comes from the Reverend Duncan McMillan. Like Belknap, McMillan secretly observes Clyde in his cell before he introduces himself and then works to bring him to confession. One of the first biblical passages he quotes is Psalm 5:6: "Thou desireth truth in the inward parts" (894). McMillan's sympathetic influence leads Clyde to wrestle with the question of his "real guilt" until, conflating divine judgment and that of the minister, he realizes the criminality of his refusal to help Roberta: "Wouldn't God—McMillan—think so?" (903–04). He confesses to McMillan, who remains troubled by "all the confusing and extenuating circumstances" (915). When asked by the governor for a reason to commute the sentence, he cannot alter his "conviction" that Clyde is guilty (922). Clyde is disturbed by McMillan's lack of sympathy and wonders, "Would no one ever understand—or give him credit for his human—if all too human and perhaps wrong hungers?" (924).

But, if the state has failed in its efforts to surveil Clyde's subconscious, Dreiser's novel has not. Stephen Greenblatt has argued that the realist novel is the ideal aesthetic form for a "power that dreams of a panopticon in which the most intimate secrets are open to the view of an invisible authority," and *An American Tragedy* seems to fulfill this project (108). While Clyde remains resistant to the social construction of his guilt by the state's disciplinary mechanisms, Dreiser's novel carefully records Clyde's complex thoughts and impulses, precisely delineating his guilt, and thereby reasserting the panoptic power of society.

❦

In 1909, Freud visited the Adirondacks, and eight years later, in his *Introductory Lectures on Psychoanalysis* (1917), he suggested that designated wilderness areas represent a withdrawal from reality. He insists that such "nature-parks" are an effort to resist the changes of modernity and preserve the "original state which everywhere else has to our regret been sacrificed to necessity. Everything, including what is useless and even what is noxious, can grow and proliferate there as it pleases. The mental realm of phantasy is just such a reservation withdrawn from the reality principle" (372).[7] Similarly, Philip Cushman connects early twentieth-century interest in the psyche to American attitudes toward wilderness areas: "Psychoanalysis provided something that was beyond the grasp of positive thinking: a new, virgin territory, an *interior frontier*. . . . Just as the American wilderness had to be settled and conquered, so too did the internal wilderness" (38–39). He argues that the focus of psychoanalysis on the "private, unconscious interior" opened up "a new terrain for enhancement and productivity" that ultimately served the needs of corporate capitalism.

Roderick Frazier Nash and Paul Sutter have pointed out that one of the primary motivations for the creation of wilderness areas was the need for spaces where cultural elites could escape the complications of modernity. Given this linkage of the psychological and the ideological, it is not surprising that early twentieth-century wilderness advocates often drew upon the language of both psychoanalysis and managerial capitalism to describe the cultural value of wild places. In "Wilderness as a Form of Land Use" (1925), Aldo Leopold argues that recreational wilderness areas will preserve the distinctive American cultural attributes: "[A] certain vigorous individualism combined with ability to organize, a certain intellectual curiosity bent to practical ends, a lack of subservience to stiff social forms, and an intolerance of drones, all of which are the distinctive characteristics of successful pioneers" (*River* 138). Of course, these are the prized values of the managerial elite. Robert Marshall, in "The Problem of the Wilderness" (1930), sees wilderness as a therapeutic release from the tensions of an urban society: "In a civilization which requires most lives to be passed amid inordinate dissonance, pressure and intrusion, the chance of retiring now and then to the quietude and privacy of sylvan haunts becomes for some people a psychic necessity" (89). Marshall invokes Freudian theory, noting that "one of the most profound discoveries of psychology has been the demonstration of the terrific harm caused by suppressed desires" and suggests that wilderness areas offer a nonmartial opportunity to indulge in the "appetite for adventure" (89).

But the emphasis on the solitude of wilderness areas leads to several problems. Since wilderness advocates have consistently seen the concept of "wilderness" in opposition to people and civilization, it demands what William Cronon has called a "thoroughgoing erasure of the history from which it sprang" ("Trouble" 79). Often, the history that is erased is the people who have been living there. In 1925, the Southern Appalachian

National Park Committee was formed to determine locations for national parks east of the Mississippi River. Their work eventually led to the creation of the Great Smoky Mountains National Park in 1934 and the Shenandoah National Park in 1935. Both parks resulted in evictions of residents who were living in those areas, just as squatters had been removed from the Adirondacks and just as Native Americans had been evicted in the creation of the western National Parks.[8] This removal of marginalized residents from wilderness areas is recreated in the effacement of the Adirondacks locals by Clyde and the wealthy tourists. In its focus on the transformation of nature through the projecting desire of the subject, *An American Tragedy* suggests the cultural mechanisms whereby populated areas were rendered empty in order to provide recreational therapy for overcivilized elites.

Concomitant with the desire for solitude was the fear that wilderness spaces have the potential to become sites of lawlessness, outside of society's panoptic gaze. Yi-fu Tuan notes that, in the Middle Ages, efforts were made to deprive criminals of hiding places by cutting down trees along roads in the countryside (130–33). In 1870, Frederick Olmsted cautioned that city parks should avoid picturesque, rugged landscape as opposed to "openness," because open areas prevent "shabbiness, disorder, indecorum, and indecency" (23). In "Wilderness as a Form of Land Use" (1925), Aldo Leopold noted, "It would be idle to discuss wilderness areas if they are to be left subject to destruction by forest fires, or wide open to abuse" (*River* 136). To counter these threats, he proposes "a very modest and unobtrusive framework of trails, telephone line and lookout stations" and insists that "such improvements do not destroy the wild flavor of the area, and are necessary if it is to be kept in usable condition" (*River* 136). Evoking the same potential wilderness subversion, in 1968, Edward Abbey argued that wilderness should be preserved as a base for guerilla actions and "a refuge from authoritarian government" (130).

Accordingly, the development of recreational wilderness areas has resulted in efforts to insure effective surveillance that penetrates the cover that nature offers for illicit activity. During the Gillette trial, the prosecutor, George Ward, argued that Chester chose South Bay for his crime because of the absence of observers. However, Ward pointed out that, paradoxically, the fewer people, the more effective the surveillance; he notes that in large summer resorts, "there is scarcely an eye watches or follows us, but when we get into the woods, just as soon as we strike the woods, every eye is on you and is marking and noting your movements" (*State of New York* 492). In addition to the gazing eyes of residents, the threat of lawlessness was countered in the Adirondacks with new technologies of social control: regulations, forest police, security guards, floodlights, fences, and fire towers.

The threat of an unmonitored wilderness has remained a concern for managers. In 2002, Brazil completed a $1.4 billion surveillance system for the Amazon rainforest. Developed by US defense contractor Raytheon, the System for the Vigilance of the Amazon (SIVAM) uses a centralized command center connected to fixed radar stations, planes, and satellites to monitor drug trafficking as well as threats to the environment from illegal logging, burning, and mining. Proponents of SIVAM argue that it will protect the threatened rainforest, guard Brazil's borders, and make possible economic development of what has been a lawless region.[9]

※

In 1925, the year that *An American Tragedy* was published, Robert Marshall, his brother George, and their guide, Herbert Clark, became the first to climb all forty-six of the Adirondack mountains that are more than four-thousand feet tall. In his book *The High Peaks of the Adirondacks*, Marshall describes the solitude of the wilderness: "The pleasure of standing on a lofty summit where only a few have ever stood before is easy to acquire in the Adirondacks. Of the forty-two high peaks only fourteen have trails up them. On certain summits, I have never seen any signs of man or heard of anyone being there" (4). Since then, the number of recreational climbers in the Adirondacks has been increasing steadily: by the 1970s, there were one hundred new "Forty-Sixers" each year; and since 2010, between three and five hundred people annually complete the challenge, so that currently there are over ten thousand Forty-Sixers. In the summer of 2017, I climbed Iroquois Peak to complete my own forty-six. My experience was quite different from Marshall's. All of the peaks were accessible by either clearly marked Department of Environmental Conservation (DEC) trails or well-established "herd paths." I encountered dozens of hikers on the trails to even the most remote peaks, and I rarely had a peak to myself. Fortunately, I contemplated no crimes against my climbing companions, for surely, I would have been caught. Indeed, the overuse of the High Peaks Wilderness has inspired a campaign by the DEC to discourage defecation on the trails, and tourists have been encouraged to visit other areas in the Adirondacks to alleviate the pressure.[10]

The changes produced by the protection of the Adirondacks has meant that over the years, individuals have described the landscape in very different ways. A 1917 New York Central Railroad brochure, published a few years after the surrounding woods were clear-cut, nevertheless describes Big Moose Lake as "a veritable tangle of mountain, lake and wilderness" (*Adirondacks* 7). Likewise, a 1922 advertising brochure for the Glennmore Hotel boasts that it is "surrounded by the unmarred beauties of nature" (*Hotel Glennmore* 14). A year later, Helen Richardson (Dreiser) described the lake as "an isolated spot, very beautiful. One felt the weight of the surrounding woods stretching for miles in every direction" (84). While they were out on the lake, she became frightened by the "hypnotic spell" of the place and worried that Dreiser might repeat Gillette's crime (85).

These varying perceptions reinforce William Cronon's point that that wilderness is "a human creation—indeed, the creation of very particular human cultures at very particular moments in human history. . . . As we gaze into the mirror it holds up for us, we too easily imagine that what we behold is Nature when in fact we see the reflection of our own unexamined longings and desires" ("Trouble" 69–70). Cronon's use of the first-person-plural pronouns suggests that wilderness is always positioned at the intersection of external, psychological, and ideological realities. At a moment when Americans were recognizing the need to preserve nature, *An American Tragedy* presents a "nature" that is mediated by both individual experience and culture.

Chapter 7

Assimilative Nature in Hurston's *Their Eyes Were Watching God*

In the fall of 1928, shortly before a hurricane devastated her home state of Florida, Zora Neale Hurston was initiated into hoodoo by Samuel Thompson, a New Orleans practitioner who claimed kinship with the legendary Marie Leveau. After a lengthy ceremony, Thompson dubbed Hurston "the Rain-Bringer" and prophesized that "The Great One" would speak to her through storms (*Mules* 200).[1] Perhaps the 1928 hurricane was a fulfillment of that prophecy, for Hurston would later use it as a model for the storm in *Their Eyes Were Watching God* (1937). In addition to inspiring the title of the novel, the hurricane leads to the death of Janie's third husband, and it drives her back to Eatonville, where she tells the story of her life to her friend. But Hurston's hurricane is more than just a convenient plot mechanism. Focusing on the novel's depiction of human efforts to control a threatening nature suggests the ways that African Americans negotiated the tensions between culture and nature during the late Progressive Era.

Previous critics have acknowledged the importance of nature in Hurston's work. As Ann Morris and Margaret Dunn note, Hurston "uses her knowledge of the plants and animals of Florida to provide realistic settings, to compose authentically natural speech for her characters, and to create central symbols" (1). Vera L. Norwood argues that "the green world of plants" empowers Janie's "dream of a way of being part of nature, yet outside the animalistic stereotypes limiting black peoples' full connection with the environment" (188). Paul Outka links *Their Eyes Were Watching God* to the effort by the writers of the Harlem Renaissance to integrate the beauty of the South with the historicized trauma engendered by that landscape. He sees the pear tree at the beginning and the hurricane at the end as moments of interpenetration of the natural and the human that reveal "both the radical promise of the natural sublime and the terrible danger of it falling into trauma" (189). Lloyd Willis argues that Hurston "offers a vision of enmeshment within an immanently physical natural world that is imbued with racial and cultural significance" (104). In 2005, Cynthia Davis objected to Hurston's absence from the ecocritical canon and insisted upon her environmental credentials: "Hurston validates environmentalism and links spiritual emptiness with materialism; she opposes rural development that destroys the local ecology, and she insists on the inviolability of nature" (154). I would argue that Hurston does indeed need to be read from an ecocritical perspective, but not because she conforms to the resistance narrative. Instead, *Their Eyes Were Watching God* is significant because it suggests a linkage between efforts to control a threatening natural world and strategies for the assimilation of African Americans.

In 1919, chemist Edwin Slosson called nature a "treacherous and unsleeping foe, ever to be feared and watched and circumvented, for at any moment and in spite of all our vigilance she may wipe out the human race by famine, pestilence or earthquake and within a few centuries obliterate every trace of its achievement" (10). But Slosson was confident that through applied science man could overcome nature and "substitute for the natural world an artificial world, molded nearer to his heart's desire" (13). In the early twentieth century, few places represented this confidence in human ability to reshape nature better than Florida.

Well into the 1920s, Florida remained relatively undeveloped, but the rich black soil of the Everglades inspired those who saw in it tremendous possibilities for agriculture. Marjorie Stoneman Douglas wrote in 1923, "The wealth of south Florida, but even more important, the meaning and significance of south Florida lies in the black muck of the Everglades and the inevitable development of this country to be the great tropic agricultural center of the world" (qtd. in Davis and Arsenault, 305). The problem was that much of the land was under a slow-moving river that flowed from Lake Okeechobee to Florida Bay. Beginning in the 1880s, this natural obstacle to development was attacked by what David McCally has called the "social epistemology of the Florida Dream": a confidence in science; a trust in negotiated political consensus and the rule of law; and an economy based on ever-increasing consumption and growth ("Everglades" 142–43). A series of private and governmental efforts began draining the Everglades, and, by the early 1920s, Lake Okeechobee was partially surrounded by a forty-seven-mile earthen dike. The subsequent drying of the land below the lake led to an agricultural boom that drew many African American migrant workers. In 1928, a headline in the *Palm Beach Post* noted that "Civilization Is Quickly Taking Backwoods Lands" (qtd. in Grunwald 191).

But the announcement of civilization's triumph was premature. The dried soil subsided more rapidly than had been anticipated; muck fires swept through the area; and, without the pressure of fresh water to keep the seawater back, aquifers were contaminated. Even more serious problems came from a series of hurricanes that struck southern Florida. In 1926, a hurricane breached the Okeechobee dike and resulted in more than three hundred deaths. Two years later, the hurricane that would inspire Hurston's novel surprised weather forecasters and destroyed twenty-one miles of the dike, resulting in more than twenty-five hundred deaths, many of them African American migrant workers. Eliot Kleinberg argues that the high death toll can be attributed to multiple causes: "a shallow lake, an inadequate dike, lack of communication, few evacuation routes, a flawed forecast" (141). Once the storm subsided, African Americans were impressed into work details, and black victims were buried in mass graves.[2]

After the 1928 hurricane, there was a demand for the federal government to become more involved in weather prediction, flood control, and disaster relief. Raymond Arsenault notes that before the twentieth century, "[s]o-called 'acts of God' came and went, and no one held out much hope that human vulnerability to such 'natural disasters' could be eliminated"; however, by the twentieth century, there was a "growing expectation that public officials should play an active role in disaster avoidance and relief" (203, 213). In early 1929, newly elected president Herbert Hoover toured the devastation in central and southern Florida. A former engineer, Hoover recognized the opportunity to use governmental resources to tame nature, and, in 1930, he signed legislation authorizing the construction of a new dike around Lake Okeechobee. In 1939, two years after the publication of *Their Eyes Were Watching God*, the US Army Corps of Engineers completed the twenty-million-dollar, eighty-five-mile-long Herbert Hoover Dike, which eventually became part of a comprehensive water control system for the Everglades.

The efforts by the Corps of Engineers to reshape nature are celebrated in their 1950s film, *Waters of Destiny*. The narrator contrasts the potential of Florida, "a land that nature always smiled upon," with the "crazed antics of the elements" and "the maddened forces of nature." Turning to Lake

Figure 7.1. Herbert Hoover Dike on Lake Okeechobee, ca. 1935.

Okeechobee, he concludes, "This monster had to be controlled," and the remainder of the film presents the triumphant story of "man's mastery of the elements."[3] But the struggle between nature and civilization was not just about hurricanes and dikes: early twentieth-century social scientists were equally interested in controlling the threatening nature represented by people of color.

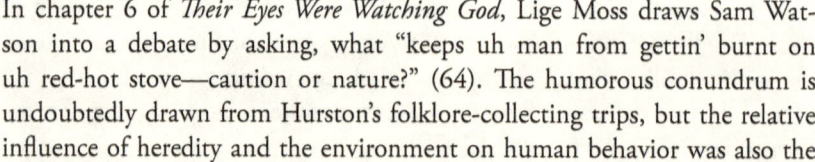

In chapter 6 of *Their Eyes Were Watching God*, Lige Moss draws Sam Watson into a debate by asking, what "keeps uh man from gettin' burnt on uh red-hot stove—caution or nature?" (64). The humorous conundrum is undoubtedly drawn from Hurston's folklore-collecting trips, but the relative influence of heredity and the environment on human behavior was also the central issue in early twentieth-century discussions of race by social scientists.

Before 1920, the relatively new discipline of anthropology was dominated by physical anthropologists and scientific racists, who saw racial types as fixed by heredity and arranged on a hierarchy from primitive to civilized.

They portrayed African Americans as barely-evolved animals, who were largely unsuccessful in the conflict with their bestial natures. In 1910, sociologist Howard W. Odum noted that when whites see a Negro as "a worthy and industrious citizen," they fail to "see him as he struggles—or more exactly does not even struggle—against the onrush of his animal nature which leads him to neglect and abuse himself, his home and his family" (14). Lacking self-control and incapable of assimilation, African Americans needed to be controlled through such Progressive Era measures as segregation, eugenics, and mental testing.

Not surprisingly, since they identified African Americans with nature, racist social scientists argued that blacks were unable to use science and technology to tame the natural world. In 1896, statistician Frederick Hoffman insisted, "The whole history of Anglo-Saxon conquest and colonization is one endless proof of race superiority and race supremacy" (314). He boasted that the white man has overcome "the very forces of nature" and "after years of struggle, gained his end and mastered the conditions of life surrounding him" (314). In 1914, sociologist John Moffatt Mecklin argued that African Americans were inferior because of their "superficial acquaintance with the mechanism of nature"; accordingly, their ignorance of science "easily gives birth to a belief in invisible forces and supernatural phenomena" (41).

By the 1920s, these racist assumptions were being contested by liberal anthropologists such as Columbia professor Franz Boas, under whom Hurston studied from 1925 to 1927. Boas challenged the validity of traditional physical markers of race, demonstrating that there was greater variation within races than among them (as part of his research, he employed Hurston to measure head dimensions in Harlem). Furthermore, instead of seeing racial characteristics as the result of biological determinism, the Boasians insisted that both physiology and psychology were shaped by environment. Daryl Scott observes, "During the interwar years, culture and the social environment replaced biology as the means of explaining black behavior. Black criminality, migration, sexual mores, and most other social developments and behaviors were no longer seen as determined by nature" (19).

Although they agreed on the role of culture, liberals disagreed about the best way to achieve an egalitarian society. Accomodationists saw blacks as a child race destined to evolve under proper nurturance; accordingly, segregation was necessary to protect them until they were ready for full participation in American civilization. Assimilationists rejected the notion of any fundamental difference between the races and predicted a speedy absorption into white culture. Meanwhile, cultural pluralists insisted upon the cultural distinctiveness of African Americans as a way of instilling racial pride in an oppressed people.⁴

This new emphasis on environment led many liberal social scientists to turn to plastic as a metaphor for human nature. Celluloid was created in 1869 as a material that could be used for billiard balls to replace the rapidly diminishing supply of ivory elephant tusks, and it was quickly followed by other synthetics such as Bakelite, polystyrene, vinyl, and nylon. Jeffrey Meikle notes that, by the early twentieth century, plastic had become a household material and was being celebrated in utopian terms "as a substance capable of transforming the material conditions that had always limited human life" (67). In 1911, Boas argued that "all the evidence is now in favor of a great plasticity of human types" as well as "a great plasticity of the mental make-up of human types" (76). Many social scientists saw African Americans as especially adaptable. In 1896 sociologist Franklin Henry Giddings asserted, "The negro is plastic. He yields easily to environing influences. Deprived of the support of stronger races, he still relapses into savagery, but kept in contact with the whites, he readily takes the external impress of civilization" (328–29). Likewise, in 1910, Howard W. Odum insisted, "The Negro shows great plasticity and much promise" (275). Representing a human triumph over the limits of nature, plastic was an ideal metaphor for those who privileged the transformative power of environment rather than the fixity of heredity.

∽

In her autobiography, *Dust Tracks in the Road* (1942), Hurston compared *Their Eyes Were Watching God* to a flood that had been "dammed up in me" (717). In the novel, Janie's ability to survive both the waters unleashed by the hurricane and the emotional flood created by her desire for intimacy demonstrates her ability to control nature and thus her potential for assimilation.

A former slave, Janie's grandmother, Nannie, sees the natural world as a threat. To escape from slavery, she hid in a swamp, where she was frightened by snakes and panthers; later, her daughter, Leafy, is raped in the woods. After Nannie is freed, she tries to "throw up a highway through de wilderness" for Leafy, and she struggles to keep her from being "used for a work-ox and a brood-sow" (16). As Outka points out, Nannie denigrates Janie's experience of the natural sublime with the pear tree because, to her, nature is associated with the trauma of slavery (189–92). Instead, she hopes that the property and possessions of the independent farmer Logan Killicks will protect Janie from degenerating into the expected role for black women as "de mule uh de world (14).

At the beginning of the novel, Janie is also distanced from nature. She is disappointed with Logan's farm, which she sees as "a lonesome place like a stump in the middle of the woods where nobody had ever been" (21–22). As he is shoveling manure, Logan looks to her like "a black bear doing some clumsy dance on his hind legs," and the end of the marriage comes when Janie realizes that Logan hopes to turn her into a mule (31). Eldridge Cleaver has pointed out that country life proved problematic for many twentieth-century African Americans, who had "come to measure their own value according to the number of degrees they are away from the soil" (58).

Janie welcomes Joe Starks as "newness and change" because he represents an urbane alternative to the grim agricultural environment of Logan's farm (32). Joe mimics white culture down to his gilded spit pot, and Janie is impressed with his confidence, which reminds her of "rich white folks" (34). When he first arrives in Eatonville, Joe is disgusted with its lack of development and dismisses the town as "nothing but a raw place in de woods," and he immediately begins to make it equal to (if separate from) white communities (34). One of his first acts is to improve upon nature by installing a gas street light, noting that artificial lighting is all that "poor weak humans" can do "if we want any light after de settin' or befo' de risin'" (45).

But distance from nature comes with a psychological cost. The townsfolk use chiasmus to suggest the unnaturalness of Joe's embrace of white culture: "It was like seeing your sister turn into a 'gator. A familiar strangeness. You keep seeing your sister in the 'gator and the 'gator in your sister, and you'd rather not" (48). Bell hooks has argued that the twentieth-century migration of African Americans to the North separated them from the natural world and "made it all the more possible for black people to internalize white-supremacist assumptions about black identity" (138). Janie quickly becomes uncomfortable with Joe's ambition and complains that it "keeps us in some way we ain't natural wid one 'nother" (46). As the marriage deteriorates, she finds Joe's promise of the trappings of white civilization less and less satisfying.

Tea Cake is appealing to Janie precisely because he is associated with nature. Janie sees him as "a bee to a blossom—a pear tree blossom in the spring" (106). He hunts, fishes, and enjoys planting a garden. Equally important, Tea Cake represents the primitive black culture that white readers would have expected from a Harlem Renaissance novel. Tea Cake's connection to nature and the primitive is demonstrated most clearly when he takes Janie to the Everglades, which are represented both as a lush Eden and as a southern, rural version of Harlem: "Big Lake Okechobee, big beans, big cane, big weeds, big everything. . . . People wild too" (129).[5] Outka sees the experience on the muck as "a portrait of an untraumatized relation between African-American subjects and the natural environment" (192–93). But the exotic natural setting also reflects culture since it inspires the music, violence, and transgressive sexuality that whites found titillating: "All night now the jooks clanged and clamored. Pianos living three lifetimes in one. Blues made and used right on the spot. . . . Work all day for money, fight all night for love. The rich black earth clinging to bodies and biting the skin like ants" (131). Anthony E. Rotundo has argued that at the turn-of-the-century white American males began to celebrate the primitive and the bestial as a source of "passions which men needed in order to be men, to struggle, survive, and dominate" (232).

However, primitive nature also has the potential for destructiveness. As in the Corps of Engineers film, the hurricane is represented as a beast that is difficult to control. As the storm develops, the wind "woke up old Okechobee and the monster began to roll in his bed" (158). At first, both whites and blacks trust the human defenses against "the senseless monster," but the lake "got madder and madder," and finally, the dikes give way: "The monstropolous beast had left his bed. . . . He seized hold of his dikes and ran forward until he met the quarters; uprooted them like grass and rushed on after his supposed-to-be conquerors" (158–62). Rachel Stein sees the hurricane as a Voodoo-like force that disrupts confidence in "progressive human dominion over nature" (78–79). Likewise, Erik D. Curren argues that the storm destroys Western rationalism's "magical belief that money and technology can conquer natural forces" (19). Lloyd Willis argues that "the power, the unruliness, the recklessness, the elemental force" of the hurricane represents the triumph of "an immanently black nature" over white exploitation (122).

But it is important to note that recognizing the limits of human efforts to control nature is not the same as repudiating those efforts. In other words, nothing in the novel suggests that the absence of dikes would have been preferable. Indeed, before the hurricane, the agricultural lands the Okechobee dike created provided Tea Cake and Janie with meaningful work, and after the storm, they return to the muck to help rebuild the dike (173). Ignoring the felicitousness of this work runs the risk of indulging in what Kimberly Ruffin calls an environmentalism "solely informed by recreation and leisure" and neglects the potential of African American literature to encourage us to "consider how work can inform an ecological outlook (21). Similarly, Dianne Glave and Mark Stoll note that African American environmental politics involve "the connection of environmental concerns to the world of work and production rather than to lifestyle choices and consumption" (20).

∽

The nature-nurture debate that preoccupied anthropology in the interwar period manifested most directly in mainstream culture through the question of African American assimilation, especially the blending of the races through interracial sexual relations. Racists insisted on the biological difference of blacks that rendered them incapable of true assimilation, even arguing that blacks were a separate species who would mongrelize the superior white race. In a 1921 speech, President Warren G. Harding argued that for the United States to attain full economic development, blacks should be granted political and economic equality, but he insisted that social equality was unthinkable because of the "fundamental, eternal, inescapable difference" between the races (11). In the early twentieth century this insistence on biological difference increasingly became inscribed in legislation, as Jim Crow segregation laws demarcated two separate Americas along the color line. Michael McGerr points out that the progressives tolerated segregation since they hoped that the separation of the races would limit the potential for violence (182–218). However, in a strictly segregated culture, the absence of physical markers of race in persons of mixed heritage led to obsessive fears of what Joel Williamson has called "invisible blackness" and resulted in further repressive legislation (98). In 1924, the Virginia Act to Preserve Racial Integrity established the "one-drop rule" that defined as black anyone possessing any black ancestor, and in the next twenty years, dozens of states followed with their own antimiscegenation laws. Walter A. Plecker, the Virginia registrar of vital statistics, used his staff to comb through records to uncover previously undetected blacks, boasting, "Few have escaped us" (qtd. in Spiro 256).

The possibility of the merging of the two races was not just threatening to racists: it was also a concern of some liberal anthropologists and members of the Harlem Renaissance. Walter Jackson notes that in the 1930s, the two most prominent students of Franz Boas disagreed on how to best promote African American equality. Ruth Benedict emphasized "cultural plasticity" and advocated "a universalist, assimilationist approach to race relations" (Jackson 121–22). On the other hand, Melville Herskovits "adhered to historical particularism, in order to recover underlying cultural patterns, in the hope of encouraging black pride and white respect for Afro-American culture" (Jackson 122). Herskovits's concerns about the American environment's ability to efface distinctions were shared by W. E. B. Du Bois. In *The Souls of Black Folk* (1903), he observes that the American Negro is conflicted by a "double-consciousness" because he refuses to "bleach his Negro soul in a flood of white Americanism" (8–9). Likewise, Langston Hughes, in "The Negro Artist and the Racial Mountain" (1926), uses a plastic metaphor to decry the "urge within the race toward whiteness, the desire to pour racial individuality into the mold of American standardization, and to be as little Negro and as much American as possible" (32). Rejecting the too-easy assimilation of the plastic Negro metaphor, Hughes insists upon black difference.

The problem that nature represented for those African Americans who wanted to be assimilated is suggested by Mrs. Turner. Of mixed race herself, she has utter contempt for dark-complected African Americans and dreams of adoption by the whites: "If it wuzn't for so many black folks it wouldn't be no race problem. De white folks would take us in wid dem" (141). When Janie suggests that whites will not want to mingle with poor blacks, Mrs. Turner argues that it is nature, not environmental factors, that is responsible for segregation: "'Tain't de poorness, it's de color and de features" (141). Insisting upon the significance of the physical markers of race that were central to early twentieth-century anthropological discussions, Mrs. Turner is resentful that she is forced to associate with blacks when "Ah got white folks' features in mah face" (142). Janie rejects Mrs. Turner's hatred of blackness and points out, "We's a mingled people and all of us got black kinfolks as well as yaller kinfolks" (141). Light-skinned herself, Janie is drawn to the black-skinned Tea Cake, and I would argue that this represents a central project of *Their Eyes Were Watching God*: the assimilation of black and white within the black community. Joel Williamson sees the Harlem Renaissance as "a conscious attempt to marry smoothly together the blackness and the whiteness inherent in Negro life in America" (163).[6]

The novel also suggests the possibility of assimilation between black and white cultures in the larger society. Janie is raised by whites and only discovers her racial identity by accident when she sees a group photograph (9).[7] When she goes to the muck, Janie is immersed in black folk culture, but during Tea Cake's illness, she consults the white doctor, a symbolic center of Western science (in contrast to Joe, who turns to a conjurer in his final illness). When Janie shoots Tea Cake, she is exonerated by a white court, and after the trial, the white women "stood around her like a protecting wall," a dike to separate her from the blacks who are angry at the verdict (188). But, eventually, she is embraced by the black community as well as the white. While the segregationists saw nature as insurmountable difference, *Their Eyes Were Watching God* suggests the assimilative potential of the natural world. After the hurricane, in one of the few scenes depicting overt white racism, Tea Cake is impressed into service burying the dead. Ordered by the guards to distinguish between the whites, who will receive coffins, and the blacks, who are destined for mass burial, he protests, "Nobody can't tell nothin' 'bout some uh dese bodies, de shape dey's in. Can't tell whether dey's white or black" (171). In other words, the forces of nature have effaced any physical markers of racial difference, and the result is a de facto assimilation.

Perhaps because of the assimilationist tendency in nature, the early twentieth century produced a curious linkage between racist segregation and progressive conservation. The leading scientific racist of the interwar period was Madison Grant, who is best known for *The Passing of the Great Race* (1916), which Adolf Hitler, in a fan letter to Grant, called "my Bible" (qtd. in Spiro 357). Grant was a central figure in eugenics, immigration restriction, and the antimiscegenation movement, helping to develop the Virginia one-drop rule. But, as Jonathan Peter Spiro notes, Grant was also a leading conservationist, who "preserved the California redwoods, saved the American bison from extinction, founded the Bronx Zoo . . . helped to create Glacier and Denali National Parks, and worked tirelessly to protect the whales in the ocean, the bald eagles in the sky, and the pronghorn antelopes on the prairie" (xii). Spiro argues that Grant's careers as a eugenicist and a conservationist are united by a commitment to preserving distinct forms of life, what he calls an effort "to save as much as possible of the old America" (qtd. in Spiro xiii).[8]

If segregationist thought could coexist with conservation, it is perhaps not surprising that *Their Eyes Were Watching God* associates assimilation with the ability to dominate nature. Amy Sickels iterates what has become the standard reading of the novel when she describes the story as that of "a black woman who reaches empowerment and self-autonomy" (61). But critics have not fully acknowledged the role that Janie's domination of nature plays in the development of her subjectivity. In one of her first spoken protests against Joe's power, Janie recognizes that she has been linked to the natural world, noting that it is easy for Joe to feel godlike "when you ain't got nothin' tuh strain against but women and chickens" (75). After Joe dies,

Janie is able to become a speaking human subject through her relationship with Tea Cake, whom Cheryl Wall has called a "natural man" (188). She hunts, fishes, plays checkers, and learns to drive a car. Immersed in the natural world of the muck, she can even tell stories.

But if Tea Cake's connection with nature can empower, it can also threaten. In 1914, John Moffatt Mecklin warned that "the more primitive and powerful instincts, which at lower levels were a help to man in his struggle for existence, are now often a constant menace in our highly civilised society" (5). While Tea Cake is clearly the best of the three men in Janie's life, his limitations have been recognized by previous critics. Michael Awkward notes that he is "a less than ideal mate" who demonstrates "traditional sexist male attitudes concerning women" (17). Especially troubling is the threatened and real violence that structures his relationship with Janie. During their initial courtship, Janie jokingly offers to give him ten pounds of "knuckle pudding," and after his disappearance in Jacksonville, she warns him that if he does it again, she will kill him (98, 124). More seriously, Janie beats Tea Cake when she is jealous, and later Tea Cake whips Janie to reassure himself that he possesses her (137, 147).

The climax of their struggle comes after Tea Cake is infected by rabies. In a Darwinian fight for survival, Janie is "a scared human being fighting for its life," and to survive, she shoots Tea Cake (184). Erik D. Curren has read Tea Cake's rabies as "a metaphor for the infection of life-affirming black folk culture by the disease of deadly white prejudices" (24). However, it is also important to recognize that the disease causes Tea Cake to degenerate into an animal. As Bill Wasik and Monica Murphy have noted, rabies "troubles the line where man ends and animal begins," and the novel makes it clear that Tea Cake has become a beast (4). Janie worries that the hospital will treat him as a "mad dog"; she sees a "ferocious look in his eyes"; and his dying gesture is to bite her arm (183–84). Thus, to save herself, Janie kills a representative of the threatening natural world.[9]

Janie's killing of Tea Cake has been recognized by critics as central to her development. Elizabeth Beaulieu argues, "Tea Cake has to die because, in the end, as long as the male-female relationship exists within a system that is defined by the man's domination—that is, marriage—the woman cannot achieve selfhood" (845–46). Or, as Melvin Dixon concludes, "although she loses Tea Cake, she gains herself" (94). But the relationship between the subordinate and main clauses of Dixon's statement needs to be explored more fully. I would argue that the losing/killing of Tea Cake is exactly what makes Janie's self-fulfillment possible because it shows her ability to dominate nature. Jeffrey Myers has argued that white American subjectivity is constructed in opposition to both African Americans and the natural world: "Both depend upon a subordination of the Other, in which the white self attempts to substantialize its own separate, superior identity by imagining the subaltern as without the will, the agency, or even the ontological status of the white subject" (12). By killing Tea Cake and taming a threatening nature, Janie has demonstrated her whiteness.

Hurston famously boasts in "How it Feels to Be Colored Me," "I am not tragically colored. There is no great sorrow dammed up in my soul. . . . I do not belong to the sobbing school of Negrohood who hold that nature somehow has given them a lowdown dirty deal" (827). Instead, she insists on the individual's ability to control nature: "I have seen that the world is to the strong regardless of a little pigmentation more or less. No, I do not weep at the world—I am too busy sharpening my oyster knife" (827). For Hurston, the tools to reshape nature, especially black nature, came from the scientific objectivity she acquired from Boas. As she notes in *Mules and Men*, the "spy-glass of Anthropology" encouraged her to see her early experiences in "the crib of negroism" from a new perspective (1). By balancing scientific and literary techniques, she was confident that she had developed a more accurate perspective on black folklore that would be interesting to a white audience. In his introduction to *Mules and Men*, Boas insists that Hurston has made a major contribution to "our knowledge of the true inner life of the Negro" (xiii). In 1928, she wrote Hughes, "I am getting inside of Negro art and lore. I am beginning to *see* really" (qtd. in Boyd 165).[10]

This focus on seeing is evident in the ending of *Their Eyes Were Watching God*. Donna Haraway has argued that "situated and embodied knowledges" represent an alternative for feminist epistemology that avoids both the "god trick" of scientific objectivity and radical constructivism (583, 581). But Haraway warns of the "serious danger of romanticizing and/or appropriating the vision of the less powerful," and she insists that "the positionings of the subjugated are not exempt from critical reexamination, decoding, deconstruction, and interpretation" (584). Janie seems to reject disembodied knowledge when she insists upon the specificity of lived experience: "It's uh known fact, Pheoby, you got tuh *go* there tuh *know* there" (192). However, this reading ignores Janie's imbrication in contemporary discourses of nature. Indeed, her final vision of Tea Cake draws upon nature nostalgia to mitigate her destruction of the natural.

After Phoebe leaves, Janie recalls the pain of killing Tea Cake, but then she imagines him diffused into nature: "Tea Cake came prancing around her where she was and the song of the sigh flew out of the window and lit in the top of the pine trees. Tea Cake, with the sun for a shawl" (193). Janie realizes that although Tea Cake is gone, she can summon his memory at will, a power strikingly similar to the nostalgic nature realism discussed at the end of chapter 1. Like the lost rivers of Twain or Dickey, the primitive, natural Tea Cake could live on in Janie's memory: "Of course he wasn't dead. He could never be dead until she herself had finished feeling and thinking" (193). Satisfied with this realization, Janie "pulled in her horizon like a great fish-net. . . . So much of life in its meshes! She called in her soul to come and see" (193). Hazel Carby argues that the fish-net image confirms "the distance between the act of representation and the subjects produced through that act of representation," and she critiques "a discourse that exists only for the pleasure of the self" (87). From an ecocritical perspective, the net image is also disturbing, suggesting an entrapment of nature in nostalgic memory. In the novel, Janie fully experiences the natural world, yet her shooting skill, her memory, and her storytelling enable her to maintain her distance and to control a dangerous nature.

In *Dust Tracks in the Road* (1942), Hurston states, "I know that destruction and construction are but two faces of Dame Nature, and that it is nothing to her if I choose to make personal tragedy out of her unbreakable laws" (795). The very title of *Their Eyes Were Watching God* makes it clear who is to blame for the destruction of the hurricane. As the storm increases in intensity, Janie is relieved when the men stop gambling since "Ole Massa is doin' *His* work now" (159). Instead of looking to the whites for answers, "six eyes were questioning *God*" (159). The storm is then personified as a monster, a manifestation of an angry nature, before its final representation as "*Him-with-the-square-toes*," a folklore image of death (168). What is missing from Hurston's novel is any indication of human culpability for the disaster.

In *Acts of God*, Ted Steinberg argues that, since the late nineteenth century, Americans have blamed natural disasters on nature or God. He points out that what gets absolved from responsibility in these constructions is human complicity in such events, especially residential development in disaster-prone areas and governmental subsidizing of such choices through flood-control projects, disaster relief, and flood insurance. Furthermore, Steinberg notes that these interpretations reinscribe unequal social structures: "by recruiting an angry God or chaotic nature to their cause, those in power have been able to rationalize the economic choices that help to explain why the poor and people of color—who have largely borne the brunt of these disasters—tend to wind up in harm's way" (xxii).

Certainly, the 1928 hurricane was not the first or the last time that people of color were disproportionally impacted by destructive acts of nature. In 1927, the Mississippi River broke through its levees and flooded twenty-seven thousand square miles, displacing more than six hundred thousand people. African Americans were conscripted to work on the levees, and the conditions in their refugee camps were inferior to those of white refugees. After the 1927 flood, public outrage at the failure of the government to protect its citizens led to the Flood Control Act of 1928, which authorized the Army Corps of Engineers to build more and higher levees. In 2005, the increased volume of water contained in this system coupled with the failure of levees weakened by cost-cutting contributed to the devastation of Hurricane Katrina, in which more than twelve hundred people died, the majority of them African Americans. Michael Dyson argues that the response of the federal government to Katrina left "poor black folk defenseless before the fury of nature" (19).[11]

Steinberg also argues that blaming nature and God diverts attention from actions that might have been done, such as better storm forecasting, higher construction standards for homes, and more effective emergency evacuation plans. Or, abandoning our confidence in human ability to tame nature, we might learn to live within the limits of the natural world. Christopher Morris has observed that the rebuilding of the dikes after Katrina illustrates the long-standing American assumption that people and nature can be separated through human ingenuity: "A hurricane or flood can only be understood, therefore, as the sudden and disastrous intrusion of the natural world into the human world" (206). *Their Eyes Were Watching God* relies on a similar confidence in an ability to separate the natural from the human as a strategy for overcoming perceived differences between the races.

Chapter 8

Environmental Stewardship in Faulkner's *Go Down, Moses*

In November of 1902, President Theodore Roosevelt accepted an invitation to go bear hunting in the Yazoo River Delta of Mississippi. The president was eager for a break from his responsibilities, especially one that involved big-game hunting; furthermore, a trip to Mississippi would give him an opportunity to ease tensions among southerners outraged by his support for antilynching laws and by his recent invitation of Booker T. Washington to a luncheon at the White House. Roosevelt's guide was Holt Collier, an ex-slave and former Confederate scout, who was famous for having killed more than three thousand bears. Early the first morning, Collier's dogs caught the scent of a bear and began the chase, which continued until the late afternoon, when the dogs trapped the bear in a water hole. Fighting for its life, the exhausted bear killed one dog and maimed another until Collier leaped into the hole and clubbed the bear senseless with his rifle. He looped a rope around the neck of the dazed bear, tied it to tree, and then blew his bugle to summon the president for the kill. When Roosevelt rode up, he was so troubled by the sight of the helpless bear that he refused to shoot it; as the president rode back to camp, Collier slit the bear's throat with a hunting knife to end its misery. The press seized upon the story, and a Brooklyn woman began marketing the first "Teddy Bear" to capitalize on Roosevelt's sportsmanship and compassion.[1]

Of course, from the bear's point of view, the question of who actually completed the kill was irrelevant; thus, Roosevelt's scruples suggest more about regional differences in hunting ethics rather than true compassion for wildlife. Correspondent Lindsay Denison pointed out that "the Mississippi bear hunt proper is a communal and not an individual sport, and that the man for whom the hunt is organized is credited with all the killing done

Figure 8.1. Roosevelt hunting bear in Mississippi (Harvard Theodore Roosevelt Collection)

by his company and the pack"; accordingly, it was "a blow to the sense of Southern hospitality . . . to find that the President had a vigorous desire to kill a bear himself" (603).

Roosevelt's Mississippi bear hunt took place nearly twenty years after the fictional bear hunt that forms the central episode of William Faulkner's *Go Down, Moses* and forty years before the publication of that novel. Written during the Depression, *Go Down, Moses* can be read as a critique of the New Deal, which Daniel T. Rodgers sees as "the defining moment of twentieth-century American progressive politics" (*Atlantic* 410). Although critics have consistently defined Faulkner's great period as beginning in

1929, with *The Sound and the Fury*, and ending in 1942, with *Go Down, Moses*, it was not until Ted Atkinson's 2006 book, *Faulkner and the Great Depression*, that anyone noticed that these dates correspond almost exactly with the years of America's worst economic crisis. As Atkinson points out, this oversight was the product of a consensus by both leftist and formalist critics that Faulkner's modernist aesthetic is fundamentally apolitical. Atkinson's revisionist analysis of Faulkner's engagement with the ideological issues of the Depression opens up an ecocritical reading of *Go Down, Moses*. At a time when progressive conservationists were endorsing statist coercion as a response to the environmental destruction caused by the laissez-faire individualism of the nineteenth century, Faulkner's novel explores the alternative of individual environmental stewardship.

Of all the novels in this study, *Go Down, Moses* has received the most attention from ecocritics, who see it as an example of resistance to environmental domination. Noting Faulkner's "evocation of a vanishing natural splendor that has been destroyed," Judith Bryant Wittenberg compares Faulkner to Aldo Leopold and argues that the novel explores "with elegiac eloquence essential questions about the interconnections between humans and their environment" (69). Similarly, Lawrence Buell claims that, in *Go Down, Moses*, "an incipient environmental ethic begins to take shape in response to regional modernization in many ways compatible with the more fully articulated environmentalism of his near-contemporary, ecologist and nature writer Aldo Leopold" (*Writing* 171). Zackary Vernon insists that the novel demonstrates "that humans' psychological health and ethical foundations depend on the preservation of the wilderness" (76). I argue that Faulkner's environmental ethic is less a critique of domination ideology than it is a response to the perceived devaluation of the individual in progressive statism.

On June 12, 1941, as Faulkner was finishing the manuscript of *Go Down, Moses*, the Weyerhaeuser Timber Company dedicated the nation's first tree farm on a cutover tract near Elma, Washington. Six months later, capitalizing on the enthusiasm generated by the event, the National Lumber Manufacturers Association created the American Tree Farms System, and by 1949, 17 million acres had been certified as tree farms. But not everyone saw this reforestation effort by the industry as entirely altruistic. US Forest Service chief Lyle Watts grumbled, "I cannot escape the conclusion that the real object of this campaign is to ward off public regulation" (qtd. in

Sharp 43–44). Watts's skepticism was legitimate since for decades the lumber industry had been aggressively fighting those who argued that governmental regulation was necessary to restore the forests that had been devastated by private lumbering.[2]

In the 1940s, the southern forests were in an especially dire condition. After lumber companies had exhausted the timber of the Great Lakes, they began buying stumpage in the South. By 1890, the federal government had sold the industry more than 2 million acres of public land, often for as little as $1.25 an acre. Between 1908 and 1915, Mississippi was the third largest lumber-producing state in the nation, with an annual yield of more than two billion board feet. Giant mills were constructed, and railroad lines were extended deep into the forests. Steam skidders destroyed everything in their path, leaving the cutover land a desolate wasteland that was prone to further degradation through fire and erosion. Such heavily capitalized projects demanded continuous production, and state tax laws encouraged rapid clear cutting and discouraged reforestation. The environmental consequences of this industrial logging are described by Nollie Hickman: "Except for a lone misshapen tree here and there, the rolling hills and flat lands appeared to be a treeless country destitute of fertility" (166). As previous critics have noted, in the opening chapter of *Light in August*, Faulkner depicts the environmental devastation caused by a lumbering operation as "a stumppocked scene of profound and peaceful desolation, unplowed, untilled, gutting slowly into red and choked ravines beneath the long quiet rains of autumn and the galloping fury of vernal equinoxes" (5).[3]

The deforestation of the South occurred amidst a growing realization that all of the nation's forests were in jeopardy. In the first three decades of the twentieth century, the threat of a national timber famine led to a debate over the relationship between private forestry and the federal government. In 1908, President Theodore Roosevelt insisted that the era of "unrestricted individualism" and "wasteful development of our natural resources" was over ("Opening Address" 10). Federal forestry began with the Forest Reserve Act of 1891, which authorized the president to create national forests, and by 1907, 150 million acres had been preserved in 159 national forests. The 1911 Weeks Act authorized the purchase of cutover lands in the East; under this legislation, an additional 19 million acres were added to the national forests, including 11 million acres of cutover land in the South. William G. Robbins points out that the lumber industry generally supported the federal acquisitions, hoping that they would ensure a steady supply of timber and bring economic stability to the chronically unstable industry (*Lumberjacks* 208).

While the national forests were managed according to the principles of sustainable forestry, the vast majority of timberland remained privately owned, and most lumbermen felt that there was little financial incentive to reforest cutover lands. Accordingly, during the interwar period, there were repeated calls from progressive conservationists for regulation of private forests. In 1919, Gifford Pinchot demanded federal intervention: "Since otherwise they will not do so, private owners of forest land must now be compelled to manage their properties in harmony with the public good" ("Lines" 900). In 1935, Chief Forester Ferdinand Silcox insisted that "if the forests are to be saved and reclaimed for the benefit of the people the government, state and federal, must assume a more direct responsibility both in greater public ownership of the forest land and in closer control over the processes of forest utilization" (200).

While lumbermen welcomed governmental subsidies and assistance for fire control, reforestation, and research, they aggressively resisted any regulation of private forestry. In 1938, George F. Jewett, a Weyerhaeuser executive who was perhaps the most strident critic of regulation, defined the issue as battling "the menace of socialism in our forests" (qtd. in Robbins, *Lumberjacks* 225). Opposition to federal control was especially strong in the South, where the ideology of states' rights remained powerful. In 1941, an executive of the Southern Pine Association warned forestry students at Duke University that "the forestry schools of the country are engaged in preparing young men for government jobs and socialistic objectives rather than in training them for the work and unlimited individualistic opportunities attainable in private forestry fields" (qtd. in L. Walker 199).

Many progressive conservationists saw the economic crisis of the Depression as an opportunity to exert federal control over private lumbering. In 1933, the National Recovery Administration (NRA) directed the lumber industry to develop a code of business practices. In addition to limits on production and regulation of workplace conditions, the Roosevelt administration insisted that the lumber code include conservation measures. Forester Raphael Zon wrote Pinchot that the code represented "the greatest opportunity we have to bring the management of private lands under control" (qtd. in Robbins, "Great Experiment" 133). However, Robbins argues that the final code represented an "empty husk" that placed most of the responsibility for conservation on such governmental initiatives as tax reform, fire prevention, and low-cost loans to the industry ("Great Experiment" 138). Indeed, most lumbermen quickly embraced the self-regulation of the code as an alternative to more coercive control. *The American Lumberman* encouraged the industry "to do its own housekeeping and thus avoid oppressive federal regulation," and David Mason of the Western Pine Association warned of "serious revolution" or "complete socialization" if the New Deal failed (qtd. in Robbins, "Great Experiment" 131, 136). According to Robbins, by the time the NRA was dissolved by the Supreme Court in 1935, this experiment in industrial self-regulation had resulted in little actual conservation ("Great Experiment" 138–39).

Although calls for governmental regulation persisted into the early 1940s, World War II ended all efforts to control private lumbering. In 1942, President Roosevelt told his advisors that until the war was over, "there should be no Federal legislation providing for Federal regulation of forestry practices on private lands" (qtd. in Robbins, *Lumberjacks* 237). But, even without regulation, the Southern forests recovered at a surprising rate. President Roosevelt was a former tree farmer, and, early in his administration, he proposed reforestation of cutover land as "a very hopeful and immediate means of relief" (654). During the 1930s, the Civilian Conservation Corps (CCC) instituted fire control measures and replanted 2.5 million acres of forest. Further reforestation was done by the Tennessee Valley Authority and through flood-control projects such as Sardis Dam, the completion of which in 1940 inundated the Tallahatchie River bottom that had inspired "The Bear." Agricultural failures resulted in the conversion of abandoned farms to forests, and the emergent pulp and paper industries found it profitable to grow and harvest trees on twenty-year cycles. In his semi-fictional history "Mississippi," Faulkner describes the "stump-pocked barrens which would remain until in simple economic desperation people taught themselves to farm pine trees" (*Essays* 21).[4]

༄

During the early twentieth century, the state also became involved in the management of wildlife. Daniel Justin Herman observes that in the nineteenth century, Americans began to embrace hunting as the embodiment of self-reliant American individualism. The popularity of hunting steadily grew, so that according to the US Bureau of the Census, in 1941, there were nearly 8 million licensed hunters (400). However, by the early twentieth century, wildlife populations were at an all-time low, and the future of hunting was threatened. Mississippi was typical in that the popularity of hunting among Mississippians, coupled with limited restrictions and the habitat loss caused by extensive lumbering, had resulted in severely depleted wildlife populations. Harmon Kallman points out that a 1932 game survey established that there were only 7,357 deer in Mississippi (357).

To ensure the continuation of hunting as a crucible of antimodern self-reliance, hunters turned to governmental regulation. Herman discusses the paradox that progressive conservationists such as Theodore Roosevelt faced: "Only by restricting the individual's right to hunt could hunting be saved as a rite of individualism. And only by strengthening government could the individual's right to hunt be effectively restricted" (225). The protective legislation that ensued significantly expanded the role of both the federal and state governments. The 1900 Lacey Act prohibited interstate trafficking in illegal game, and the 1913 Weeks-McLean Act and the 1918 Migratory Bird Act granted the federal government the right to regulate the hunting of migratory birds (including loons). By 1920, most states had created game commissions with paid wardens and had passed laws that restricted seasons, hunting methods, and bag limits. In 1871, Mississippi counties were given the power to regulate hunting, and, in 1906, the first statewide game law establishing licenses and bag limits was passed. Shooting does was banned in 1915, but bag limits remained among the highest in the country (until 1928 Mississippians could legally kill five deer yearly). The Mississippi Game and Fish Commission was created in 1932, but public acceptance of its authority remained inconsistent until after World War II.[5]

The new laws were accompanied by a wildlife bureaucracy that rested upon a progressive ideology of scientific management and professionalism. The Biological Survey was originally created in 1885 to conduct scientific research on wildlife, but, as Congress began to pass protective legislation, the Survey became responsible for enforcing those laws, and game management developed into a profession. Committed to increasing game populations for hunters, game managers viewed wildlife as a crop that could be managed for maximum yield. But the crop proved to be difficult to control, and deer populations fluctuated wildly. Thomas R. Dunlap argues that by the 1930s such failures as the irruption and subsequent crash of the deer populations on Arizona's Kaibab Game Preserve led managers to turn to ecology as a way to legitimize their discipline through scientific quantification (76).

The influence of ecology on game management is best illustrated in the career of Aldo Leopold, whom Lawrence Buell and others have linked to Faulkner. Leopold began his career in 1915 with the Forest Service, but he became increasingly interested in the protection of wildlife. In 1933, he accepted a chair in game management at the University of Wisconsin, and that same year, his book *Game Management* was published, which became the standard textbook in the field. During the early years of his career, Leopold had confidence in the regulatory power of the federal government. In his 1924 essay "Pioneers and Gullies," he insisted that the final step in controlling soil erosion is to implement governmental inspection and "force all owners to conserve their lands to the extent that is found reasonable and practicable. If they fail to do so, the Government must install the necessary controls and assess the landowner with the cost" (*River* 113). Likewise, in 1923, when a conflict developed between the Forest Service and the state of Arizona over the management of the deer herd in the Kaibab National Forest, Leopold saw it as an opportunity to demonstrate "the truth that in the long run the States will retain only such authority as they earn by their competency in game management" (qtd. in Falder 86).

However, by the mid-1930s, Leopold had become disenchanted with statist conservation. Julianne Lutz Newton notes that although Leopold was involved with several New Deal projects, he objected to their lack of integration and their focus on symptoms rather than causes (145–76). In the essays he wrote during this period, Leopold touted individual responsibility as the solution to environmental problems. In "Conservationist in Mexico" (1937), he concluded, "[W]e seem ultimately always thrown back on individual ethics as the basis of conservation policy. It is hard to make a man, by pressure of law or money, do a thing which does not spring naturally from his own personal sense of right and wrong" (*River* 243–44). Likewise, in "Land-Use and Democracy" (1942), Leopold rejected our reliance on the "vicarious conservation" of the government and proposed instead "self-government as a cure for land abuse" (*River* 298–99). Leopold's famous call for a land ethic in *A Sand County Almanac* (1949) is based on a recognition of the limits of external control. After admitting that most of his life had been spent working for governmental conservation, he expressed doubt that taxpayers would continue to fund the massive projects that were necessary. Given those limits, his answer was "a land ethic, or some other force which assigns more obligation to the private landowner" (213). Rather than legal restrictions, the land ethic would be enforced through "social approbation for right actions: social disapproval for wrong actions" (225). Throughout the book, he emphasized the role of the responsible individual: landowners who practice husbandry and hunters who voluntarily exercise the ethical restraint of sportsmanship.[6]

Previous biographers of Leopold have represented his career as an evolution towards a deeper awareness of the significance of ecology. Lisa Mighetto aptly describes this narrative as "one of the most famous stories in American environmental history" (101). However, this interpretation overlooks the extent to which Leopold's career also reflects the anxiety that many Americans in the 1930s felt over the increased power of a centralized, regulatory government. John Milton Cooper notes that the repression of dissidents during World War I "drove many erstwhile Progressives and even radicals to recoil from the concentration of government power" (171). Alan Brinkley observes that by Roosevelt's second term, the rise of totalitarian regimes in Europe and Roosevelt's own political missteps had led to fears that the New Deal could result in a dictatorship (154–64).

In 1934, historian James Truslow Adams reassured readers of *The New York Times Magazine* that the New Deal would not result in either communism or fascism; instead, he predicted that the country was moving toward a "higher" individualism based on "the exercise of self-control, cooperation and social intelligence" (11). The historical development of forestry and game management suggests that by the late 1930s many Americans were troubled by both laissez-faire individualism and coercive regulation by the state. *Go Down, Moses* explores the possibility of individual responsibility as a middle ground between those extremes and in the process shifts the focus of conservation from wilderness to the farm.

Go Down, Moses depicts the environmental and human consequences of unrestrained individualism. Ike McCaslin denounces the plantation system as an edifice "founded upon injustice and erected by ruthless rapacity and carried on even yet with at times downright savagery not only to the human beings but the valuable animals too" (285). During the summer camps, the "proven hunters" shoot turkeys with pistols "for wagers or to test their marksmanship" (196). After Ben has been killed, Major DeSpain rejects a plan to maintain the land as a hunting preserve, and instead sells his property to the lumber companies, guaranteeing its devastation. Fittingly, "The Bear" section ends with an image of the rampant individualism that has destroyed the wilderness. While hunting, Ike comes across Boon Hogganbeck sitting under a tree full of squirrels. Although Boon's gun is in pieces (and even if it were not, he is incapable of hitting anything), he snarls at Ike, "Get out of here! Dont touch them! Dont touch a one of them! They're mine!" (315).

This individualistic possessiveness is also the cause of the human suffering in the novel. Ike's decision to repudiate his family's plantation is driven by his discovery that his grandfather, Carothers McCaslin, used his economic power and social freedom to commit incest with one of his slaves. As Ike explains his decision to Cass Edmonds, he struggles to repudiate "that evil and unregenerate old man who could summon, because she was his property, a human being because she was old enough and female, to his widower's house and get a child on her and then dismiss her because she was of an inferior race" (281).

The modern welfare state that emerged during the New Deal is represented as equally problematic. Roth Edmonds runs the McCaslin plantation during the 1930s and often expresses opposition to New Deal agricultural controls. He sees Lucas Beauchamp as even more trouble and conflict than "the federal government," and when Roth is with other farmers, he adds "his voice to the curses at governmental interference" (112–13, 119). In "Delta Autumn," he seems to equate the New Deal with fascism, asking rhetorically what will be left of the country "after Hitler gets through with it? Or Smith or Jones or Roosevelt or Willkie or whatever he will call himself in this country?" (322). Roth goes on to attack the loss of freedom and responsibility engendered by the welfare state: "Half the people on public dole that wont work and half that couldn't work even if they would. Too much cotton and corn and hogs, and not enough for people to eat and wear. The country full of people to tell a man how he cant raise his own cotton whether he will or wont" (323).[7]

Roth's rants would be easier to dismiss if they did not echo Faulkner's own critiques of the government. In a 1952 address to the Delta Council, Faulkner presented himself as a farmer who had spent fifteen years "trying to cope not only with the Lord but with the federal government too" (*Essays* 127). In that speech, he went on to identify the enemy of freedom as the welfare state that "faces us now from beneath the eagle-perched domes of our capitols and from behind the alphabetical splatters on the doors of welfare and other bureaus of economic or industrial regimentation" (132). As Charles S. Aiken notes, throughout these complaints about the New Deal is a recurring emphasis on the loss of personal responsibility (*William Faulkner* 156).

An alternative to both rampant individualism and governmental coercion is a society of individuals who act ethically without external control. In the novel, Ike McCaslin seems to be such an individual. Trained by Sam Fathers in the code of the hunt and the wilderness, Ike refuses to benefit from the sins of his individualistic forefathers, and he envisions his repudiation of the family plantation as part of the unfolding of God's plan for the South, America, and humanity. However, Ike fails to integrate his mythic wilderness experiences into everyday life in a way that would alleviate the human and environmental problems of the modern South.[8]

Perhaps the cause of Ike's failure is those mythic wilderness experiences and the view of nature they engender. In 1935, just before Faulkner began working on *Go Down, Moses*, Leopold and seven other conservationists gathered in Washington, DC, to organize the Wilderness Society in an effort to preserve primitive public lands. Thirty years later, the Society's efforts resulted in the Wilderness Act of 1964, which legislatively defined wilderness as "an area where the earth and its community of life are untrammeled by man, where man himself is a visitor who does not remain" (qtd. in Callicott, *Great New* 121). Since the early 1990s, some environmental historians have insisted that this conception of wilderness as a place distinct from civilization has problematic implications. In "The Trouble with Wilderness," William Cronon argues that thinking of wilderness areas as separate from civilization represents an "escape from history" and creates "the false hope of an escape from responsibility, the illusion that we can somehow wipe clean the slate of our past and return to the tabula rasa that supposedly existed before we began to leave our marks on the world" (80).[9]

Certainly, Ike's education under Sam Fathers involves a repression of history through mystifications of the true power relationships that have produced the wilderness setting for that education. As Sam narrates stories of the "dead and vanished" Native Americans, they become mythically real to Ike, "as if they were still happening" (165). This, of course, glosses over the reality of the displacement of Native Americans by Ike's white ancestors. Ike's experiences with nature also blur the proprietorship of the McCaslin farm. He consistently denies that anyone can possess the land: "[A]lthough it had been his grandfather's and then his father's and uncle's and was now his cousin's and someday would be his own land . . . their hold upon it actually was as trivial and without reality as the now faded and archaic script in the chancery book in Jefferson which allocated it to them" (165). Perhaps in some mystical sense this is true, but the question of whose name is in the chancery book has a real impact on the lives of the people living on land in post–Civil War Mississippi. As Bart Welling observes, Ike's wilderness experience depends on "his sole imaginative possession of it, a kind of ownership based on its *insulation* from what he imagines to be the tainting blackness of his family/plantation" (488).

Ike's wilderness education likewise obscures the environmental impact of the hunters. Repeatedly, he emphasizes the puniness of the men, which makes them no threat to the more powerful woods, which are "not quite inimical because [the hunters] were too small" (170). After he has killed his first buck, the memory of that experience makes the forest "less than inimical now and never to be inimical again," and he realizes that Sam has "consecrated and absolved him from weakness and regret" for the slain animals (171, 175). By the time of "The Bear," Ike begins to represent the wilderness as "doomed," but he continues to insist on its mythic permanence (185). His stand is virtually virgin as if "frail and timorous man had merely passed without altering it, leaving no mark or scar," and Ike feels abject, with "a sense of his own fragility and impotence against the timeless woods" (194, 192). In "Lion," the story that evolved into "The Bear," the main character is Quentin Compson, who seems to recognize that such feelings of fragility are absurd. When he is placed at his stand for the bear hunt, Quentin is scared until he realizes that his fear is "mindless and superstitious" because he is armed: "I was telling myself that black bears are not dangerous, they won't hurt a man unless they are cornered, when all of a sudden I thought, with a kind of amazed surprise, *Besides, I have a gun. Why, I have a gun!*" (192).

Ike also ignores his own participation in the exploitation of the wilderness. As he matures, Ike grows increasingly competent in the woods and worries because he "found himself becoming so skillful so fast that he feared he would never become worthy because he had not learned humility and pride" (282). On the day that Ben is killed, General Compson assigns Ike to the mule, thereby giving him the best chance to kill the bear, because he recognizes that Ike is the best woodsman among them. Much like Theodore Roosevelt, Ike passes up opportunities to shoot Ben himself, but he is still part of the group that kills the bear. He comforts himself with a belief in the fatality of Ben's death: "It was the beginning of the end of something, he didn't know what except that he would not grieve. He would be humble and proud that he had been found worthy to be a part of it too or even just to see it too" (216–17).

Fifty years later, when he returns to the Delta, Ike contrasts the diminished wilderness of the present with his memory of past hunts and notes that there used to be bear and so much game that "a man shot a doe or a fawn as quickly as he did a buck" (319). But, despite his acknowledgment of the scarcity of game in the present, Ike remains an effective and relentless killer: "[H]e still shot almost as well as he ever had, still killed almost as much of the game he saw as he ever killed; he no longer even knew how many deer had fallen before his gun" (320). Ike's sustained slaughter is in contrast to the hunting of Faulkner himself, who, as Joseph Blotner notes, discovered in his fifties that although he still loved to go to hunting camp, he no longer liked to kill animals (*Faulkner* 2: 1519).[10]

By the time of "Delta Autumn," Ike's views of both nature and race relations are troubling. Upon arrival at the Delta, Ike is able to transcend his sadness over the dwindling wilderness because he recognizes that it was "still wilderness. There was some of it left" (326). He continues to see man's domination of nature in teleological terms: "He had watched it, not being conquered, destroyed, so much as retreating since its purpose was served now and its time an outmoded time" (326). As it turns out, there is just enough wilderness left for Ike: "He seemed to see the two of them—himself and the wilderness—as coevals . . . the two spans running out together, not toward oblivion, nothingness, but into a dimension free of both time and space" (337). In this mythic fantasy of a permanent wilderness, there would be room for Ike, his old hunting friends, and the "tall unaxed trees and sightless brakes where the wild strong immortal game ran forever" (337–38). Clearly, this is the same nature nostalgia that surfaces in Twain, Hurston, and Dickey.

At the end of "Delta Autumn," the racist implications of such nostalgia are made apparent. When he realizes that Roth has repeated the family sins of miscegenation and incest, Ike falls into in a nightmarish vision that conflates the destruction of the wilderness and his fears of racial amalgamation: "This Delta. *This land which man has deswamped and denuded and derivered in two generations so that . . . Chinese and African and Aryan and Jew, all breed and spawn together until no man has time to say which one is which nor cares. . . .* No wonder the ruined woods I used to know dont cry for retribution! . . . The people who have destroyed it will accomplish its revenge" (347). Like progressive conservationists such as Charles Goethe or Madison Grant, Ike equates the elimination of the wilderness with the loss of clear distinctions between the races.

When he is drawn into a discussion of game laws, Ike emphasizes the individualistic nature of wilderness ethics. He rejects Roth Edmonds's pessimistic view that the reason they do not kill does is "because there is a man with a badge to watch us" (331). One of the party instantly comprehends Ike's affirmation of individual responsibility: "We dont kill does because if we did kill does in a few years there wouldn't even be any bucks left to kill" (331). Ike explains that God created the wilderness to give man the opportunity to learn responsibility and restraint: "He said, 'I will give him his chance. I will give him warning and foreknowledge too, along with the desire to follow and the power to slay. The woods and fields he ravages and the game he devastates will be the consequence and signature of his crime and guilt, and his punishment'" (332). In *A Sand County Almanac*, Leopold similarly celebrates sport hunting because it encourages the hunter to become his own observer: "A peculiar virtue in wildlife ethics is that the hunter ordinarily has no gallery to applaud or disapprove of his conduct. Whatever his acts, they are dictated by his own conscience, rather than by a mob of onlookers" (178).

In an 1895 article in *Science* magazine, Bernhard Fernow, the chief of the US Division of Forestry dismissed as naïve the belief that without regulation the individual will "develop the social instinct, will desire the common good even at the expense of his own good, and finally, will seek voluntarily cooperation as a result of superior intelligence" (255). The ethical failures of Ike McCaslin would seem to reinforce Fernow's skepticism. Despite an education that should have produced a responsible individual capable of working toward the common good, Ike retreats into escapist wilderness nostalgia, rejecting his ethical obligation to manage the land and the people on it. When asked about Ike's decision to repudiate his inheritance, Faulkner replied that there were three possible responses to racial injustice. The first two involve a withdrawal from society, similar to what Ike does: "This is rotten, I don't like it, I can't do anything about it, but at least I will not participate in it myself, I will go off into a cave or climb a pillar to sit on" (qtd. in Gwynn 246). Faulkner went on to suggest that a better alternative was to challenge the injustice through concrete actions: "The third says, This stinks and I'm going to do something about it. . . . What we need are people who will say, This is bad and I'm going to do something about it" (qtd. in Gwynn 246).

A major focus of the progressive movement was the restructuring of rural life. In 1916, President Theodore Roosevelt created the Country Life Commission to investigate farm conditions and make recommendations for improvement. The chair of that committee, Cornell agriculture professor Liberty Hyde Bailey, saw the farmer as the ideal balance between "needful individualism and social crystallization" (*Essential* 82). Daniel T. Rodgers argues that the New Dealers viewed the Depression as an opportunity to revive progressive rural reform projects as "a new set of social and solidaristic forms, less anarchic and individualistic than in the past" (*Atlantic* 449). But, despite their efforts, the emphasis of agricultural reform remained centered on individual choice. The Agriculture Adjustment Act of 1933 sought to stabilize prices by paying farmers to voluntarily reduce production—the target of Roth's complaints about the government telling "a man how he cant raise his own cotton whether he will or wont" (323). The Roosevelt administration also educated farmers on more efficient agricultural techniques, such as contour plowing to conserve soil. Anthony J. Badger notes that the New Dealers wanted "to reverse the traditional exploitative, individualistic attitude to the land" by encouraging farmers to voluntarily rely on the advice of agricultural experts (169). But he points out that, ultimately, these efforts had little impact on the forces that were changing modern agriculture: mechanization and the rise of giant agribusiness farms (189).

When asked at the University of Virginia about the destruction of the wilderness depicted in *Go Down, Moses*, Faulkner indicated that we should feel compassion for the "obsolete" wilderness (qtd. in Gwynn 277). But then he argued that if a "wise person" takes charge of the environmental change to prevent a purely mercenary exploitation, the loss of the wilderness could be positive if it "makes more education for more people, and more food for more people, more of the good things in life" (qtd. in Gwynn 277). In other words, under the guidance of a responsible individual, the loss of the wilderness would be acceptable if the resulting increased agriculture supported the life-enhancing goals of the biopolitical state. *Go Down, Moses* represents farmers as responsible individualists who can conserve both the land and the people living on it.

Despite Faulkner's frequent assertions in the 1940s and 1950s that farming was his primary occupation, critics have paid less attention to the novel's representation of agriculture than they have to its wilderness hunting scenes.[11] From 1938 to the 1950s, Faulkner raised mules and horses and grew cotton and corn on a 320-acre farm in northeastern Lafayette County that he named Greenfield. When asked in a 1957 interview what he liked to do, Faulkner replied, "Farming, I suppose. I'm a farmer by profession. I've bullocks, horses, farmhouses—all sorts. I like moving in the field" (qtd. in Inge 152). Indeed, one might usefully compare Faulkner's work at Greenfield to Aldo Leopold's 1935 purchase of a rundown farm in Wisconsin, which he described as a "refuge from too much modernity" (*Sand County* viii).[12]

Since Ike repudiated the McCaslin plantation, the possession of the farm with "its benefits and responsibilities" went to Cass Edmonds and his descendants, Zach and Roth (44). If "The Old People" depicts Ike's initiation into wilderness ethics through the killing of his first deer, it is worth noting that Cass was also baptized by Sam Fathers. When Ike insists that he saw the spirit buck, Cass reassures him, "Steady. I know you did. So did I. Sam took me in there once after I killed my first deer" (180). After Buck and Buddy McCaslin die in 1870, twenty-year-old Cass takes over the farm, and by the 1880s, his commitment to the wilderness seems to be compromised by his responsibilities to the plantation. Arguing that Ike should be allowed to stay in the woods with the dying Sam Fathers, General Compson negatively contrasts Cass with Ike. Cass has "one foot straddled into a farm and the other foot straddled into a bank" and doesn't have a "good hand-hold where this boy was already an old man long before you damned Sartorises and Edmondses invented farms and banks" (240). Yet, under Cass's administration, the plantation is "solvent and efficient and, more than that: not only still intact but enlarged, increased" (285). As Nancy Drew Taylor notes, this would have been "quite a feat" given the economic circumstances of the late nineteenth century (187). Cass also demonstrates care for the human inhabitants, building a house for Lucas and allotting him acreage to farm (106). Even Fonsiba's Yankee husband patronizingly admits that "in your way, according to your lights and upbringing" Cass has treated Fonsiba (and presumably the other tenants) well (263).[13]

Cass dies in the 1890s, leaving the plantation to Zack. Although he appears less frequently than any of the Edmondses, the brief references in "The Fire and the Hearth" suggest a complicated but positive relationship with his tenants. Daniel J. Singal correctly interprets his struggle with Lucas over Molly as "a hopelessly tangled web of causation, arising directly from the South's tangled racial past, that Zack, for all his good intentions, could never hope to decipher" (272). In addition to honoring the family commitment to Lucas, in his will, he arranges for Molly to be cared for in perpetuity (98).

When Zach dies in 1921, twenty-three-year-old Roth inherits the farm. He is a problematic character, perhaps because he is a composite of different characters appearing in the stories that became *Go Down, Moses*. The relations of Roth with the people of the plantation are not ideal, but they are not entirely flawed either. His interactions with Lucas reveal a racist paternalism, but also a sincere desire to work cooperatively with him. Despite his near-constant frustration with his oldest tenant, Roth posts bail for Lucas and represents his interests in the court. As David Paul Ragan notes, "Roth remains a participant in life—fulfilling his obligations to the land and to his tenants; he remains involved and vulnerable in a way Ike does not" (305). From an environmental perspective, the worst that can be said about Roth is that he presumably illegally kills a doe in "Delta Autumn" (348).[14]

Lucas represents another alternative to Ike's escapist repudiation. There is no indication that he ever accompanied the hunters to the Big Woods, but, as a boy, Lucas hunts small game on the plantation with Zach, much as young Ike did (111). However, by the time of "The Fire and the Hearth," he has given up hunting "because he felt that the pursuit of rabbits and 'possums for meat was no longer commensurate with his status" (36). Instead, his experience of nature has come primarily from agricultural work in the pastoral middle ground between wilderness and civilization. His reflections on farming echo Faulkner's: "He had liked it; he approved of his fields and liked to work them, taking a solid pride in having good tools to use and using them well, scorning both inferior equipment and shoddy work" (42). Lucas's pride is parallel to Rider's satisfaction with his work at the lumber mill in "Pantaloon in Black" and invites comparison to Kimberly Ruffin's insistence on the centrality of work in African Americans' experience of nature (21).[15]

Lucas also poses a critique of modern farming technologies. Roth complains that Lucas continues "to farm his acreage in the same clumsy old fashion which Carothers McCaslin himself had probably followed, declining advice, refusing to use improved implements, refusing to let a tractor so much as cross the land" (113). This passage is especially intriguing since, shortly after buying Greenfield Farm, Faulkner purchased a used Fordson tractor. As Charles S. Aiken points out, Henry Ford's Fordson was one of the first mass-produced tractors; thus, "Symbolically, Faulkner participated in the introduction of the machine into American cotton production" ("Faulkner" 16). Zach also refuses to allow tractors on the farm, so Lucas's opposition seems driven more by antimodern rejection of the new rather than any awareness of the environmental problems of mechanized agriculture (43). Lucas also spurns the modern technology of aerial spraying, "refusing even to allow the pilot who dusted the rest of the cotton with weevil poison, even fly his laden aeroplane through the air above it," a stance that does seem to anticipate contemporary concerns about toxicity (113). Edmund Russell points out that although aerial crop dusting for boll weevils with chemicals that had been developed in World War I for use against the enemy was commonplace, many southern hunters were concerned about the effect on wildlife, and sharecroppers feared that they might be poisoned (67, 80).

The land stewardship of the Edmondses and Lucas can be contrasted to the Arkansas farm of Fonsiba's husband. Despite his own rejection of responsibility to the land, Ike has nothing but contempt for its unkempt appearance: he sees it as "a farm only in embryo, perhaps a good farm, maybe even a plantation someday, but not now, not for years yet and only then with labor, hard and enduring and unflagging work and sacrifice" (265). In contrast to Ike, the Edmondses do not turn to a mythical wilderness to evade responsibility; instead, they attempt to negotiate the complicated physical and social terrain of the post–Civil War South by managing the plantation based on careful stewardship of the land and respect for the people living on it, rather than individual rapacity or governmental control. Likewise, Lucas does not join the African American migration north, but instead remains on the land, farming it in his fiercely independent fashion.[16]

Go Down, Moses does not resist the human domination of the wilderness; instead, the novel suggests that the taming of the wilderness by the farmer represents an example of responsible environmental stewardship. The relative neglect by ecocritics of farming in *Go Down, Moses* perhaps reflects what Dana Phillips has described as their suspicion of pastoralism because of its compromises with civilization: "Many of them subscribe to the questionable idea that wilderness is the chief repository or savings bank of value insofar as the natural world is concerned, since it is the one place supposed to be forever wild and hence forever true" (147). But, in his critique of traditional views of wilderness, Kenneth R. Olwig imagines a usage of nature that "emphasizes sustainable reciprocity rather than domination and makes of nature not a spectacle but something to be dwelled within" (380).

In 1935, Faulkner and two friends organized the Okatoba Hunting and Fishing Club in an attempt to preserve the area where he had hunted since the 1920s. Faulkner sought help from the state Game and Fish Commission, explaining his plan to hire a deputy game warden "to protect the game which is fast being exterminated in that section" (qtd. in Blotner, *Faulkner* 1: 879). A more ambivalent attitude toward governmental regulation of wildlife is suggested by his encounter with a state game warden while hunting ducks in the Tallahatchie River bottom. When asked to produce his hunting license, Faulkner was forced to admit that he didn't have one.[17]

Richard Gray, in *The Life of William Faulkner*, draws upon Bakhtin's concept of the polyphonic novel to argue that Faulkner's great novels are dialogic: "Throughout his life . . . he was involved in argument (with all that term implies by way of agreement and conflict) with a series of sociohistorical positions and events, cultural traditions and allegiances, that were his peculiar destiny" (12). Certainly, one of those arguments involved the role of the government. Atkinson sees Faulkner as part of a class of Southern Democrats who were conflicted by the social upheaval of the Depression and the changes instituted by the New Deal: "Experiencing high anxiety, the dominant class in the Depression longed for an overarching sense of stability and security and yet remained heavily invested in fundamental tenets of classical liberalism: self-reliance, state and local control, and private property rights" (12).

This conflict is evident in the representation of both hunting and farming in *Go Down, Moses*. The novel presents a range of possibilities, from unrestrained individualism to state control; ultimately, however, individual stewardship seems to emerge as a tenuous answer to the environmental and social problems in the South. Faulkner's comments on race in the 1950s and 1960s reveal a similar emphasis on personal responsibility rather than governmental coercion. In his 1956 "Letter to a Northern Editor," he opposed those forces "which would use legal or police compulsion" to eliminate the problem of racism: "I was against compulsory segregation. I am just as strongly against compulsory integration" (*Essays* 86). For Faulkner, the alternative to statist coercion is responsible whites who take up their burden. At the University of Virginia in 1958, Faulkner paternalistically explained that the role of whites is to teach "the responsibilities of equality" to blacks (*Essays* 157).

Individual environmental stewardship has remained a popular conservative ideology. In March 2012, Representative Bob Goodlatte, a Republican from Virginia, introduced legislation that would limit the authority of the Environmental Protection Agency (EPA) over the clean-up of the Chesapeake Bay. Goodlatte praised individual farmers who are making "good faith efforts" and denounced the EPA for ignoring the "voluntary measures" being undertaken by farmers (E329). Similarly, Ted Steinberg discusses the shift in contemporary environmentalism from the regulation of corporations to personal responsibility in antilitter campaigns, Earth Day celebrations, and the climate change movement (*Down to Earth* 229, 254, 290). *Go Down, Moses* suggests that the roots of this confidence in the responsible individual can be found in the 1930s reaction against progressivism and the New Deal.[18]

Epilogue

In 1913, the progressive agrarian Liberty Hyde Bailey called upon farmers to become part of "the physical conquest of the earth" (*Country-Life* 58). Praising the "social brotherhood" that was displayed during the construction of the Panama Canal, he insisted that although the era of militarism was ending, Americans still had opportunities to develop "the finest spirit of conquest" and thus avoid racial weakness: "There are mountains to pierce, sea-shores to reclaim, vast stretches of submerged land to drain, millions of acres to irrigate and many more millions to utilize by dry-farming, rivers to canalize, the whole open country to organize and subdue by means of local engineering work" (57–58). The past century of American environmental history suggests that we have indeed taken up Bailey's challenge.

One impulse for pursuing this project came a few years ago when I was lecturing on what I call (after Stephen Greenblatt) "The Swerve" in American views of nature. As I was explaining the rise of less-anthropocentric views of nature at the turn of the twentieth century, a student asked me why this environmental perspective did not immediately become the mainstream view. Subsequently, as I examined the roots of contemporary environmentalism, it became clear that the belief that nature must be subdued persisted well into the twentieth century. In an article written the year after the passage of the 1964 Wilderness Act, Robert Wernick argues that the wilderness "is precisely what man has been fighting against since he began his painful, awkward climb to civilization. It is the dark, the formless, the terrible, the old chaos which our fathers pushed back, which surrounds us yet, which will engulf us all in the end. It is held at bay by constant vigilance, and when the vigilance slackens it swoops down for a melodramatic revenge" (12). Writing just three years before the first Earth Day celebration in 1970, Earl Finbar Murphy insisted, "The ambition of man has always been to control completely not only his immediate environment but all of nature," and he predicted that "a total control of nature is possible in a not very distant future" (3, 11). Alfred Hitchcock's *The Birds* (1963), a nightmarish vision of a threatening nature, was released the year after *Silent Spring* was published. Nor did the dominance paradigm end in the 1970s with the birth of contemporary environmentalism. As Samuel Hays has discussed in *Beauty, Health, and Permanence*, a central part of the Reagan revolution of the 1980s was resistance to the gains of the environmental movement, and that conservative reaction has been deeply embedded in the politics of the twenty-first century.

It is always tempting to read contemporary discourses into texts written during a different era and thus uncover the embryonic beginnings of our modern perspective. In his excellent *Witnesses to a Vanishing America* (1981), Lee Clark Mitchell invokes the resistance narrative by pointing out that "issues that we assume are modern—conservation, protection of endangered species, native rights, and questioning of the price of progress—actually originated early in the nineteenth century" (xiv). More recently, in *The Myth of Silent Spring* (2018), Chad Montrie has challenged "the *Silent Spring* origin story of environmentalism" by tracing the beginnings of the movement to nineteenth-century working-class environmental concerns (60).[1] Indeed, our views seem more authentic if we can trace them back to enlightened seers of an earlier era. Thus, it is not surprising that ecocritics have discovered continuity with contemporary environmental thought in turn-of-the-century works of literature. But it is important to recognize that literary texts are always entangled with the ideologies that were present at the time they were written and that this imbrication complicates any attempt to see history as progressive evolutionary change. The environmental attitudes of Kate Chopin might well be similar to those of Terry Tempest Williams, but they probably more closely resemble the views of Gifford Pinchot.

Of course, my own work is likewise a product of its cultural moment. During the writing of this book, Progressive Era issues have been ubiquitous, as Americans have debated immigration restriction, the regulation of business, social welfare, regulatory environmentalism, and the politics of inclusion. Indeed, it is tempting to hear an echo of Theodore Roosevelt's critique of the "nature fakers" in President Trump's attack on "fake news." Meanwhile, a series of natural disasters have devastated some of the same regions I have been writing about, yet many Americans remain reluctant to connect these problems to human activity: the Yale Program on Climate Change Communication indicates that in 2016 only 53 percent of Americans believe that global warming is caused by anthropogenic factors, and 42 percent are not worried about the risks (Marlon, et al.). These contexts have undoubtedly contributed to my skepticism about the progressive narrative of American environmentalism.

For these reasons, tracing the genealogy of contemporary environmentalism is a complicated project. Historians have seen the beginnings of the movement in George Perkins Marsh's *Man and Nature* (1864) or in the writings of Thoreau and Muir. Others point to the Progressive Era conservation of Pinchot and Roosevelt, Carson's *Silent Spring*, or the first Earth Day in 1970. *Reconciling Nature* suggests that modern environmentalism developed in the decades surrounding the turn of the century from a complicated tangle of ideologies of nature. My readings of these novels indicate that after the American Civil War, individuals did begin to see the nonhuman world in less anthropocentric ways, but this environmental awareness was complicated by a persistent discourse of domination that was intimately connected to anxieties about human as well as natural threats. Environmentalism in what historians have begun calling "the long Progressive Era" was largely a response by white middle-class Americans to the social transformations that were produced by the emergence of modern industrial capitalism.[2] Focusing on the representation of nature in these novels reveals a series of intertwined efforts to reconcile those anxieties by manipulating the natural world and by controlling others through nature.

One anxiety that surfaces in these texts is the tension between the individual and the state that developed from the significantly stronger national government that emerged after the Civil War. The progressives relied on this newly empowered state to address the serious environmental and social problems of the era, and women and African Americans turned to the federal government for social justice and empowerment. But, by the 1930s, many Americans were concerned that the individual was being lost to the collective, and a reaction against statism surfaced. The novels of Crane, Chopin, Sinclair, and Austin recognize the diminishment of individual autonomy resulting from the interdependence of the city. Twain's frontier and Dreiser's wilderness park are sites of potential lawlessness that require state intervention. Both Austin and Hurston seem to embrace the state's pursuit of social justice even if it means a loss of individuality. Only Faulkner, writing at the end of the New Deal, insists on the responsible individual as an alternative to statist coercion.

Another concern during this period was the assimilation of individuals and groups perceived as different into mainstream American culture. The emancipation of the slaves, the massive immigration from southern and eastern Europe, the subjugation of the Native Americans, and women's growing demand for equality left native-born cultural elites concerned about a potential loss of authority. For many progressives, Darwin's theories established a clear hierarchy of species, races, and genders, and they worried that modern society intermingled the less evolved with the more highly civilized. The progressives also believed that nature could serve an educational or even a disciplinary role as it socialized the lower classes, women, immigrants, and people of color. However, since these groups were seen as already closer to the natural, the use of nature to assimilate them involved potential risks and demanded careful surveillance and management by experts.

Written at the beginning of the period, Twain's *Huckleberry Finn* remains ambivalent yet hopeful about the possible inclusion of African Americans into American society. Crane's *Maggie* is more pessimistic, emphasizing the need for police power to control the lower classes in the unnatural environment of the city. Likewise, Chopin's *The Awakening* explores the problems that unmanageable nature represented for women, difficulties that might be alleviated by experts in psychology. Sinclair and Austin shared the progressives' confidence in their ability to control both the natural world and the problematic nature of immigrants and social radicals through scientific management and eugenics. Influenced by Freud, Dreiser shifts attention to the threatening nature of the individual subconscious. In a society obsessed over racial difference, Hurston sought assimilation of those who could demonstrate the ability to control nature. Writing at the end of the period, when a reaction against progressivism had emerged, Faulkner's unease with statist environmentalism seems strikingly similar to his distaste for government-enforced integration.

Anxieties over the threats to human life that were posed by natural catastrophes could be alleviated by progressive confidence in science and technology. The decades surrounding the end of the nineteenth century introduced a domination of the external world that was previously unimaginable. Technological developments in flood control, irrigation, and weather prediction seemed to make humans less vulnerable to the vicissitudes of the natural world. The scientific management of nature is most evident in the work of Chopin, Austin, and Hurston. All three personally experienced the negative consequences of a threatening nature, and their novels express little reservation about human efforts to control the natural world. As this domination led to the diminishment of wild areas, regret over the lost wilderness became widespread, but that sense of loss was reconciled by a belief that the changes of modernity could be embraced or at least tolerated as long as the wild persisted in nostalgic imaginative reconstruction or in legislatively preserved remnants. Thus, the creation of national parks and wilderness areas is paralleled by Twain's evocation of the Mississippi River Valley, by Chopin's restoration of Grande Isle, by Hurston's preservation of rural black folklore, and by Ike McCaslin's escape into a mythical wilderness.

During this time, many Americans began to see nature as an antimodern protest against the overcivilization and the unnatural conditions of the city, and they sought a more natural experience by going on camping trips, moving to the suburbs, and reading nature stories. However, this anti-urban impulse conflicted with a growing fascination with the city. By the early twentieth century, American cities had become symbols of modernism, while rural life was increasingly viewed as benighted. As William Cronon notes in *Nature's Metropolis*, "If the city was unfamiliar, immoral, and terrifying, it was also a new life challenging its residents with dreams of worldly success, a landscape in which the human triumph over nature had declared anything to be possible" (13). The novels in this study suggest that the back-to-nature movement produced ambivalence about the socializing potential of nature and the danger of reversion to the primitive. While Crane saw hope in transplanting children from the city to rural environments, both Twain and Sinclair seem to recognize that such excursions to the wilderness were themselves entangled in industrial civilization. Similarly, Edna Pontellier's vacation at the beach alienates her from civilization; Clyde Griffiths discovers that the Adirondacks are not a safe space to indulge his fantasies; and Ike McCaslin's wilderness experiences render him incapable of contributing to the environmental and social problems of the South.

Written at a time of environmental crisis (perhaps this is always the case), these novels reveal a variety of creative strategies to reconcile anxiety over a disappearing natural world with the need to control and develop a threatening nature. Their engagement with both the newfound respect for nature and the continued impulse to dominate the natural help account for their ongoing popularity. Rejecting simplistic reductions, these authors explored the tensions embedded in their society's views of nature. A similar engagement with the Progressive Era's complex views of nature can be seen among those scientists and public figures associated with America's use of atomic weapons.

On November 10, 1950, eight years after *Go Down, Moses* was published, Faulkner was notified that he had been awarded the 1949 Nobel Prize for Literature. Reluctant to travel to Sweden to accept the award, Faulkner evaded the issue by retreating to deer camp. Eventually, however, he succumbed to pressure from his family and the State Department and agreed to go to Stockholm, where he delivered a 557-word speech that has subsequently been acknowledged as one of the best of the Nobel acceptance addresses.[3]

In his speech, Faulkner proclaims his faith in the human ability to triumph over the fear caused by the atomic era. Just over a year before, the USSR exploded its first nuclear weapon, thereby initiating an arms race that would continue through the century. Thus, Faulkner begins by observing, "Our tragedy today is a general and universal physical fear so long sustained by now that we can even bear it. There are no longer problems of the spirit. There is only the question: When will I be blown up?" (*Essays* 119). Faulkner then suggests that the fear of nuclear holocaust has led to a diminished literature that ignores the "old universal truths" and "the problems of the human heart in conflict with itself" (119–20). Instead, today's writer focuses on ephemeral, naturalistic subjects: "He writes not of love but of lust. . . . He writes not of the heart but of the glands" (120). Faulkner concludes by encouraging writers to reject the role of spectator to the impending "end of man" (120). Instead they must be the "props" to help humanity "endure and prevail" (120). While endurance is a long-standing Faulknerian virtue (usually attributed to African Americans and women), in the Nobel Prize speech, he insists on more than mere animal survival. James B. Carothers argues that the final paragraph of the speech "represents a conscious choice for Faulkner, a manifesto against the despair, cynicism, pessimism, and solipsism he recognized in the Cold War *zeitgeist*" (29–30).

Faulkner's affirmative conclusion also aligns with an official project in the late 1940s to soothe American fears of nuclear war. In *By the Bomb's Early Light* (1985), Paul Boyer describes the efforts of the Atomic Energy Commission to naturalize the atom by "playing down the bomb's dangers and discrediting those who continued to warn of such dangers" (303). Faulkner's alignment with this goal is perhaps not surprising given his subsequent diplomacy for the State Department, efforts which Catherine Gunther Kodat has called "his career as one of America's first Cold War cultural celebrities" (157). Likewise, Faulkner's emphasis on prevailing rather than just surviving can be seen as a reflection of the focus on "quality-of-life" issues that Thomas Robertson has identified in discussions of overpopulation in the 1950s. He notes that as the population continued to grow, many Americans became concerned about not only survival, but also threats to "freedom, creativity, clean air, space, and solitude" (79).

Faulkner's decision to structure his speech around the possibility of atomic apocalypse seems especially appropriate since the award he was receiving was funded by Alfred Nobel, the inventor of dynamite. Nobel hoped that his stable explosive would be a tool that would enhance human control of nature in areas such as mining, but it did not take long for the military potential of dynamite to be developed. Nobel did not see a conflict between his explosives and world peace: in 1892 he wrote fellow pacifist Bertha von Suttner, "My factories may end war sooner than your congresses. The day when two army corps will be able to destroy each other in one second, all civilized nations will recoil from war in horror and disband their armies" (qtd. in Sohlman and Schück 227). Needless to say, Nobel's prophecy that the threat of mutually assured destruction would end warfare proved to be naive. On August 6, 1945, five years before Faulkner's speech, the United States dropped an atomic bomb equivalent to approximately eleven thousand tons of Nobel's dynamite on Hiroshima, Japan, leveling the city and killing more than 140,000 people. Three days later, a bomb equivalent to approximately nineteen thousand tons of dynamite was dropped on Nagasaki, killing another 70,000 Japanese.[4]

The debate among historians over the decision to use atomic weapons against Japan has been contentious. The orthodox view insists that the bombs were militarily necessary to end the war quickly and save the casualties that would have resulted from an invasion of the mainland. Revisionists argue that President Harry Truman and his advisers knew that the Japanese were nearly defeated and could be induced to surrender by either Russian involvement in the war (which occurred three days after Hiroshima) or by a modification of the unconditional surrender terms to allow for the continuance of the emperor (as was eventually conceded). These historians claim that the decision to use the bomb was driven by a desire to intimidate the Soviet Union through atomic diplomacy, as well as by a racist impulse to punish the hated Japanese. An ecocritical reading of the development and deployment of the first atomic bombs is unlikely to settle this debate, but it does suggest that the ideologies of nature that have been the focus of this book might have provided a deep structure for the decisions that were made, the rationales that were offered for those decisions, and the American public's response to the bombings.[5]

The reverse side of the Nobel Prize medal for Physics and Chemistry depicts the goddess Science lifting the veil (and exposing the breasts) of the goddess Nature, who carries a cornucopia; on the edge of the medal is a Latin motto that translates, "They who bettered life on earth by new-found mastery" (Larsson 31). Apart from strategic considerations, the construction of the atomic bomb represents an apotheosis of the human effort to master and dominate the natural world through technology. A few months after the war, physicist Robert Oppenheimer, the director of the Los Alamos laboratory, insisted upon the morality of his efforts: "If you are a scientist you believe that it is good to find out how the world works; that it is good to find out what the realities are; that it is good to turn over to mankind at large the greatest possible power to control the world" (qtd. in Rhodes 761). Similarly, Willard Libby, another physicist who worked on the Manhattan Project, boasted, "Man's place in the physical universe is to be its master . . . and by controlling the natural forces with his intelligence, to put them to work to suit his purposes, and to build a future world in his own image" (17). Physicist Edward Teller is best known for encouraging the development of the hydrogen bomb, which he predicted "will allow us to extend our power over natural phenomena far beyond anything we can at present imagine" (qtd. in Rhodes 758). Nonscientists were equally impressed: Secretary of War Henry Stimson thought the bomb "constitutes merely a first step in a new control by man over the forces of nature too revolutionary and dangerous to fit into the old concepts" (qtd. in Alperovitz 427). And science-fiction writer Philip Wylie exulted, "What greater challenge than to wrestle the fundamental powers of the universe into submission!" (qtd. in Boyer, *Bomb's* 137).

But this sense of mastery over nature also raised concerns about the future of humanity. Writing a few days after the bombing, *Saturday Review of Literature* editor Norman Cousins noted that any elation over the end of the war was tempered by fear, "a primitive fear, the fear of the unknown, the fear of forces man can neither channel nor comprehend" (5). Boyer demonstrates that after a war in which the American mainland escaped destruction, the atomic bomb suddenly made Americans feel terribly vulnerable. While individual death has always been a possibility, the power of the new weapons threatened to bring the extinction of the human race, or even the end of nature itself (*Bomb's* 276–81). Boyer notes that some felt that scientists had gone too far in uncovering nature's secrets: "In powerful counterpoint to the almost desperate faith in scientists as technological wonder-workers and political sages, one also finds strong currents of fear, mistrust, and disillusionment" (*Bomb's* 268–69). Oppenheimer himself admitted in a 1945 speech to the American Philosophical Society that by creating such a "terrible weapon," scientists have "raised again the question of whether science is good for man, of whether it is good to learn about the world, to try to understand it, to try to control it, to help give to the world of men increased insight, increased power" (7). Not surprisingly, his answer was "an unalterable *yes*," but others were less confident (7). Herbert Hoover, an engineer at heart, saw the wastefulness of the atomic bomb as both immoral and a violation of scientific efficiency; he reflected sadly, "The use of the atomic bomb, with its indiscriminate killing of women and children, revolts my soul" (qtd. in Alperovitz 635).

Despite their commitment to the cult of technology, the scientists involved in the bomb project were not immune to the anti-urban return to the natural. In *The Republic of Nature*, Mark Fiege challenges the assumption that the "atomic scientists had no affinity for the wonder and power of nature"; instead he argues that that they "sought to understand nature, and they found great intellectual and emotional satisfaction in their study of it" (283, 306). Certainly, the scientists who developed the bomb often turned to the natural world for therapy and recreation. To overcome his boyhood sickliness, Oppenheimer spent a summer at a dude ranch in New Mexico, not far from the eventual site of Los Alamos Laboratory. Richard Rhodes notes that "like Eastern semi-invalids in frontier days, Oppenheimer's encounter with wilderness, freeing him from overcivilized restraints, was decisive, a healing of faith" (121). Oppenheimer's familiarity with the area enabled him to suggest the Los Alamos location, which was the site of a private outdoor school for boys, modeled after the Boy Scouts (William S. Burroughs was a graduate). Rhodes notes that while working on the bomb, the scientists relaxed through horseback riding, mountain climbing, and fly fishing (however, Enrico Fermi took the ethical stand of insisting on using worms since he felt that the trout's final meal should be authentic). Rhodes also recounts that during the construction of the Trinity site in southern New Mexico, the army MPs hunted antelopes with machine guns to provide fresh meat for the scientists (567–68, 654).

Another nature-loving physicist, Albert Einstein, was vacationing in the Adirondacks when he heard that the bomb had been dropped. In an interview with the *Albany Times Union*, Einstein reassured the reporter of the weapon's naturalness: "In developing atomic or nuclear energy, science did not draw upon supernatural strength, but merely imitated the reaction of the sun's rays. Atomic power is no more unnatural than when I sail my boat on Saranac Lake" (qtd. in Stager 239). Seeing nuclear energy as natural helped reconcile American fears of the bomb, and the public quickly became intrigued with the potential of the new technology to control an unruly nature. The US Air Force considered using atomic bombs to deflect tornados from Florida, and others proposed using nuclear power to improve agriculture, dig canals, and blast open mountain chains (Steinberg, *Acts of God* 128–29; Boyer, *Bomb's* 113). Boyer notes that one idea that generated substantial interest was using atomic bombs to melt the polar icecaps, thereby raising ocean levels, improving the climate, and opening lands for development; however, a 1946 article in *Science Digest* cited scientists who argued that such a project would be too expensive (*Bomb's* 111, 115).

The development of the bomb was made possible by Depression-era conservation projects designed to control a threatening nature. Oak Ridge, Tennessee, and Hanford, Washington, were chosen to produce enriched uranium and plutonium because they had access to electricity from hydroelectric dams built in the 1930s by the Tennessee Valley Authority and the Army Corps of Engineers. Indeed, some of the Oak Ridge residents who were forced to evacuate had already been twice transplanted: once by the development of the Smoky Mountains National Park and once by the construction of the Norris Dam. Conservation ideology also influenced plans for postwar reconstruction. Douglas Brinkley points out that Roosevelt believed that conservation could be the basis of peace, and he planned to create a deindustrialized, pastoral postwar Germany (*Rightful Heritage* 549–51, 560). Furthermore, peacetime uses of atomic energy drew upon positive views of nature to ease the public's fears of the atom. John Wills explores the similarities that link the nuclear landscapes of testing grounds and reactors to the creation, management, and cultural significance of national parks; he notes that in the 1960s and 1970s, "corporations located nuclear plants amidst newly created 'nature reserves,' hoping that local wildlife would freely congregate alongside reactors and thus show their support of the atom" (460).

The deeply rooted American uneasiness with the city also influenced the response to nuclear weapons. Gar Alperovitz notes that Admiral Lewis Strauss proposed demonstrating the power of the bomb to the Japanese by dropping one over a cryptomeria forest near Nikko, a place that he had visited before the war (333). Cryptomeria is a Japanese cedar that grows up to seventy yards tall and two yards in diameter, and Strauss felt that the flattening of the trees would convince the Japanese of the bomb's potential. Instead, the two bombs were dropped on the cities of Hiroshima and Nagasaki. According to Alperovitz, the targets were chosen primarily for their potential to have a spectacular psychological effect on the Japanese (524). However, it seems possible that on some level American anti-urbanism influenced the choice of targets. In a December 15, 1945, speech, Truman contrasted the natural and the urban when he explained that when he made the decision, "It occurred to me that a quarter of a million of the *flower* of our young manhood was worth a couple of Japanese *cities*, and I still think they were and are" (my italics, qtd. in Alperovitz 516). At Los Alamos, the army turned the unpopulated high desert into a city, so the scientists could create a weapon that would turn cities into deserts. After the blast, a survivor observed that Hiroshima was "no longer a city, but a burnt-over prairie" (qtd. in Alperovitz 416). Paul Boyer notes that one of the effects of the bomb was to revitalize the prestige of city-planning experts, who urged that decentralizing American cities would make them less vulnerable to nuclear attack and solve other chronic urban problems (176). Elmer T. Peterson, in his 1946 anthology of anti-urbanism, *Cities Are Abnormal*, asks, "[D]oes not modern warfare (specifically the atomic bomb) advise us to scatter rather than to gather in dense clusters of humanity?" (11).[6]

Edmund Russell has argued that in the early twentieth century chemical warfare and pest control produced not only a consilience of technologies, but also a shared ideological framework: "[P]est control created a set of values that warriors used to argue for combatting and even annihilating

Figure E.1. Hiroshima, 1945 (Wikimedia Commons)

human enemies. War created a powerful motive and rationale for a huge leap in the scale on which people controlled insects" (3–4). Perhaps the most controversial aspect of the debate over the decision to drop the bomb is the question of whether it was driven by racist views of the Japanese. Anti-Asian sentiment in America was deeply rooted, and once war broke out, the Japanese enemy was seen as different from the Germans. Shortly after Pearl Harbor, more than 110,000 Japanese Americans were forcibly relocated to internment camps (one major camp was Manzanar, in Mary Austin's Owens Valley). John Dower, in *War without Mercy*, argues that "webs of perception" in both Japan and the United States led to atrocities and war crimes that in turn reinforced those stereotypes (73). While Americans recognized that there were "good Germans," the "Japs" were seen as a homogenous, subhuman species. He notes that before and during the war, governmental officials, soldiers, and the general public represented the Japanese as rabid dogs, ants, vermin, and, most commonly, savage apes or monkeys (81–85).

Journalist John Hersey noted that "the Japs are like animals. Against them you have to learn a whole new set of physical reactions. You have to get used to their animal stubbornness and tenacity. They take to the jungle as if they had been bred there, and like some beasts you never see them until they are dead" (qtd. in Rhodes 519). Popular war correspondent Ernie Pyle observed, "In Europe we felt that our enemies, horrible and deadly as they were, were still people. But out here I soon gathered that the Japanese were looked upon as something subhuman and repulsive; the way some people feel about cockroaches or mice" (qtd. in Dower 78). Dower notes that this 'linguistic softening of the killing process" relied on two metaphors: hunting and exterminating pests (89). Thus, a 1943 article in the Marine magazine *Leatherneck* described Guadalcanal as a "hunter's paradise . . . teeming with monkey-men" (qtd. in Dower 90). In August 1945 a letter to the editor in the *Milwaukee Journal* complained that the United States had stopped dropping atomic bombs on Japan, asking, "When one sets out to destroy vermin, does one try to leave a few alive in the nest?" (qtd. in Boyer, *Bomb's* 185).

In *"Society Must be Defended,"* Michel Foucault argues that such racism enables the biopolitical state, whose ostensible purpose is not only to "make live" by regulating populations, but also to wage war and thus "expose not only its enemies but its own citizens to the risk of death" (254). Racism establishes a break or "caesura" in "the biological continuum addressed by biopower" by defining some groups as inferior and worthy of extermination (255). Coevally, a positive relation is established, whereby "the death of the other, the death of the bad race, of the inferior race (or the degenerate, or the abnormal) is something that will make life in general healthier" (255). Thus, war becomes not only a destruction of the inferior enemy, but "a way of regenerating one's own race" (257). In *The Descent of Man* (1871), Darwin predicted that in the future "the civilized races of man" would exterminate and replace both "the savage races" and anthropomorphous apes (132). Americans in 1945 saw the Japanese as both savage and simian; accordingly, the decision to use nuclear weapons was that much easier. Two days after the Nagasaki bomb, Truman insisted: "When you deal with a beast you have to treat him as a beast" (qtd. in Weingartner 563).

Of course, mass slaughter of racial others did not begin at Hiroshima. Boyer notes a "divergence" in how Americans responded to the ethical questions raised by the atomic bombings and the Holocaust (225). He points out that "some ethical writers addressed the Jewish Holocaust; others addressed the potential world holocaust of atomic war or the actual holocaust visited upon two Japanese cities," but few writers addressed both (226). The metaphorical beastialization of the Japanese underscores the linkage between the Holocaust and Hiroshima. David Smith in *Less than Human* (2011) has explored the ways that the Nazis used subhuman imagery to justify the holocaust by depicting Jews as "apes, pigs, rats, worms, bacilli, and other nonhuman creatures" (145).

The use of nonhuman metaphors to render genocide and nuclear weapons psychologically possible also suggests a third pole in this ethical triangle—the animal slaughterhouse. In 2002, People for the Ethical Treatment of Animals (PETA) unveiled a controversial display entitled *Holocaust on Your Plate*, which featured images of the Holocaust juxtaposed with images of slaughterhouse animals. Cary Wolfe observes that speciesist discourse is always critical because "those who fall outside the frame, because they are marked by differences of race, or species, or gender, or religion, or nationality, are always threatened with 'a non-criminal putting to death'" (*Before* 9).

∽

In *Beauty, Health, and Permanence* (1987), Samuel Hays sees the origins of contemporary environmentalism in the postwar search for a clean and healthful environment as a quality of life amenity. He argues that despite the media image of environmentalists as obsessed with "impending catastrophe," they were actually "purveyors of optimism," who refused to accept the limits on environmental improvement imposed by managers of regulatory agencies

(542). But Hays's optimism narrative has been challenged by other historians of environmentalism. In *Nature's Economy* (1994), Donald Worster states that the explosion of the first atomic bomb initiated the "Age of Ecology" (342). He argues that the threat of nuclear annihilation "cast doubt on the entire project of the domination of nature that had been at the heart of modern history. It raised doubts about the moral legitimacy of science, about the tumultuous pace of technology, and about the Enlightenment dream of replacing religious faith with human rationality as the basis of material welfare and virtue" (343). Similarly, Robertson in *The Malthusian Moment* (2012) links the birth of environmentalism to post–World War II "apocalyptic anxieties" (225). He argues that two important books published in 1948—Fairfield Osborn's *Our Plundered Planet* and William Vogt's *Road to Survival*—drew upon prewar ecological concerns with carrying capacity, environmental degradation, and limits to Keynesian economic growth.

Worster's and Robertson's focus on apocalyptic fear suggests that the strongest link between contemporary and turn-of-the-century environmentalism was anxiety. If environmentalism developed from a desire for an improved quality of life, these novels indicate that it also emerged from a widely felt sense of loss and fear. In the modern era, Americans worried about the disappearance of forests and game animals, and they feared the destructive effects of nature from storms, droughts, and diseases. Resistance to the culture of domination was largely driven by Americans who were anxious about vanishing wild areas and game animals; who mourned the loss of country ways as they grappled with the chaos of the city; and who were troubled by the threats to hegemony from immigrants, women, and people of color. And, as Faulkner's speech suggests, after 1945, Americans feared that scientific efforts to control nature could lead to the extermination of the human race. If there is a clear distinction between early and contemporary environmentalism, it seems to be an intensifying of fears caused by the threat of nuclear war. No longer could anxiety over environmental degradation be evaded by seeing it as a regional problem.

The role that fear of atomic apocalypse played in the development of contemporary environmentalism is perhaps best illustrated in the career of Howard Zahniser, author of the 1964 Wilderness Act. One month after the bombs were dropped, Zahniser resigned his position at the US Department of Agriculture and became the editor of the Wilderness Society's magazine, *Living Wilderness*. His biographer, Mark Harvey, attributes the move to Zahniser's deep concern about nuclear war: "He was shocked not only by the violence of the bombs but also by the astonishing prospect of humankind breaking up nature. The splitting of the atom was for Zahniser a deep violation of the ethical code to which he subscribed, a code that obligated mankind to understand nature before manipulating it" (253). In October 1945, Zahniser discussed the atomic bomb in an essay in *Living Wilderness*. Noting that humans have retained the "animal drives" of their evolutionary past, he warns that "now this lord of all creatures, with the old unsuppressed fish brain, knows how to drop from the air a small accumulation of matter containing exploding atoms that can pulverize a city, and blow its structures and inhabitants into a cloud of dust" (41). Harvey notes that Zahniser hoped that recreation in wilderness areas could be an antidote to the pervasive fear of the bomb (67).

Nuclear anxiety was also central to the development of Rachel Carson's environmentalism. Carson began her writing career by depicting the natural world in popular books such as *The Sea Around Us* (1951). But, by the early 1950s, she had become concerned that the atomic bomb could destroy that world. Her biographer, Linda Lear, notes, "By focusing on the immutable forces of nature, *The Sea Around Us* calmed atomic fears in others. But for Carson, the Bikini Island tests in the Pacific, the spread of nuclear arms among nations, and the war in Korea had fundamentally altered her private belief in the ultimate sanctity of nature" (220). In a 1958 letter to a friend, she mourned the death of the old idea "that much of Nature was forever beyond the tampering reach of man" (qtd. in Lear 310). The opening pages of *Silent Spring* (1962) link concerns about pesticides to fears about radiation: "In this now universal contamination of the environment, chemicals are the sinister and little-recognized partners of radiation in changing the very nature of the world—the very nature of its life" (6). One reviewer complained, "It isn't enough to have the threat of atomic warfare, a population explosion, communist aggression, irreligion, youth dereliction and other menaces . . . [W]e must also face the prediction that chemical warfare against insects is contaminating our air and sea and ground" (qtd. in Lear 428).[7]

Thus, the two central thrusts of modern environmentalism—wilderness preservation and control of toxins—can be associated with the threats posed by nuclear weapons. So perhaps it is not surprising that a critique of fearmongering has become a part of the conservative reaction against environmentalism. In a 1971 speech to the American Petroleum Industry, Ronald Reagan attacked the "Doomsday syndrome" of environmentalists (114). Similarly, in 1992, Rush Limbaugh accused environmentalists of trying to increase support for their efforts through "crisis mongering" (168).

Certainly, anyone who receives mailings from the mainstream environmental organizations must admit the role that fear plays in contemporary environmentalism. I suspect that these organizations would insist that focusing on the real threats to nature is a necessary strategy to motivate people to make the personal and cultural changes necessary to mitigate human damage to the environment.

But the strategy of inducing environmental phobia is problematic. In "The Farmer as Conservationist" (1939), Aldo Leopold noted, "I have no hope for conservation born of fear" (*River* 258). If too persistently invoked—especially if the possibility of remediation seems unlikely—fear can be repressed or the concerns dismissed as unrealistic. In Melville's "Bartleby, the Scrivener," the narrator is emotionally hardened when he realizes the full tragedy of Bartleby's mental condition. He insists that his coldness is not due to insensitivity or selfishness, but rather "a certain hopelessness of remedying excessive and organic ill. To a sensitive being, pity is not seldom pain. And when at last it is perceived that such pity cannot lead to effectual succor, common sense bids the soul be rid of it" (653). In *Beyond Ecophobia* (1996), David Sobel warns that a curriculum that emphasizes environmental crises (rainforest destruction, oil spills, global warming) might cause children to disassociate from nature. Instead, he recommends "that children have an opportunity to bond with the natural world, to learn to love it and feel comfortable in it, before being asked to heal its wounds" (10). The danger of a fear-driven environmentalism is especially apparent when anthropogenically altered nature itself is represented as the threat (as it is in natural horror films such as *Godzilla*). The film version of Al Gore's *An Inconvenient Truth* (2006) features images of Hurricane Katrina's destruction to illustrate the potential for more frequent, climate-change-induced storms. However, as some of the novels discussed in this book suggest, if nature is a threat, one response might be to develop better human strategies for controlling it.

My intention has not been to write an expose of environmentally incorrect views in classic American literature (along the lines of "Shakespeare the Sexist" or "Crane the Racist"). Such cultural policing seems anachronistic. Nevertheless, it does seem important to recognize that domination of nature is deeply embedded in our cultural past. This desire to subdue nature was not eliminated by fears of diminishing resources, desire for escape from urban problems, or greater leisure time spent in nature. Indeed, a pessimist might argue that the need to dominate nature is too deeply hardwired into our species to be overcome. In *Civilization and Its Discontents*, Freud identifies the "superior power of nature" and "the feebleness of our own bodies" as fundamental sources of human unhappiness (86). In any case, while revisiting the classics of American literary history, it is important to resist the urge to sanitize their ideas to make them align more closely with contemporary environmentalism.

⁂

One final anecdote suggests the imbrication of industrial capitalism with American views of nature in this period. In *The Summit of the Years* (1913), John Burroughs recognized the danger of our pursuit of control over the natural world, observing, "We cannot vault into the saddle of the elemental forces and ride them and escape the danger of being ridden by them" (68). Shortly after he wrote this, Burroughs began enjoying car camping expeditions with three of the leading industrialists of the era: Henry Ford, Thomas Edison, and Harvey Firestone. Burroughs and Ford had met in 1913 when the nature-loving automobile manufacturer became disturbed by Burroughs's critique of modernism in *The Summit of the Years*. Frustrated by Burroughs's attacks, Ford decided to give the naturalist a Model T so that he could "know nature better" (*My Life* 237). After a few accidents, Burroughs learned to appreciate the automobile since, according to Ford, "it helped him to see more" (237).

In 1913, the new friends drove to Concord, where they camped and visited the sites associated with transcendentalism. The following year, Ford introduced Burroughs to Edison on a trip to the inventor's winter home in Florida, and the three explored the Everglades. In 1916 Burroughs, Edison, and Firestone went auto camping in the Adirondacks (Ford was unable to join them), and they continued the tradition with trips to the Great Smoky Mountains in 1918 and to New England in 1919. Burroughs's biographer, Edward Renehan, notes that Ford provided a fleet of cars that carried such comforts as gasoline-powered electricity generators; a refrigerator; a dining tent that seated twenty; and private tents outfitted with cots, mattresses, blankets, sheets, and pillows (273). Burroughs admits that these antimodern excursions were "luxuriously equipped," but he insists that the campers still endured hardships, as they sought a deeper connection to the external world: "We react against our complex civilization, and long to get back for a time to first principles. We cheerfully endure wet, cold, smoke, mosquitoes, black flies, and sleepless nights, just to touch naked reality once more" (*Under the Maples* 121–22).[8]

Intriguingly, this putative experience with naked reality led Burroughs to a heightened recognition of the civilized nature of his wealthy friends. Noting that Ford "is as tender as a woman and much more tolerant," Burroughs observes that despite his practical abilities, the manufacturer is "through and through an idealist" (123). He insists that Ford has created a new ideal for businessmen, "that of a man whose devotion to the public good has been a ruling passion, and whose wealth has inevitably flowed from the depth of his humanitarianism" (124). Similarly, Burroughs notes of Edison, "[H]is first and leading thought has been, What can I do to make life easier and more enjoyable to my fellow-men?" (124).

For all of these nature lovers, their social commitment typically meant the domination of nature. Noting that Ford was indifferent to the aesthetics of scenery, Burroughs points out that, "His interest in the stream is in its potential water-power. He races up and down its banks to see its fall, and where power could be developed. He never ceases to lament so much power going to waste, and points out that if the streams were all harnessed, as they could easily be, farm labor everywhere, indoors and out, could be greatly lessened" (*Under the Maples* 122). Firestone notes that Edison "would dam

Figure E.2. Edison, Burroughs, Ford and Firestone camping, 1918 (The Collections of The Henry Ford)

every suitable stream in the country just to get the power" (226). Nor did Burroughs object to this instrumental approach to nature: on their 1916 trip, he gushes, "When Edison gets his foundry perfected for extracting potash on a commercial scale out of the granite rocks, what an inexhaustible supply the Adirondacks will afford him" (qtd. in Firestone 200).

Burroughs's enthusiasm for these camping trips suggests how easily respect for nature could be reconciled to the rise of modernity in America. As Americans learned to appreciate and to protect nature, they also learned how to accept its transformation into resources and commodities, thereby making it less threatening. We are still struggling to reconcile those divergent views of the natural world.

Notes

Introduction

1. In addition to Burroughs's account in *Signs and Seasons*, the loon hunt is described in Clara Barrus's *John Burroughs, Boy and Man* (322–23). A young John Muir also shot a loon; he kept the wounded bird as a pet (*Story* 76–78).

2. In *Wake-Robin* (1877), Burroughs offers the following advice to novice ornithologists: "First, find your bird; observe its ways, its song, its calls, its flight, its haunts; then shoot it (not ogle it with a glass), and compare with Audubon. In this way the feathered kingdom may soon be conquered" (231). Many of Burroughs's essays suggest an ambivalence about the scientific domination of nature. Thus, in a discussion of laboratory experimentation, he observed that we put an animal "through a sort of inquisitorial torment in the laboratory, we starve it, we electrocute it, we freeze it, we burn it, we incarcerate it, we vivisect it, we press it on all sides and in all ways, to find out something about its habits or mental processes that is usually not worth knowing" (*Summit* 51–52).

3. For similar interpretations of the development of pre-1945 environmentalism, see Philip Shabecoff's *A Fierce Green Fire* (1993) and Steven Stoll's *U.S. Environmentalism since 1945* (2007). Stephen Fox, in *The American Conservation Movement* (1985), sees the history of environmentalism as a tension between idealistic amateurs like Muir and professional conservationists such as Pinchot; writing in the early 1980s, he dismisses the rumors of an environmental backlash (329).

4. In 1999, Scott Slovic stated that "not a single work anywhere utterly defies ecocritical interpretation, is off-limits to green reading" (1103). In their 2000 anthology, *Reading Under the Sign of Nature*, John Tallmadge and Henry Harrington argue that ecocritics have begun to move "beyond the romantic Euroamerican canon and its nature writers like Muir and Thoreau toward other traditions, including those of oriental and Native American cultures" (x). Glen Love (2003) argues that ecocriticism needs "to reexamine and reinterpret the depictions of nature in the canonical works of the past," pointing specifically to literary naturalism as a site requiring such interpretation (34–35).

5. For the turn-of-the-century interest in nature, see Peter J. Schmitt's *Back to Nature*, Kevin C. Armitage's *The Nature Study Movement*, William L. Bowers's *The Country Life Movement in America 1900–1920*, and Dona Brown's *Back to the Land*.

6. Recently, ecocritics such as Simon C. Estok have explored the concept of "ecophobia" as a way of explaining negative human interactions with nature. America's fascination with apocalyptic entertainment is discussed in John F. Kasson's *Amusing the Million* (71–72).

7. For discussions of views of the naturalness of women, African Americans, and immigrants during this period, see George M. Fredrickson's *The Black Image in the White Mind*, and Marianna Torgovnik's *Gone Primitive*. McCann's book is an exceptionally negative reading of progressivism: he argues that progressive philosophy is "not distinguishable from that of the fascist movement in Europe" and compares Franklin Roosevelt's use of social art to that of Hitler, Stalin, and Mussolini (224–25, 114). Benjamin Heber Johnson presents the movement more sympathetically, arguing that it "laid the basis for real and lasting environmental improvements" (4). He notes that progressive conservation "was no more tainted by eugenics than was any other political movement that enjoyed substantial support among the native-born white population of the country" and that it "was neither less nor more racist than native-born white American society as a whole" (93, 227).

8. Bruno Giberti's *Designing the Centennial*, and Robert W. Rydell's *All the World's a Fair* are excellent histories of the Philadelphia Centennial.

9. While most historians see the Progressive Era as beginning in 1890 and ending in 1920, histories of turn-of-the-century reform include the ranges 1870–1920 (McGerr), 1877–1920 (Wiebe), 1890–1940 (Hofstadter), and 1900–1928 (Graham, *Great Campaigns*).

10. The introduction of Mikko Saikku's *This Delta, This Land* offers a clear introduction to environmental history (5–25). My own approach is especially influenced by what he describes as "the historiography of human ideas on the environment, or the study of how humans have viewed the natural world in their science, religion, arts, and ethics" (9).

11. W. Barksdale Maynard's *Walden Pond* discusses the pastry allegations against Thoreau (85–86).

Chapter 1

1. Derek Traversi sees Eliot's river as a symbol of "racial experience" and links it to Conrad's *Heart of Darkness*; furthermore, he argues that the river is "a witness to the history of man's continually expanding domination over his environment" (153).

2. See Alan Gribben, *Mark Twain's Library* (2: 744–45). Other popular late nineteenth-century outdoor guidebooks include Francis Galton, *The Art of Travel* (1855); John K. Lord, *At Home in the Wilderness* (1876); John M. Gould,

How to Camp Out (1877); W. Hamilton Gibson, *Camp Life in the Woods* (1881); and "Nessmuk" [George Washington Sears], *Woodcraft* (1884). Gribben notes that Gibson's *Camp Life* was in Twain's library (1: 256). In 1901, Twain vacationed in the Adirondacks; for an interview with him during that trip, see Gary Scharnhorst, *Mark Twain: The Complete Interviews* (394–400).

3. In *Tom Sawyer* (1876), Tom, Huck, and Joe Harper decide to become pirates and camp on Jackson's Island for several days (chapters 13–17). In contrast to *Huckleberry Finn*, the boys steal significantly fewer provisions (meat, a skillet, and tobacco), and, except for occasional bouts of homesickness, they thoroughly enjoy the freedom from civilization's restraints. I am grateful for Professor John Bird's suggestion at the 2017 SAMLA conference that I examine the camping excursion in *Tom Sawyer*.

4. For a discussion of Twain's revisions of this passage, see Victor Fischer and Lin Salamo (471–79).

5. The outfit for their western trip is described in "Huck Finn and Tom Sawyer among the Indians" (38). Michael Patrick Hearn notes that such outfits were expensive (443). Previous critics have recognized that the ending of the novel shows Huck's entanglement in civilization. Nina Baym notes that at the end Huck "has still not made his break" (132). Schulman argues that Huck cannot light out because he "carries the divisions of the dominant society within his own consciousness, quite aside from the violence and acquisitiveness he will find in the territory" (44). Twain's own ambivalence about the ending might be suggested by his inability to continue what he intended to be a trilogy. Immediately after finishing *Huck Finn*, Twain began "Huck Finn and Tom Sawyer among the Indians," but he was unable to complete it. Another false start is represented by an 1891 notebook entry describing a story where "Huck comes back sixty years old, from nobody knows where—and crazy" (qtd. in Hearn cxvii).

6. David M. Wrobel's *The End of American Exceptionalism* is an excellent history of frontier anxiety.

7. For nineteenth-century attitudes towards African Americans and Native Americans, see George Fredrickson, *The Black Image in the White Mind*; Thomas F. Gossett, *Race: The History of an Idea in America*; and Frederick E. Hoxie, *A Final Promise: The Campaign to Assimilate the Indians, 1880–1920*.

8. Charles Dudley Warner depicts the Adirondack guide as a "primitive man" who is "unimpaired by the refinements of an artificial culture" and thus can enjoy "a special communion with nature" (49). William Murray praises Adirondack guides as "bronzed and hardy, fearless of danger, eager to please, uncontaminated with the vicious habits of civilized life" (38).

9. Interestingly, the education that Huck and Tom offer Jim is liberal: history, religion, literature, modern languages. By the 1880s most white Americans had rejected the idea of liberal education for both blacks and Indians; instead, they were to be trained in the industrial arts to prepare them for their lowly position in

society. In his personal life, Twain seems to have rejected this limited view: Philip Butcher points out that in 1885 he offered to help pay the expenses of an African American student at Yale Law School.

10. David E. E. Sloane has argued that Huck's comment to the Duke is a "disguise" and that his response to Aunt Sally is his "ultimate covering response" (78–79). However, Sacvan Bercovitch insists that Huck's reply to Aunt Sally is "profoundly racist" and "gratuitous, totally unnecessary" (107–08).

11. Harold Beaver presents a convincing case for seeing Jim as manipulative. Twain's ambivalence about the potential assimilation of nonwhites is evident in the view of Native Americans presented in "Huck Finn and Tom Sawyer among the Indians." The central theme of the unfinished work is the dangerous naivete of a romantic view of Native Americans. Influenced by James Fenimore Cooper's novels, Tom is convinced that "Injuns" are "the noblest human beings that's ever been in the world," but the Native Americans they encounter quickly turn out to be treacherous murderers and rapists (35).

12. William A. Gleason suggests that Huck would reject the technology celebrated at the Centennial (although he agrees that Twain would be more intrigued), and he argues that Twain's praise of "the link between art and industry" in the final section of *Life on the Mississippi* represents his own Centennial Exposition (92).

13. Maxine Benson's *Martha Maxwell* is an excellent discussion of Maxwell's life and work. She points out that in the 1870s habitat displays were still new, and most museum exhibits consisted of "rows of specimens placed side by side against white backgrounds so that they could be compared with one another" (140). Bruno Giberti sees this shift from comparative to contextual displays as the transition from the objective gaze of the Enlightenment to the modern subjective glance (99–101, 203–04). He argues that Maxwell's willingness to be photographed as part of the display reflected this more subjective model of perception: "[M]an had lost his unique position as the observing subject and had himself become an observed object of scientific scrutiny" (147–48).

14. For bison at the Centennial, see Ingram (106, 141, 374). In *Roughing It* (1871), Twain presents a tall-tale version of a buffalo hunt (569–73).

15. Lloyd Willis discusses the preservationist impulse of nature nostalgia, noting that what matters for Emerson "is not that nature endures in any viable physical sense, but that an 'impression' of it endures for 'the human mind'" (22).

16. Fiedler's reading was first presented in "Come Back to the Raft Ag'in, Huck Honey!" (1948).

Chapter 2

1. For the starling's introduction into America, see Susan Woodward and Joyce Quinn, *Encyclopedia of Invasive Species* (237–40).

2. In the introduction of *Toward a Literary Ecology* (2103), Karen E. Waldron notes that the ecologies of the slum have an "interrelated impact on Maggie's brief life" (xxiv).

3. The environmental conditions of the slums are discussed in Paul Boyer, *Urban Masses and Moral Order in America, 1820–1920*; and Roy LuBove, *The Progressives and the Slums*.

4. The best history of American nativism is John Higham's *Strangers in the Land*.

5. Nonfiction exposés of the slum include Benjamin Orange Flower's *Civilization's Inferno* (1893), Jacob Riis's *How the Other Half Lives* (1890) and *The Children of the Poor* (1892). Literary depictions include Edgar Fawcett's *The Evil that Men Do* (1889), James Sullivan's *Tenement Tales of New York* (1895), and Edward Townsend's *A Daughter of the Tenements* (1895).

6. For the history of ecology, see Robert McIntosh, *The Background of Ecology*; Sharon Kingsland, *The Evolution of American Ecology, 1890–2000*; and Donald Worster, *Nature's Economy*. Dana Phillips offers an intriguing critique of the contemporary misuses of ecology in *The Truth of Ecology*.

7. In *A Stephen Crane Encyclopedia*, Stanley Wertheim revisits the Pizer thesis: "Maggie's downfall is attributable less to the pressures of the external environment than to the projection by herself and her family of theatrical romantic illusions and middle-class moral values on the atavistic world of the slums" (212). In 2006, James Nagel noted the influence of Pizer's reading of *Maggie*.

8. For a history of the sweatshop, see Daniel E. Bender, *Sweated Work, Weak Bodies*.

9. The segregation of vice districts is discussed in Ruth Rosen, *Lost Sisterhood* (6–7), and Timothy J. Gilfoyle, *City of* Eros (97–23).

10. The neighborhoods involved in Maggie's final walk are discussed in Andrew Lawson's "Class Mimicry in Stephen Crane's City" and Stanley Wertheim's "The New York City Topography of *Maggie* and *George's Mother*."

11. Stanley Wertheim discusses the repeated incidents (*Stephen Crane Encyclopedia*, 213).

12. For the creation of Central Park, see Matthew Gandy, *Concrete and* Clay (77–113).

13. Robert Woods's 1898 anthology *The City Wilderness* seems to be the first usage of a metaphor that has remained powerful. In 1967, Senator Robert Kennedy warned, "We confront an urban wilderness more formidable and resistant and in some ways more frightening than the wilderness faced by the Pilgrims or the pioneers" (qtd. in "Troubled Cities" 43). Carolyn Merchant discusses the city as wilderness metaphor in *American Environmental History* (118–20).

14. Christopher Wilson argues that in the Tenderloin sketches Crane wrote for the *New York Journal* in 1896, he exemplifies "an emerging middle-class ambivalence about the kind of power turn-of-the-century policing represented" (55). In

The Chicago Gangster Theory of Life, Andrew Ross argues that environmental cultural studies should include such issues as "freedom from police surveillance and harassment" (103).

15. See Marilyn Irvin Holt, *The Orphan Trains*, and Julia Guarneri, "Changing Strategies for Child Welfare, Enduring Beliefs about Childhood."

16. For a history of the 1964 riot, see Janet L. Abu-Lughod's *Race, Space, and Riots in Chicago, New York, and Los Angeles* (159–94).

Chapter 3

1. There have been several excellent discussions of the influence of hurricanes on *The Awakening*. Barbara C. Ewell notes that the novel is set in 1892, a year before the Great October Storm: "In situating her characters in a place whose destruction was imminent, Chopin must have recognized the poignancy she was adding to Edna's short-lived awakening" (22). Amanda Lee Castro challenges the reading of the islands as a place of freedom from naturalistic restriction; she argues that the novel's readers would have been aware of the devastation caused by the 1893 storm and thus would have recognized the island's utopianism as tenuous. See also Barbara C. Ewell and Pamela Glenn Menke, "*The Awakening* and the Great October Storm of 1893."

2. Chopin's struggles with nature are described in Emily Toth's *Kate Chopin* (30–31, 130, 139, 158–59).

3. For the turn-of-the-century reception of Emerson and Thoreau, see Charles E. Mitchell, *Individualism and Its Discontents*; Robert Habich, *Building Their Own Waldos*; Gary Scharnhorst, *Henry David Thoreau*; and Fritz Oehlschlaeger and George Hendrick, *Toward the Making of Thoreau's Modern Reputation*. For Ford's interest in transcendentalism, see Neil Baldwin, *Henry Ford and the Jews* (44–47), and Edward J. Renehan, Jr., *John Burroughs* (271–76).

4. The standard biography of Hall is Dorothy Ross's *G. Stanley Hall*.

5. Donald A. Ringe sees Edna's choice of reading material as evidence of her romanticism (581). Other critics, such as Elizabeth Nolan, have argued that since Edna falls asleep while she is reading Emerson, Chopin is critiquing the inadequacy of Transcendentalism (130). For Emerson's influence on Chopin, see Kathleen Nigro, "Mr. Emerson Comes to St. Louis."

6. Max Oelschlaeger reads this passage as indicative of the Emersonian view of nature that is coterminous with anthropocentric manipulation: "[N]ature is mere putty in human hands, bestowed by God upon his most favored creation, *man*" (135).

7. According to Toth, Chopin's moods were often driven by the weather (87, 90–91).

8. Historians of the Progressive Era have acknowledged the centrality of scientific management by experts. Robert H. Wiebe notes that the rise of an edu-

cated middle class and the professionalization of the disciplines led to an increased emphasis on "continuous, expert management of indeterminate processes" (193). Samuel P. Hays discusses the "gospel of efficiency" that drove progressive conservation, whereby "experts, using technical and scientific methods, should decide all matters of development and utilization of resources" (271). Daniel T. Rodgers sees an emphasis on "efficiency, rationalization, and social engineering" as one of the primary discourses of progressivism ("In Search" 126).

9. For Chopin's relationship with Kolbenheyer, see Toth (131–32, 174–75, 258–61).

10. Tara Parmiter notes that Mandelet "fails to acknowledge that Edna's actions are a legitimate response to an oppressive social structure" (11–12). Cheryl L. Rose Jacobsen argues that a comparison of Dr. Mandelet to turn-of-the-century marriage and health advice manuals demonstrates "the basic subversiveness of Chopin's novel" (117). She sees Mandelet as a mix of conventional and progressive ideologies: he "offers a sympathetic understanding of both female sexuality and the social constraints which simultaneously initiate the birth of Edna's autonomous identity and ultimately cause its stillbirth," but he "lapses at times into the most conservative cultural voice" (101–02).

11. Perhaps because it complicates the narrative of Mitchell's patriarchal oppression of Gilman, discussion of his Camp Cure has been relatively scant in comparison to his more famous Rest Cure. The best analyses are David G. Schuster's *Neurasthenic Nation* (134–38) and Helen Horowitz's *Wild Unrest* (124, 135). Jennifer Tuttle argues that Mitchell's Rest Cure and his West Cure (a treatment that sent male patients to the West to recuperate) "were complimentary parts of one process through which normative gender identities were constructed and reinforced" (105). In a footnote, Tuttle acknowledges that the Camp Cure made outdoor experience "attainable by many women," but she insists that it "does not entirely undermine his early gendering of the Rest and West cures" (120). Barbara Will also concedes in a footnote that Mitchell "modified his ideas about the gendered division of 'Rest Cure' and 'West Cure,'" but she incorrectly dates the modification as developing after "Gilman's story had achieved some measure of fame," rather than in 1888, four years *before* the publication of the story (310). It is also worth noting that even in the 1874 version of the Camp Cure, Mitchell allowed that camping provided charm for "all men, and indeed for many women" (*Nurse* 60). It is tempting to speculate as to why Mitchell prescribed the Rest Cure to Gilman rather than his West or Camp Cures. Perhaps he saw her case as requiring extreme measures. In *Lectures on Diseases* (1881) Mitchell noted that the Rest Cure "is a plan never to be used where exercise, outdoor life, tonics, or change have not been thoroughly tested" (232–33). Prior to seeking Mitchell's help, Gilman had gone to California for several months, and the exposure to rugged nature led to a temporary recovery. But when she returned to her husband and child, she relapsed; accordingly, Mitchell perhaps felt that her case was serious enough to require the Rest Cure.

Equally puzzling is his permanent ban on Gilman's writing. In his writings on the Rest Cure, Mitchell is clear that he only prohibited writing for the duration of the actual treatment (four to five weeks), and in *Doctor and Patient* he presents writing as useful therapy. It is possible that Mitchell altered his typical prescription for Gilman because he recognized the centrality of writing to her struggle to reject domesticity. However, as Horowitz argues, it is also conceivable that Gilman misunderstood or even distorted Mitchell's advice in her subsequent accounts (140–41). Julie Bates Dock notes that in Gilman's retellings of her experience with Mitchell, she created other myths, including the story that the publication of "The Yellow Wall-paper" led him to abandon the Rest Cure.

Chapter 4

1. In 1874, George P. Marsh discussed the problem of nonnative species in *The Earth as Modified by Human Action* (56–147). For recent accounts, see Kim Todd, *Tinkering with Eden*, and Peter Coates, *American Perceptions of Immigrant and Invasive Species*. Robert J. Spear notes that in the twentieth century, the federal government continued the war against the gypsy moth; after World War II, DDT was used until the publication of Rachel Carson's *Silent Spring* led to the end of blanket aerial spraying (254–60).

2. Harvard geologist Nathaniel Southgate Shaler, who served as one of the gypsy moth commissioners, warned that the moths "might break down our civilization" by destroying the forests that had made America great (qtd. in Spear 72). As vice president of the Anti-Immigration League, he used similarly apocalyptic language to describe the new immigration as "a distinct danger to the state" (*United States* 613).

3. There are several excellent histories of the Chicago meat industry: Louise Carroll Wade's *Chicago's Pride* (1987), William Cronon's *Nature's Metropolis* (1991), Wilson J. Warren's *Tied to the Great Packing Machine* (2007), and Dominic A. Pacyga's *Slaughterhouse* (2015).

4. The novel's composition and publication are discussed in Sinclair's *Autobiography* (117–35) and Anthony Arthur's *Radical Innocent* (40–84). Although significantly shorter than the *Appeal to Reason* serialization, the 1906 Doubleday, Page text has become standard. Quotes from both texts are from the Norton Critical Edition of *The Jungle*, which includes excerpts from the *Appeal* version.

5. For a good discussion of reform Darwinism, including its influence on Gilman, see Gary Scharnhorst's *Charlotte Perkins Gilman* (46–48). An introduction to Ward's thought can be found in Charles R. McCann Jr. (32–58).

6. In *The Book of Life*, Sinclair explains that man's higher evolution comes because he is the creator who improves upon the natural world through technology. Nevertheless, many still believe in the "immutable" laws of nature, insisting on Malthusian pessimism when modern birth control provides an alternative or

on "the diminishing returns of agriculture," which intensive agriculture renders meaningless (1:24–25).

7. Michael Brewster Folsom finds Jurgis's conversion to socialism "psychologically unconvincing" and notes that it "is a psychic event, not a social or economic one, and not so much rational or logical in its development as it is emotional" (40, 36). Rosendale sees the experience "as an encounter with a wilderness more genuine than the jungle with which he is so familiar" (72). Michael Lundblad argues that Jurgis remains "animalized throughout the novel" (113).

8. For a good overall history of eugenics, see Daniel J. Kevles, *In the Name of Eugenics*. Donald K. Pickens's *Eugenics and the Progressives* is somewhat dated but still useful. Diane B. Paul's *The Politics of Heredity* has an excellent chapter on leftist eugenics (11–35). A thorough analysis of Sinclair's interest in eugenics can be found in Alison Pasinella, "Becoming (Post) Human" (139–50).

9. See Betty Keller for Seton's meeting with Kropotkin (163–64). Lisa Mighetto discusses the influence of Kropotkin on the nature writers (20).

10. The definitive history of the Nature Faker controversy is Ralph H. Lutts's *The Nature Fakers*.

11. Lundblad insists that despite any intended farce, "the hog-squeal passage maintains an ability to evoke tremendous sympathy for the pigs themselves" (109). I would argue that this passage had less emotional effect on Sinclair's audience than perhaps it should have.

12. Alexandra Minna Stern notes that "Goethe invested in what he understood as the comprehensive betterment of the biota, a grand goal that could be attained through the enlightened management of the earth's multitudinous and interrelated species, particularly those he deemed hardy, supple, and righteous" (158).

Chapter 5

1. Some previous critics have recognized that Austin's relationship to the resistance tradition is complicated. Anna Carew-Miller sees two voices in Austin's nature writing: a confident voice that critiques the "traditional (male) relationship to nature as a power struggle through which men try to control nature" and a fearful voice that recognizes the violence and indifference of nature (90). David N. Cassuto recognizes that *The Ford* represents a conflict between Austin's progressive commitment to reclamation ideology and her proto-ecofeminist worldview (52). Nicolas S. Witschi argues that Austin is less a nature writer than a realist who pursued "a morally inflected cultural criticism"; he sees the novel "wrapping the problem of knowledge within the representation of a struggle for natural resources in general and for water in particular" (116, 128).

2. William L. Kahrl's *Water and Power* (1982) and John Walton's *Western Times and Water Wars* (1992) are the best accounts of the California water wars.

For the role played by the Austins, see Abraham Hoffman, "Mary Austin, Stafford Austin, and the Owens Valley," and Susan Goodman and Carl Dawson, *Mary Austin and the American West* (53–56).

3. For Austin's experiences in New York, see Goodman and Dawson (119–71).

4. The best analysis of Wright's rarely-read novel is Phillip H. Round's *The Impossible Land* (51–68).

5. David N. Cassuto argues that *The Ford* anticipates ecofeminism "by linking the subjugation of women with that of the land and merging the two into a potent force for social change" (51). However, Anne Raine correctly points out that "unlike some later ecofeminists, Austin objects not to the men's desire to own and develop the land, but to the lack of 'organizing capacity' that prevents them from doing so effectively" (257).

6. Anne Raine sees Anne as "the novel's real heroine" and admires her "liberal feminist critique of Kenneth's romantic agrarianism" (256). She argues that Austin does not see "the managerial and entrepreneurial gaze" of Rickart and Anne as "automatically a desecration of the land"; instead, that mode of vision is the key to Anne's "conservationist practice" (252, 260). David N. Casutto insists that "her philosophy contains much that would later become ecofeminism" (52). Stacy Alaimo argues that Anne "proposes that ownership of the land should be determined not by capital, but by affinity," thereby suggesting that "land is not an utterly malleable resource but a force of its own" (77).

7. For the development of scientific testing, see Joel Spring.

8. John Walton argues that Austin depicts the settlers as "precarious entrepreneurs anxious for commercial development. The men, at least, were progressives in the spirit of Roosevelt's expansive regime. They welcomed federal intervention that promised regional development and later quarreled with Los Angeles mainly over their right to share in the fruits of growth" ("Foreword," xiv).

9. Surprisingly, no one has pointed out the possible influence of Austin's novel on Upton Sinclair's *Oil!* (1927). George H. Nash notes that Herbert Hoover was deeply involved as a financier of several California oil businesses from 1909 through 1914, the time frame in which Austin befriended the Hoovers (447–74).

10. In *California: The Land of the Sun* (1914), Austin describes the oil fields near Bakersfield as "half-formed prehistoric creatures come up out of the ground to see what men are about" (132).

11. Benay Blend argues that Austin hoped that irrigation projects in Arizona would "lead to ideal village patterns embracing small-scale communalism, local integrity, and self-sufficiency," thus avoiding the unrestrained development of modernism, such as what she had seen in California ("Mary Austin," 20). Blend concludes, "What concerned her most was not preservation of pristine wilderness but an emerging ideology that ignored the repercussions of unlimited mastery over the environment" (25).

12. For the postaqueduct history of the Owens Valley, see William L. Kahrl, *Water and Power*; John Walton, *Western Times and Water Wars*; and Rebecca Fish Ewan, *A Land Between*.

13. In *Rivers of Empire*, Donald Worster argues that both Van Dyke and Austin "spoke for an alternative side of modern America: one against domination, instrumentalism, the power of capital and technique; one in favor of freedom, wild, untrammeled grandeur, and human humility" (74). Susan Goodman and Carl Dawson are more dismissive of Van Dyke, arguing that Austin recognizes that the land is "inextricably linked with human life," in contrast to Van Dyke, who sees public lands as "middle-class adventure parks or outdoor museums reserved for the discerning few" (58). Furthermore, they argue that while Van Dyke and Jack London represent the desert "as a battle for dominance," Austin "presents the natural world as at once unforgiving or indifferent *and* nurturing" (59).

Chapter 6

1. The best accounts of the Gillette-Brown incident are Craig Brandon, *Murder in the* Adirondacks; and Joseph W. Brownwell and Patricia W. Enos, *Adirondack Tragedy*.

2. For Dreiser's trip to the Adirondacks, see his *American Diaries* (400–02) and Helen Dreiser's *My Life with Dreiser* (83–85).

3. For histories of tourism in the region, see Jane A. Barlow, ed., *Big Moose Lake in the Adirondacks*, and William L. Scheffler and Frank Carey, *Big Moose Lake, New York in Vintage Postcards*.

4. The Dexter murder is described in Neal S. Burdick's "Who Killed Orrando P. Dexter?"

5. The best history of interwar wilderness preservation is Paul Sutter's *Driven Wild*. He argues that the movement was primarily motivated by a desire to create outdoor recreational space free from the intrusion of automobiles and roads.

6. In addition to detailing Freud's influence on Dreiser, Moers discusses Clyde's distortions, noting "the growing unreality" of his perceptions (237). John Clendenning has also explored Dreiser's use of Freud in *An American Tragedy*. He sees the novel both as an "oedipal tragedy in which Clyde is tempted, then punished by the patriarchal order" and a "pre-oedipal tragedy" in which Clyde is "fixated in the archaic maternal dyad" (33). Joseph Karaganis discusses the novel's emphasis on observation from a Lacanian perspective.

7. Freud's visit to the Adirondacks is described in George Prochnik's *Putnam Camp*.

8. For discussions of the removal of residents from the national parks, see Alfred Runte, *National Parks* (115–17); Darwin Lambert, *The Undying Past of*

Shenandoah National Park (227–55); Daniel Pierce, *The Great Smokies* (154–73); and Chris J. Magoc, *Yellowstone* (138–48).

9. E. Peter Wittkoff discusses the Amazon surveillance system in "Brazil's SIVAM: Surveillance Against Crime and Terrorism."

10. Statistics on the Forty-Sixers can be found on the Adirondack Forty-Sixers website (http://www.adk46er.org/). Mike Lynch discusses the overuse of the High Peaks Wilderness.

Chapter 7

1. For Hurston's initiation, see her "Hoodoo in America" (359) and Robert Hemenway's *Zora Neale Hurston* (117–23).

2. The environmental history of south Florida is presented in Jack Davis and Raymond Arsenault, *Paradise Lost*; David McCally, *The Everglades*; Michael Grunwald, *The Swamp*; and Eliot Kleinberg, *Black Cloud*. Anna Lillios discusses Hurston's use of the 1928, 1929, and 1935 hurricanes. John Lowe suggests that Hurston might have been influenced by previous "hurricane-genre" novels (202–03).

3. My discussion of *Waters of Destiny* is indebted to Grunwald (219–23).

4. For views of race in the early twentieth century, see George Fredrickson; *The Black Image in the White Mind*; Vernon Williams, *Rethinking Race*; Daryl Scott, *Contempt and Pity*; Lee D. Baker, *From Savage to Negro*; and Jerry Gershenhorn, *Melville J. Herskovits and the Racial Politics of Knowledge*.

5. Lloyd Willis observes that Hurston describes the Everglades as "Harlem without patronage and race leadership and with some measure of financial self-sufficiency" (121).

6. Daryl Scott points out that, in the mid-1930s, scholars had begun to discuss racial self-hatred as one of the consequences of racism. Nellie McKay argues that Janie's "positive black self-concept at the end of her narrative" suggests "Hurston's rejection of black self-hate" (63). John Lowe sees Mrs. Turner as "Hurston's surrogate for all those critics who accused *her* of cuttin' the monkey for white folks" (185).

7. It is intriguing to speculate whether Janie's discovery of her race was influenced by Ruth Horowitz's 1939 research in which she showed African American children pictures of white and black children and asked them to identify the picture that represented them. Another possible source is the Tarzan novels or movies: in *Tarzan of the Apes* (1912), Tarzan is raised by apes and only realizes his difference when he sees his reflection in a pool of water. For a discussion of Tarzan, see Marianna Torgovnick (47–48).

8. Donald K. Pickens discusses the eugenicists' interest in conservation as well as their "chronic antiurban bias" (136, 191–96).

9. Robert Haas explores the historical and scientific context of rabies. Paul Outka points out that Tea Cake is infected with both rabies and "the terrible white supremacist history that transformed black men into the Black Beast" (198).

10. For discussions of Hurston as an anthropologist, see Suzanne Clark and Alice Gambrell.

11. Discussions of the 1927 and 2005 floods and the governmental responses to those floods can be found in Christopher Morris and John Barry.

Chapter 8

1. For Roosevelt's hunt, see Minor Ferris Buchanan, *Holt Collier* (151–83); and Douglas Brinkley, *Wilderness Warrior* (431–45). Charles S. Aiken notes that by 1940 Faulkner was hunting on the Big Sunflower River, about twenty miles northeast of Roosevelt's camp (*William Faulkner* 158–74).

2. For the tree farm movement, see Paul Sharp.

3. Histories of lumbering in the South can be found in Mikko Saikku, *This Delta, This Land*; Michael Williams, *Americans and Their Forests*; Lawrence Walker, *The Southern Forest*; and Nollie Hickman *Mississippi Harvest*.

4. Neil Maher's superb history of the CCC, *Nature's New Deal*, discusses Roosevelt's connections with forestry (20–29). For the Sardis Dam project, see Wiley C. Prewitt (214). In *Big Woods*, Ike McCaslin mourns that his former hunting grounds are "*now thirty feet below the surface of a government-built flood-control reservoir whose bottom was rising gradually and inexorably each year on another layer of beer cans and bottle tops and lost bass plugs*" (170).

5. For the development of hunting regulations, see Thomas R. Dunlap, *Saving America's Wildlife*; Harmon Kalman, *Restoring America's Wildlife*; and Aldo Leopold, *Report on a Game Survey of Mississippi*.

6. Benjamin Heber Johnson discusses Leopold's distrust of bureaucratic conservation (252–53).

7. Joseph Blotner notes that while revising the magazine version of "Delta Autumn" for the novel, Faulkner changed Roth's list of potential dictators, substituting Roosevelt and Willkie for Pelley and Yokohama (*Uncollected Stories* 695). Wendell Willkie was Roosevelt's Republican opponent in the 1940 presidential election. William Pelley was an American admirer of Hitler who was the Christian party's candidate for president in 1936.

8. Although some early critics saw Ike positively, most readers have been more critical. Francis Lee Utley sees him as a Christlike figure who "has the courage to make the initial repudiation, and to sustain it in spite of the demonic temptation offered by his greedy and hysterical wife" (186). David H. Stewart insists, "What he achieves is little more than cheap self-satisfaction, cheap because his basic urge is to gain peace

and to escape, which prevents him from finding solutions that really satisfy or that are really meaningful" (216). Olga W. Vickery argues that the values Ike learned in the wilderness "should have been asserted within the context of civilization" (212). Michael Millgate suggests that "Ike's attempt to carry over into the practical workaday world the lessons Sam Fathers taught him in the wilderness was bound to fail" (232). For Erik Dussere, Ike's repudiation "is ultimately an empty gesture, a failure" (22).

9. For the controversy over wilderness, see J. Baird Callicott and Michael P. Nelson, *The Great New Wilderness Debate* and *The Wilderness Debate Rages On*. Other ecocritics have recognized the problems with Ike's view of the wilderness. Louise Westling sees Ike as one of the many American literary heroes who excuse their mistreatment of the landscape "by retreating into a nostalgia that erases their real motives, displaces responsibility, and takes refuge in attitudes of self-pitying adoration" (5). Albert J. Devlin concludes that both Sam and Ike "reject the passional life to embrace a wilderness whose fantasy of unrestricted movement in time and space can hardly be resisted" (195). Christopher Rieger criticizes Ike's "dualistic thinking that artificially opposes wilderness and civilization" and argues that "Ike's conception of the wilderness as beyond time is revealed as a sentimental fantasy" (142).

10. Jill Faulkner Summers recalls that her father "liked to be in the woods. He didn't like killing things. . . . And he very seldom brought deer back from the deer hunts that he went on down in the Delta" (qtd. in Bezzerides 94).

11. A few critics have explored the role of agriculture in *Go Down, Moses*, but they typically see it as an example of the resistance narrative. In *William Faulkner and the Southern Landscape*, Aiken discusses cotton plantation farming in the late 1930s in Mississippi; he notes that in *Go Down, Moses*, "the tenant farmer theme is overpowered by more potent ones" (*William Faulkner* 139). Lutwack argues that in "The Bear" section, "the value of the wilderness is explicitly set over against farming, and the emphatic conclusion is that cotton culture was accomplished only at the price of shamefully exploiting both land and people, whereas wilderness experience is the source of true pride, humility, courage" (169). Richard Godden's *William Faulkner* explores the struggles of white landowners who are attempting to come to terms with the departure of the black labor force that resulted from the agricultural modernization of the New Deal. Wittenberg sees a critique of capitalist domination of land and people in Faulkner's depiction of the plantation, in contrast to the "high value" he places on wilderness (63). John T. Matthews agrees that the plantation is rooted in dominance: "To plant is to conquer nature; to cultivate a plantation is to 'translate' the wilderness; to make a profit, to commandeer labor; to exercise authority, to dominate the landless, slaves, women, and children" (38).

12. Dona Brown discusses the back-to-the-land movement of the 1930s (141–201).

13. Annette Bernert, who also notes that Cass has seen the phantom buck, sees him as "a man divided against himself, a socially responsible individual whose idealism and analytical intelligence have driven him, unwillingly, into cynicism" (185).

14. While Roth appears in two of the stories that became "The Fire and the Hearth" ("Gold Is Not Always" and "A Point of Law"), in "Delta Autumn," the Roth character is named Don Boyd. Nancy Drew Taylor points out that Roth inherits the farm during an economic crisis caused by the fall in cotton prices (66). Cleanth Brooks notes that Roth "comes off rather well in his dealings with the aged Lucas and his wife Molly" (274). Karl F. Zender argues that Roth shows "a paternal regard for the well-being of all of his tenants," and he sees similarities between Roth and Faulkner: "[L]ike Faulkner in the early 1940s, Roth is a man driven almost to distraction by the demands, both social and economic, being made on him by the people among whom he lives" (*Crossing* 74, 65). Godden sees Roth as a landowner capable of recognizing "that his identity forms on both sides of the structure of oppression which he administers" (82).

15. Wittenberg sees Lucas as "a greedy would-be landowner" and a "striving entrepreneur" (62). Zender defends Lucas's decision to remain on the farm and challenges the postmodern "skeptical view of the accommodation Lucas Beauchamp reaches with the plantation social order" (*Faulkner* 85).

16. Although they are not farmers, Gavin Stevens and Miss Worsham in "Go Down, Moses" represent other possibilities of what Ike might have become. While paternalistic, their efforts to help Molly Beauchamp in the "Go Down, Moses" section still represent a better response to the racial problems in the South than Ike's withdrawal. Bernard W. Bell notes that Stevens "demonstrates the social interdependency of Southern whites and blacks, the system of paternalism and noblesse oblige" (232). Thadious M. Davis argues that Miss Worsham assumes "what the role of whites must continue to be in the lives of blacks—that is, paternalistic and, in part, a moral response to the legacy of property" (230).

17. For the Okatoba Club and the incident with the game warden, see Aiken (*William Faulkner* 166) and Blotner (*Faulkner* 1: 879).

18. The conservative backlash against environmental regulation is discussed in Samuel P. Hays, *Beauty, Health, and Permanence*. In *Loving Nature, Fearing the State*, Brian Allen Drake explores the "middle ground between postwar environmentalism and antistatism" (182).

Epilogue

1. Montrie provides a useful reminder of what previous scholars have uncovered about working-class contributions to environmentalism, but his critique of the historical significance of Carson's book ignores her role in the emergence of the widespread popular environmental movement of the 1970s. As my book notes, in the nineteenth century, there was indeed recognition of the vulnerability of the environment, but these concerns were contained by cultural fears of a threatening nature and the continued confidence in human ability to control nature and make

it useful. I argue that Carson and the other originators of contemporary environmentalism were able to reach a larger audience and have a more sustained impact because the threats to the environment (pesticides, radiation) were no longer limited to specific areas.

2. Rebecca Edwards seems to have coined the phrase "long Progressive Era" in her book *New Spirits: Americans in the Gilded Age, 1865–1905* (7). As I note in the introduction, the dates of progressivism have been debated by historians.

3. For the story of Faulkner's Nobel Prize speech, see Joseph Blotner's *Faulkner* (2: 1337–71). Mark LaVoi's rhetorical analysis puts the speech in the historical context of nuclear anxiety; he demonstrates that "Faulkner offered a language that helped ameliorate fear, retain hope, and champion life in a world of atomic worry" (200).

4. An account of Nobel and his prize can be found in Burton Feldman's *The Nobel Prize*. John Burroughs also believed in the potential of science to end war: in 1913 he observed, "Science now promises to make war so deadly that it will practically abolish it" (*Summit* 67). The explosive yields and casualties are from Richard Rhodes (711, 734, 740).

5. For a recent review of the debate over the use of the bomb, see Michael Kort's *The Columbia Guide to Hiroshima and the Bomb* (2007).

6. Raymond Williams argues that a central theme in negative depictions of the modern city is exposure "to kinds of physical mass attack, as in the obliteration bombing of the Second World War and, at its peak, the destruction of cities by atomic bombs" (*Country* 275).

7. In "Chemical Fallout," Ralph H. Lutts discusses the significance of concerns about radioactivity in *Silent Spring*. J. R. McNeill and Peter Engelke summarize the environmental problems associated with nuclear weapons (160–68).

8. The most thorough account of the camping trips is Norman Brauer's *There to Breathe the Beauty* (1995).

Works Cited

Abbey, Edward. *Desert Solitaire: A Season in the Wilderness*. Simon & Schuster, 1968.
Abu-Lughod, Janet L. *Race, Space, and Riots in Chicago, New York, and Los Angeles*. Oxford UP, 2007.
Adams, James Truslow. "'Rugged Individualism' Analyzed." *New York Times Magazine*, 18 Mar. 1934, pp. 1–2, 11.
Addams, Jane. *A New Conscience and an Ancient Evil*. MacMillan, 1912.
The Adirondacks. New York Central Lines, [1917]. Adirondack Museum Collection, Blue Mountain Lake, NY.
Agamben, Giorgio. *Homo Sacer: Sovereign Power and Bare Life*. 1995. Stanford UP, 1998.
Aiken, Charles S. "Faulkner and the Passing of the Old Agrarian Culture." *Faulkner and Material Culture*, edited by Joseph R. Urgo and Ann J. Abadie, UP of Mississippi, 2007, pp. 3–19.
———. *William Faulkner and the Southern Landscape*. U of Georgia P, 2009.
Alaimo, Stacy. *Undomesticated Ground: Recasting Nature as Feminist Space*. Cornell UP, 2000.
Alperovitz, Gar. *The Decision to Use the Atomic Bomb and the Architecture of an American Myth*. Alfred A. Knopf, 1995.
Armbruster, Karla, and Kathleen R. Wallace, editors. *Beyond Nature Writing: Expanding the Boundaries of Ecocriticism*. UP of Virginia, 2001.
Armitage, Kevin C. *The Nature Study Movement: The Forgotten Popularizer of America's Conservation Ethic*. UP of Kansas, 2009.
Arsenault, Raymond. "The Public Storm: Hurricanes and the State in Twentieth-Century America." *Paradise Lost?: The Environmental History of Florida*, edited by Jack E. Davis and Raymond Arsenault, UP of Florida, 2005, pp. 201–32.
Arthur, Anthony. *Radical Innocent: Upton Sinclair*. Random House, 2006.
Askins, Justin. "Thankfully, the Center Cannot Hold." *Sharp Eyes: John Burroughs and American Nature Writing*, edited by Charlotte Zoë Walker, Syracuse UP, 2000, pp. 251–64.

Atkinson, Ted. *Faulkner and the Great Depression: Aesthetics, Ideology, and Cultural Politics*. U of Georgia P, 2006.
Austin, Mary. *California: The Land of the Sun*. Adam and Charles Black, 1914.
———. "The Colorado River Controversy." *The Nation*, vol. 125, 9 Nov. 1927, pp. 510–12.
———. *Earth Horizon: Autobiography*. 1932. U of New Mexico P, 1991.
———. *The Ford*. 1917. U of California P, 1997.
———. *The Land of Little Rain*. 1903. Penguin Books, 1997.
———. "The Owens River Water Project." *San Francisco Chronicle*, 3 Sept. 1905, p. 19.
———. "The Tremblor: A Personal Narration." *The California Earthquake of 1906*, edited by David Starr Jordan, A. M. Robertson, 1907, pp. 339–60.
———. "Why I am a Progressive." *Beaver County Times*, 21 Oct. 1912, p. 4.
Awkward, Michael, "Introduction." *New Essays on Their Eyes Were Watching God*, edited by Michael Awkward, Cambridge UP, 1990, pp. 1–27.
Badger, Anthony J. *The New Deal: The Depression Years, 1933–40*. Farrar, Straus and Giroux, 1989.
Bailey, Liberty Hyde. *The Country-Life Movement in the United States*. Macmillan, 1913.
———. *Essential Agrarian and Environmental Writings*. Edited by Zachary Michael Jack, Cornell UP, 2008.
Baker, Lee D. *From Savage to Negro: Anthropology and the Construction of Race, 1896–1954*. U of California P, 1998.
Baldwin, Neil. *Henry Ford and the Jews: The Mass Production of Hate*. Public Affairs, 2001.
Banfield, Edward C. *The Unheavenly City: The Nature and the Future of Our Urban Crisis*. Little, Brown, 1970.
Barlow, Jane A., editor. *Big Moose Lake in the Adirondacks: The Story of the Lake, the Land, and the People*. Syracuse UP, 2004.
Barrow, Mark V., Jr. *Nature's Ghosts: Confronting Extinction from the Age of Jefferson to the Age of Ecology*. U of Chicago P, 2009.
———. *A Passion for Birds: American Ornithology After Audubon*. Princeton UP, 1998.
Barrus, Clara. *John Burroughs, Boy and Man*. Doubleday, Page, 1920.
Barry, John M. *Rising Tide: The Great Mississippi Flood of 1927 and How It Changed America*. Simon & Schuster, 1997.
Baym, Nina. "Melodramas of Beset Manhood: How Theories of American Fiction Exclude Women Authors." *American Quarterly*, vol. 33, no. 2, 1981, pp. 123–39.
Beard, Daniel Carter. *The Outdoor Handy Book: For Playground, Field, and Forest*. 1896. Skyhorse, 2008.
Beaulieu, Elizabeth, editor. *Writing African American Women: An Encyclopedia of Literature by and about Women of Color*, vol. 1, Westport: Greenwood, 2006.

Beaver, Harold. "Run, Nigger, Run." *The Critical Response to Mark Twain's Huckleberry Finn*, edited by Laurie Champion, Greenwood, 1991, pp. 187–94.

Bederman, Gail. *Manliness & Civilization: A Cultural History of Gender and Race in the United States, 1880–1917.* U of Chicago P, 1995.

Beer, Janet. "Walking the Streets: Women out Alone in Kate Chopin's New Orleans." *Kate Chopin's* The Awakening: *A Sourcebook*, edited by Janet Beer and Elizabeth Nolan, Routledge, 2004, pp. 92–97.

Bell, Bernard W. "William Faulkner's 'Shining Star': Lucas Beauchamp as a Marginal Man." *Critical Essays on William Faulkner: The McCaslin Family*, edited by Arthur F. Kinney, G. K. Hall, 1990, pp. 224–33.

Bell, Hamilton Wright. *The Winning of Barbara Worth.* Book Supply, 1911.

Bender, Daniel E. *Sweated Work, Weak Bodies: Anti-Sweatshop Campaigns and Languages of Labor.* Rutgers UP, 2004.

Bennett, Michael. "From Wide Open Spaces to Metropolitan Places: The Urban Challenge to Ecocriticism." *The ISLE Reader: Ecocriticism, 1993–2003*, edited by Michael P. Branch and Scott Slovic, U of Georgia P, 2003, pp. 296–317.

———, and David W. Teague, editors. *The Nature of Cities: Ecocriticism and Urban Environments.* U of Arizona P, 1999.

Benson, Maxine. *Martha Maxwell: Rocky Mountain Naturalist.* U of Nebraska P, 1986.

Bercovitch, Sacvan. "Deadpan Huck: Or, What's Funny about Interpretation." *Kenyon Review*, vol. 24, nos. 3–4, 2002, pp. 90–134.

Bergon, Frank. "'Sensitive to the Verge of the Horizon': The Environmentalism of John Burroughs." *Sharp Eyes: John Burroughs and American Nature Writing*, edited by Charlotte Zoe Walker, Syracuse UP, 2000, pp. 19–25.

Bergthaller, Hannes. "Introduction: Ecocriticism and Environmental History." *ISLE*, vol. 22, no. 1, 2015, pp. 5–8.

Bernert, Annette. "The Four Fathers of Isaac McCaslin." *Critical Essays on William Faulkner: The McCaslin Family*, edited by Arthur F. Kinney, G. K. Hall, 1990, pp. 181–89.

Beveridge, Albert J. "The March of the Flag." *The Meaning of the Times and Other Speeches*, Bobbs-Merrill, 1908, pp. 47–57.

Bezzerides, A. I. *William Faulkner: A Life on Paper.* UP of Mississippi in cooperation with Mississippi Authority for Educational Television, 1980.

Blend, Benay. "Mary Austin and the Western Conservation Movement: 1900–1927." *Journal of the Southwest*, vol. 30, no. 1, 1988, pp. 12–34.

———. "A Victorian Gentlewoman in the Rocky Mountain West: Ambiguity in the Work of Mary Hallock Foote." *Reading Under the Sign of Nature: New Essays in Ecocriticism*, edited by John Tallmadge and Henry Harrington, U of Utah P, 2000, pp. 85–100.

Blotner, Joseph. *Faulkner: A Biography.* Random House, 1974. 2 vols.

———, editor. *Uncollected Stories of William Faulkner.* Random House, 1979.

Boas, Franz. *Changes in Bodily Form of the Descendants of Immigrants (Final Report)*. Government Printing Office, 1911.
Bowers, Fredson. "Textual Introduction." *The Works of Stephen Crane:* Bowery Tales. Edited by Fredson Bowers, vol. 1, UP of Virginia, 1969, pp. liii–xcviii.
Bowers, William L. *The Country Life Movement in America, 1900–1920*. Kennikat, 1974.
Bowler, Peter J. *The Norton History of the Environmental Sciences*. W. W. Norton, 1992.
Boyd, Valerie. *Wrapped in Rainbows: The Life of Zora Neale Hurston*. Scribner, 2003.
Boyer, Paul. *By the Bomb's Early Light: American Thought and Culture at the Dawn of the Atomic Age*. Pantheon Books, 1985.
———. *Urban Masses and Moral Order in America, 1820–1920*. Harvard UP, 1978.
Branch, Michael P. "Before Nature Writing: Discourses of Colonial American Natural History." *Beyond Nature Writing: Expanding the Boundaries of Ecocriticism*, edited by Karla Armbruster and Kathleen R. Wallace, UP of Virginia, 2001, pp. 91–107.
———, Rochelle Johnson, Daniel Patterson, and Scott Slovic, editors. *Reading the Earth: New Directions in the Study of Literature and the Environment*. U of Idaho P, 1998.
———, and Scott Slovic, editors. *The ISLE Reader: Ecocriticism, 1993–2003*. U of Georgia P, 2003.
Brandon, Craig. *Murder in the Adirondacks:* An American Tragedy *Revisited*. North Country Books, 1986.
Brauer, Norman. *There to Breathe the Beauty: The Camping Trips of Henry Ford, Thomas Edison, Harvey Firestone, John Burroughs*. Norman Brauer, 1995.
Brinkley, Alan. *The End of Reform: New Deal Liberalism in Recession and War*. Alfred A. Knopf, 1995.
Brinkley, Douglas. *Rightful Heritage: Franklin D. Roosevelt and the Land of America*. Harper, 2016.
———. *The Wilderness Warrior: Theodore Roosevelt and the Crusade for America*. HarperCollins, 2009.
Brooks, Cleanth. *William Faulkner: The Yoknapatawpha Country*. 1963. Louisiana State UP, 1990.
Brown, Dona. *Back to the Land: The Enduring Dream of Self-Sufficiency in Modern America*. U of Wisconsin P, 2011.
Brownwell, Joseph W., and Patricia W. Enos. *Adirondack Tragedy: The Gillette Murder Case of 1906*. Nicholas K. Burns, 2003.
Buchanan, Minor Ferris. *Holt Collier: His Life, His Roosevelt Hunts, and the Origin of the Teddy Bear*. Centennial, 2002.
Buell, Lawrence. *Writing for an Endangered World*. Harvard UP, 2001.
Bulmer, Martin. *The Chicago School of Sociology: Institutionalization, Diversity, and the Rise of Sociological Research*. U of Chicago P, 1984.

Burdick, Neal S. "Who Killed Orrando P. Dexter?" *Adirondack Life*, May/June 1982, pp. 23–49.

Burkett, Paul. *Marx and Nature: A Red and Green Perspective*. St. Martins, 1999.

Burroughs, John. "Real and Sham Natural History." 1903. *The Wild Animal Story*, edited by Ralph H. Lutts, Temple UP, 1998, pp. 129–43.

———. *Signs and Seasons*. 1886. Barnes and Noble, 2008.

———. *The Summit of the Years*. Houghton Mifflin, 1913. The Riverby Edition of the Writings of John Burroughs, vol. 17.

———. *Under the Maples*. Houghton Mifflin, 1921.

———. *Wake-Robin*. 2nd ed., Riverside, 1877.

Butcher, Philip. "Mark Twain's Installment on the National Debt." *Southern Literary Journal*, vol. 1, no. 2, 1969, pp. 48–55.

Calkins, Raymond. *Substitutes for the Saloon*. 1901. 2nd ed., Houghton Mifflin, 1919.

Callicott, J. Baird, and Michael P. Nelson, editors. *The Great New Wilderness Debate*. U of Georgia P, 1998.

———. *The Wilderness Debate Rages On*. U of Georgia P, 2008.

Carby, Hazel. "The Politics of Fiction, Anthropology, and the Folk: Zora Neal Hurston." *New Essays on Their Eyes Were Watching God*, edited by Michael Awkward, Cambridge UP, 1990, pp. 71–93.

Carew-Miller, Anna. "Mary Austin's Nature: Refiguring Tradition through the Voices of Identity." *Reading the Earth: New Directions in the Study of Literature and the Environment*, edited by Michael P. Branch, Rochelle Johnson, Daniel Patterson, and Scott Slovic, U of Idaho P, 1998, pp. 79–95.

Carothers, James B. "'In Conflict with Itself': The Nobel Prize Address in Faulknerian Contexts. *Faulkner and Formalism: Returns of the Text*, edited by Annette Trefzer and Ann J. Abadie, UP of Mississippi, 2012, pp. 20–40.

Carroll, Charles. *The Negro a Beast: Or, In the Image of God*. American Book and Bible House, 1900.

Carson, Rachel. *Silent Spring*. 1962. Mariner, 2002.

Carter, Susan B., Scott Sigmund Gartner, Michael R. Haines, Alan L. Olmstead, Richard Sutch, and Gavin Wright, editors. *Historical Statistics of the United States: Earliest Times to Present*. Millennial ed., vol. 1, Cambridge UP, 2006.

Cassuto, David N. *Dripping Dry: Literature, Politics, and Water in the Desert Southwest*. U of Michigan P, 2001.

Castro, Amanda Lee. "Storm Warnings: The Eternally Recurring Apocalypse in Kate Chopin's *The Awakening*." *Southern Literary Journal*, vol. 47, no. 1, Fall 2014, pp. 68–80.

Cervetti, Nancy. *S. Weir Mitchell, 1829–1914: Philadelphia's Literary Physician*. The Pennsylvania State UP, 2012.

Chadwick-Joshua, Jocelyn. *The Jim Dilemma: Reading Race in Huckleberry Finn*. UP of Mississippi, 1998.

Chopin, Kate. *The Awakening*. 1899. Edited by Margaret Culley, W. W. Norton, 1976.

———. *Kate Chopin's Private Papers*. Edited by Emily Toth and Per Seyersted, Indiana UP, 1998.

Claghorn, Kate Holladay. "Foreign Immigration and the Tenement House in New York City." *The Tenement House Problem*, edited by Robert W. DeForest and Lawrence Veiller, vol. 2, Macmillan, 1903, pp. 67–90.

Clark, Suzanne. "Narrative Fitness: Science, Nature, and Zora Neale Hurston's Folk Culture." *Restoring the Connection to the Natural World: Essays on the African American Environmental Imagination*, edited by Sylvia Mayer, Transaction, 2003, pp. 45–71.

Cleaver, Eldridge. *Eldridge Cleaver: Post-Prison Writings and Speeches*. Edited by Robert Scheer, Random House, 1969.

Clendenning, John. "Desire and Regression in Dreiser's *An American Tragedy*." *Dreiser Studies*, vol. 25, no. 2, 1994, pp. 23–35.

Coates, Peter. *American Perceptions of Immigrant and Invasive Species: Strangers on the Land*. U of California P, 2006.

Colten, Craig E. *An Unnatural Metropolis: Wresting New Orleans from Nature*. Louisiana State UP, 2005.

Cooper, John Milton. "From Promoting to Ending Big Government: 1912 and the Progressives' Century." *The Progressives' Century: Political Reform, Constitutional Government, and the Modern American State*, edited by Stephen Skowronek, Stephen M. Engel, and Bruce Ackerman, Yale UP, 2016, pp. 157–73.

Cousins, Norman. "Modern Man Is Obsolete." *Saturday Review of Literature*, 18 Aug. 1945, pp. 5–9.

Crane, Stephen. *The Correspondence of Stephen Crane*. Edited by Stanley Wertheim and Paul Sorrentino, Columbia UP, 1988. 2 vols.

———. *Maggie: A Girl of the Streets*. 1893. Edited by Thomas A. Gullason, W. W. Norton, 1979.

Croker, Robert A. *Stephen Forbes and the Rise of American Ecology*. Smithsonian Institution, 2001.

Cronon, William. *Nature's Metropolis: Chicago and the Great West*. W. W. Norton, 1991.

———. "A Place for Stories: Nature, History, and Narrative." *Journal of American History*, vol. 78, no. 4, March 1992, pp. 1347–76.

———. "The Trouble with Wilderness; or, Getting Back to the Wrong Nature." *Uncommon Ground: Rethinking the Human Place in Nature*, edited by William Cronon, W. W. Norton, 1996, pp. 69–90.

———. *Uncommon Ground: Rethinking the Human Place in Nature*. W. W. Norton, 1996.

Curren, Erik D. "Should Their Eyes Have Been Watching God?: Hurston's Use of Religious Experience and Gothic Horror." *African American Review*, vol. 29, no. 1, 1995, pp. 17–25.

Cushman, Philip. "Psychotherapy to 1992: A Historically Situated Interpretation." *History of Psychotherapy: A Century of Change*, edited by Donald K. Freedheim, American Psychological Association, 1992, pp. 21–64.

Darwin, Charles. *The Annotated Origin: A Facsimile Edition of the First Edition of* On the Origin of Species. Harvard UP, 2009.

———. *Descent of Man and Selection in Relation to Sex*. 1871. Barnes & Noble, 2004.

Davis, Cynthia. "The Landscape of the Text: Locating Zora Neale Hurston in the Ecocritical Canon." *Florida Studies: Proceedings of the 2005 Annual Meeting of the Florida College English Association*, edited by Steve Glassman, Karen Tolchin, and Steve Brahlek, Cambridge Scholars, 2006, pp. 149–56.

Davis, Jack E., and Raymond Arsenault, editors. *Paradise Lost?: The Environmental History of Florida*. UP of Florida, 2005.

Davis, Thadious M. *Games of Property: Law, Race, Gender, and Faulkner's* Go Down, Moses. Duke UP, 2003.

Dawkins, Richard. *River Out of Eden: A Darwinian View of Life*. Basic, 1995.

Deluzio, Crista. *Female Adolescence in American Scientific Thought, 1830–1930*. Johns Hopkins UP, 2007.

Denison, Lindsay. "President Roosevelt's Mississippi Bear Hunt." *Outing*, vol. 41, no. 5, Feb. 1903, pp. 603–10.

Derrick, Scott. "What a Beating Feels Like: Authorship, Dissolution, and Masculinity in Sinclair's *The Jungle*." *Studies in American Fiction*, vol. 23, no. 1, 1995, pp. 85–100.

Deverell, William. "Conquest to Convalescence: Nature and Nation in United States History." *The Oxford Handbook of Environmental History*, edited by Andrew C. Isenberg, Oxford UP, 2014, pp. 644–67.

Devlin, Albert J. "History, Sexuality, and the Wilderness in the McCaslin Family Chronicle." *Critical Essays on William Faulkner: The McCaslin Family*, edited by Arthur F. Kinney, G. K. Hall, 1990, pp. 189–98.

Dewey, John. "My Pedagogic Creed." *John Dewey: The Early Works, 1882–1898*. Edited by Jo Ann Boydston, vol. 5, Southern Illinois UP, 1972, pp. 84–95.

———. "The School as Social Centre." *John Dewey: The Middle Works, 1899–1924*. Edited by Jo Ann Boydston, vol. 2, Southern Illinois UP, 1976, pp. 80–93.

Dickey, James. *Deliverance*. 1972. Delta, 1994.

Dixon, Melvin. *Ride Out the Wilderness: Geography and Identity in Afro-American Literature*. U of Chicago P, 1987.

Dixon, Terrell F. "Nature, Gender, and Community: Mary Wilkins Freeman's Ecofiction." *Beyond Nature Writing: Expanding the Boundaries of Ecocriticism*, edited by Karla Armbruster and Kathleen R. Wallace, UP of Virginia, 2001, pp. 162–76.

Dock, Julie Bates, editor. *Charlotte Perkins Gilman's "The Yellow Wall-paper" and the History of Its Publication and Reception: A Critical Edition and Documentary Casebook*. Pennsylvania State UP, 1998.

Dower, John W. *War Without Mercy: Race and Power in the Pacific War*. Pantheon Books, 1986.

Dowling, Robert M. *Slumming in New York: From the Waterfront to Mythic Harlem*. U of Urbana P, 2007.

Drake, Brian Allen. *Loving Nature, Fearing the State: Environmentalism and Antigovernment Politics before Reagan*. U of Washington P, 2013.

Dreiser, Helen. *My Life with Dreiser*. World, 1951.

Dreiser, Theodore. *American Diaries, 1902–1926*. Edited by Thomas P. Riggio, James L.W. West III, and Neda M. Westlake, U of Pennsylvania P, 1983.

———. *An American Tragedy*. 1925. Library of America, 2003.

———. "Remarks." *The Psychoanalytic Review*, vol. 18, 1931, p. 250.

Du Bois, W. E. B. *The Souls of Black Folk*. Edited by Brent Hayes Edwards, Oxford UP, 2007.

Dunlap, Thomas R. *Saving America's Wildlife: Ecology and the American Mind, 1850–1990*. Princeton UP, 1988.

Dussere, Erik. *Balancing the Books: Faulkner, Morrison, and the Economies of Slavery*. Routledge, 2003.

Dyson, Michael Eric. *Come Hell or High Water: Hurricane Katrina and the Color of Disaster*. Basic Civitas Books, 2006.

Edwards, Rebecca. *New Spirits: Americans in the Gilded Age, 1865–1905*. Oxford UP, 2006.

Eliot, T. S. "The Boy and the River: Without Beginning or End." *Adventures of Huckleberry Finn: A Case Study in Critical Controversy*, edited by Gerald Graff and James Phelan, Bedford/St. Martin's, 2004, pp. 285–89.

———. "The Dry Salvages." *Collected Poems, 1909–1962*. Harcourt, Brace & World, 1963, pp. 191–99.

Emerson, Ralph Waldo. *Nature*. *Ralph Waldo Emerson: Essays & Lectures*. Edited by Joel Porte, Library of America, 1983, pp. 5–49.

Engels, Frederick. *Dialectics of Nature*. Translated and edited by Clemens Dutt, International, 1940.

Erdheim, Cara Elana. "Is There a Place for Ecology in *An American Tragedy*? Wealth, Water, and the Dreiserian Struggle for Survival." *Studies in American Naturalism*, vol. 3, no. 1, 2008, pp. 3–21.

Estok, Simon C. *The Ecophobia Hypothesis*. Routledge, 2018.

Evernden, Neil. *The Social Creation of Nature*. Johns Hopkins UP, 1992.

Ewan, Rebecca Fish. *A Land Between: Owens Valley, California*. Johns Hopkins UP, 2000.

Ewell, Barbara C. "Storm Stories: Chopin and Faulkner in New Orleans—and on the Gulf Coast." *Faulkner and Chopin*. Edited by Robert W. Hamblin and Christopher Rieger, Southeast Missouri State UP, 2010, pp. 17–34.

———, and Pamela Glenn Menke. "*The Awakening* and the Great October Storm of 1893." *Southern Literary Journal*, vol. 42, no. 2, 2010, pp. 1–11.

Faulkner, William. *Big Woods*. Random House, 1955.

———. *Essays, Speeches, and Public Letters*. Edited by James B. Meriwether, Random House, 1965.

———. *Go Down, Moses*. 1942. Vintage International, 1990.

———. *Light in August*. 1932. Vintage International, 1990.

———. "Lion." *Uncollected Stories of William Faulkner*. Edited by Joseph Blotner, Random House, 1979, pp. 184–200.

Feldman, Burton. *The Nobel Prize: A History of Genius, Controversy, and Prestige*. Arcade, 2000.

Fernow, B[ernhard]. E. "The Providential Functions of Government with Special Reference to Natural Resources." *Science*, vol. 2, no. 35, 30 Aug. 1895, pp. 252–65.

Fiedler, Leslie. "Come Back to the Raft Ag'in, Huck Honey!" *Partisan Review*, vol. 15, June 1948, pp. 664–71.

Fiege, Mark. *The Republic of Nature: An Environmental History of the United States*. U of Washington P, 2012.

Firestone, Harvey S. *Men and Rubber: The Story of Business*. Doubleday, Page, 1926.

Fischer, Victor, and Lin Salamo, editors. *Adventures of Huckleberry Finn*. U of California P, 2010.

Fiske, George Walter. *Boy Life and Self Government*. Association, 1912.

Flader, Susan L. *Thinking Llike a Mountain: Aldo Leopold and the Evolution of an Ecological Attitude toward Deer, Wolves and Forests*. U of Wisconsin P, 1974.

———, and J. Baird Callicott. "Introduction." *The River of the Mother of God and Other Essays by Aldo Leopold*. Edited by Susan L. Flader and J. Baird Callicott, U of Wisconsin P, 1991, pp. 3–31.

Flower, B[enjamin]. O[range]. *Civilization's Inferno*. Arena, 1893.

Foerster, Norman. "The Nature Cult Today." *The Nation*, vol. 94, 11 Apr. 1912, pp. 357–59.

Folsom, Michael Brewster. "Upton Sinclair's Escape from *The Jungle*: The Narrative Strategy and Suppressed Conclusion of America's First Proletarian Novel." *Upton Sinclair's* The Jungle, edited by Harold Bloom, Chelsea House, 2002, pp. 21–47.

Ford, Henry. *My Life and Work*. Garden City, 1922.

Foucault, Michel. *The History of Sexuality. Volume 1: An Introduction*. Pantheon Books, 1978.

———. *"Society Must be Defended": Lectures at the Collège de France, 1975–76*. Edited by Mauro Bertani and Alessandro Fontana, Picador, 2003.

Fox, Stephen. *The American Conservation Movement: John Muir and His Legacy*. U of Wisconsin P, 1985.

Fredrickson, George M. *The Black Image in the White Mind: The Debate on Afro-American Character and Destiny, 1817–1914*. Harper and Row, 1971.

Freud, Sigmund. *Civilization and Its Discontents*. 1930. Hogarth, 1961. The Standard Edition of the Complete Psychological Works of Sigmund Freud, general editor James Strachey, vol. 21, pp. 64–145.

———. "'Civilized' Sexual Morality and Modern Nervous Illness." 1908. Hogarth, 1959. The Standard Edition of the Complete Psychological Works of Sigmund Freud, general editor James Strachey, vol. 9, pp. 177–204.

———. "Lecture 23: The Paths to the Formation of Symptoms." *Introductory Lectures on Psychoanalysis.* 1916–17. Hogarth, 1963. The Standard Edition of the Complete Psychological Works of Sigmund Freud, general editor James Strachey, vol. 16, pp. 358–72.

Freund, Ernst. *The Police Power: Public Policy and Constitutional Rights.* U of Chicago P, 1904.

Gambrell, Alice. *Women Intellectuals, Modernism, and Difference: Transatlantic Culture, 1919–1945.* Cambridge UP, 1997.

Gandal, Keith. *The Virtues of the Vicious: Jacob Riis, Stephen Crane, and the Spectacle of the Slum.* Oxford UP, 1997.

Gandy, Matthew. *Concrete and Clay: Reworking Nature in New York City.* MIT Press, 2003.

Garrard, Greg. *Ecocriticism.* Routledge, 2004.

George, Henry. *Social Problems.* Belford, Clarke, 1883.

Gershenhorn, Jerry. *Melville J. Herskovits and the Racial Politics of Knowledge.* U of Nebraska P, 2004.

Giberti, Bruno. *Designing the Centennial: A History of the 1876 International Exhibition in Philadelphia.* UP of Kentucky, 2002.

Giddings, Franklin Henry. *The Principles of Sociology.* Macmillan, 1896.

Gifford, Terry. *Green Voices: Understanding Contemporary Nature Poetry.* Manchester UP, 1995.

Gilfoyle, Timothy, J. *City of Eros: New York City, Prostitution, and the Commercialization of Sex, 1790–1920.* W. W. Norton, 1992.

Gilman, Charlotte Perkins. *The Living of Charlotte Perkins Gilman: An Autobiography.* 1935. U of Wisconsin P, 1990.

Gilmore, Michael T. "Revolt Against Nature: The Problematic Modernism of *The Awakening.*" *New Essays on* The Awakening, edited by Wendy Martin, Cambridge UP, 1988, pp. 59–87.

Giorcelli, Cristina. "Edna's Wisdom: A Transitional and Numinous Merging." *New Essays on* The Awakening, edited by Wendy Martin, Cambridge UP, 1988, pp. 109–48.

Glave, Dianne D., and Mark Stoll, editors. *"To Love the Wind and the Rain": African Americans and Environmental History.* U of Pittsburg P, 2006.

Gleason, William A. *The Leisure Ethic: Work and Play in American Literature, 1840–1940.* Stanford UP, 1999.

Glotfelty, Cheryll. "Introduction: Literary Studies in an Age of Environmental Crisis." *The Ecocriticism Reader: Landmarks in Literary Ecology*, edited by Cheryll Glotfelty and Harold Fromm, U of Georgia P, 1996, pp. xv–xxxvii.

Godden, Richard. *William Faulkner: An Economy of Complex Words.* Princeton UP, 2007.

Goodlatte, Bob. *Congressional Record.* 112th Congress, 2nd Session. Vol. 158, issue 37, 7 Mar. 2012. www.gpo.gov/fdsys/granule/CREC-2012-03-07/CREC-2012-03-07-pt1-PgE329/content-detail.html. Accessed 23 Dec. 2016.

Goodman, Susan, and Carl Dawson. *Mary Austin and the American* West. U of California P, 2008.

Gosling, F. G. *Before Freud: Neurasthenia and the American Medical Community, 1870–1910.* U of Illinois P, 1987.

Gossett, Thomas F. *Race: The History of an Idea in America.* Southern Methodist UP, 1963.

Gougeon, Len. "Looking Backwards: Emerson in 1903." *Nineteenth-Century Prose,* vol. 30, nos. 1–2, 2003, pp. 50–73.

Graham, Otis L., Jr. *An Encore for Reform: The Old Progressives and the New Deal.* Oxford UP, 1967.

———. *The Great Campaigns: Reform and War in America, 1900–1928.* Prentice-Hall, 1971.

Gray, Richard J. *The Life of William Faulkner.* Blackwell, 1994.

Greenblatt, Stephen. "Invisible Bullets: Renaissance Authority and Its Subversion." *New Historicism and Renaissance Drama,* edited by Richard Wilson and Richard Dutton, Longman, 1992, pp. 83–108.

Gribben, Alan. *Mark Twain's Library: A Reconstruction.* G. K. Hall, 1980. 2 vols,

Grunwald, Michael. *The Swamp: The Everglades, Florida, and the Politics of Paradise.* Simon & Schuster, 2006.

Guarneri, Julia. "Changing Strategies for Child Welfare, Enduring Beliefs about Childhood: The Fresh Air Fund, 1877–1926." *Journal of the Gilded Age and Progressive Era,* vol. 11, no. 1, January 2012, pp. 27–70.

Gwynn, Frederick L., and Joseph L. Blotner, editors. *Faulkner in the University: Class Conferences at the University of Virginia, 1957–1958.* U of Virginia P, 1959.

Haas, Robert. "Might Zora Neale Hurston's Janie Woods Be Dying of Rabies? Considerations from Historical Medicine." *Literature and Medicine,* vol. 19, no. 2, 2000, pp. 205–28.

Habich, Robert D. *Building Their Own Waldos: Emerson's First Biographers and the Politics of Life-Writing in the Gilded Age.* U of Iowa P, 2011.

Haeckel, Ernst. *The Evolution of Man: A Popular Scientific Study.* Vol. 1, G. P. Putnam's Sons, 1905.

Hall, A[lfred]. D[aniel]. "Some Aspects of Vegetarianism." *Harper's New Monthly Magazine,* vol. 123, July 1911, pp. 208–13.

Hall, G. Stanley. *Adolescence.* D. Appleton, 1904. 2 vols.

———. "Some Practical Results of Child Study." *The Work and Words of the National Congress of Mothers.* Appleton, 1897, pp. 165–71.

Hamlin, Kimberly A. "Sexual Selection and the Economics of Marriage: 'Female Choice' in the Writings of Edward Bellamy and Charlotte Perkins Gilman." *America's Darwin: Darwinian Theory and U.S. Literary Culture*, edited by Tina Gianquitto and Lydia Fisher, U of Georgia P, 2014, pp. 151–80.

Haraway, Donna. "Situated Knowledges: The Science Question in Feminism and the Privilege of Partial Perspective." *Feminist Studies*, vol. 14, no. 3, 1988, pp. 575–99.

Hardin, Garrett. "The Tragedy of the Commons." *Science*, vol. 162, 13 Dec. 1968, pp. 1243–48.

"Harding Says Negro Must Have Equality in Political Life." *New York Times*, 27 Oct. 1921, pp, 1, 11.

Hartness, James. *The Human Factor in Works Management*. McGraw-Hill, 1912.

Harvey, Mark. *Wilderness Forever: Howard Zahniser and the Path to the Wilderness Act*. U of Washington P, 2005.

Hays, Samuel P. *Beauty, Health, and Permanence: Environmental Politics in the United States, 1955–1985*. Cambridge UP, 1987.

———. *Conservation and the Gospel of Efficiency: The Progressive Conservation Movement, 1890–1920*. 1959. U of Pittsburgh Press, 1999.

Heap, Chad. *Slumming: Sexual and Racial Encounters in American Nightlife, 1885–1940*. U of Chicago P, 2009.

Hearn, Michael Patrick, editor. *The Annotated* Huckleberry Finn. W. W. Norton, 2001.

Hemenway, Robert E. *Zora Neale Hurston: A Literary Biography*. U of Illinois P, 1977.

Herman, Daniel Justin. *Hunting and the American Imagination*. Smithsonian Institution Press, 2001.

Herrick, Robert. *The Gospel of Freedom*. Macmillan, 1898.

Hickman, Nollie. *Mississippi Harvest*. U of Mississippi P, 1962.

Higham, John. *Strangers in the Land: Patterns of American Nativism, 1860–1925*. 2nd ed., Rutgers UP, 1988.

"Hobbling Back to Nature. *The Nation*, 21 Mar. 1907, pp. 258–59.

Hoffman, Abraham. "Mary Austin, Stafford Austin, and the Owens Valley." *Journal of the Southwest*, vol. 53, no. 3–4, 2011, pp. 305–22.

Hoffman, Frederick L. *Race Traits and Tendencies of the American Negro*. Macmillan, 1896.

Hofstadter, Richard. *The Age of Reform*. Vintage, 1960.

Holt, Marilyn Irvin. *The Orphan Trains: Placing Out in America*. U of Nebraska P, 1992.

hooks, bell. *Sisters of the Yam: Black Women and Self-Recovery*. South End, 2005.

Horowitz, Helen Lefkowitz. *Wild Unrest: Charlotte Perkins Gilman and the Making of "The Yellow Wall-Paper."* Oxford UP, 2010.

Horwitz, Howard. "Maggie and the Sociological Paradigm." *American Literary History*, vol. 10, no. 4, 1998, pp. 606–38.

Hotel Glennmore. Big Moose Lake, NY: Hotel Glennmore Corporation, [circa 1914]. Adirondack Museum Collection, Blue Mountain Lake, NY.

———. Big Moose Lake, NY: Hotel Glennmore Corporation, 1922. Adirondack Museum Collection, Blue Mountain Lake, NY.

Hoxie, Frederick E. *A Final Promise: The Campaign to Assimilate the Indians, 1880–1920*. U of Nebraska P, 1984.

Hughes, Langston. "The Negro Artist and the Racial Mountain." 1926. *The Collected Works of Langston Hughes*. Edited by Christopher C. DeSantis, vol. 9, U of Missouri P, 2002, pp. 31–36.

"Hunt Dexter's Slayer." *Plattsburgh Sentinel and Clinton County Farmer*, 25 Sept. 1903, p. 5.

"The Hunter's Camp." *Forest and Stream*, vol. 6, no. 21, 29 June 1876, pp. 333–34.

Huntington, Ellsworth. *Civilization and Climate*. Yale UP, 1915.

Hurston, Zora Neale. *Dust Tracks in the Road*. 1942. *Zora Neale Hurston: Folklore, Memoirs, and Other Writings*. Edited by Cheryl A. Wall, Library of America, 1995, pp. 557–808.

———. "Hoodoo in America." *The Journal of American Folklore*, vol. 44, no. 174, 1931, pp. 317–417.

———. "How It Feels to Be Colored Me." *Zora Neale Hurston: Folklore, Memoirs, and Other Writings*. Edited by Cheryl A. Wall, Library of America, 1995, pp. 826–29.

———. *Mules and Men*. HarperCollins, 2008.

———. *Their Eyes Were Watching God*. HarperCollins, 2006.

Hussman, Lawrence E. "The Fate of the Fallen Woman in *Maggie* and *Sister Carrie*." *The Image of the Prostitute in Modern Literature*. Edited by Pierre L. Horn and Mary Beth Pringle, Frederick Ungar, 1984, pp. 91–100.

Inge, M. Thomas, editor. *Conversations with William Faulkner*. UP of Mississippi, 1999.

Ingram, J. S. *The Centennial Exposition*. Hubbard Bros., 1876.

Jackman, Wilbur S. *Nature Study for the Common Schools*. Henry Holt, 1892.

Jackson, Walter. "Melville Herskovits and the Search for Afro-American Culture." *Malinowski, Rivers, Benedict and Others*, edited by George W. Stocking, Jr., U of Wisconsin P, 1986, pp. 95–126.

Jacobsen, Cheryl L. Rose. "Dr. Mandelet's Real Life Counterparts and Their Advice Books: Setting a Context for Edna's Revolt." *Perspectives on Kate Chopin:Proceedings from the Kate Chopin International Conference, April 6, 7, 8 1989*, Northwestern State UP, 1990, pp. 101–25.

Jacoby, Karl. *Crimes against Nature: Squatters, Poachers, Thieves, and the Hidden History of American Conservation*. U of California P, 2001.

James, William. "The Moral Equivalent of War." *William James: Writings 1902–1910*. Library of America, 1987, pp. 1281–93.

Johnson, Benjamin Heber. *Escaping the Dark, Gray City: Fear and Hope in Progressive-Era Conservation*. Yale UP, 2017.

Johnson, Lyndon Baines. "Speech to the Nation on Civil Disorders." 27 July 1967. http://millercenter.org/president/lbjohnson/speeches/speech-4040. Accessed 28 Dec. 2016.

Kahrl, William L. *Water and Power: The Conflict over Los Angeles' Water Supply in the Owens Valley*. U of California P, 1982.

Kallman, Harmon, editor. *Restoring America's Wildlife: The first 50 years of the Federal Aid in Wildlife Restoration (Pittman-Robertson) Act*. US Fish and Wildlife Service, 1987.

Karaganis, Joseph. "Naturalism's Nation: Toward *An American Tragedy*." *American Literature*, vol. 72, no. 1, 2000, pp. 153–80.

Kasson, John F. *Amusing the Million: Coney Island at the Turn of the Century*. Hill & Wang, 1978.

Keller, Betty. *Black Wolf: The Life of Ernest Thompson Seton*. Douglas & McIntyre, 1984.

Kellogg, J[ohn] H[arvey]. *Shall We Slay to Eat?* Good Health, 1899.

Kern, Robert. "Ecocriticism: What Is It Good For?" *The ISLE Reader: Ecocriticism, 1993–2003*, edited by Michael P. Branch and Scott Slovic, U of Georgia P, 2003, pp. 258–81.

Kevles, Daniel J. *In the Name of Eugenics: Genetics and the Uses of Human Heredity*. Alfred A. Knopf, 1985.

Kingsland, Sharon E. *The Evolution of American Ecology, 1890–2000*. Johns Hopkins UP, 2005.

Kingsolver, Barbara. *Prodigal Summer*. HarperCollins, 2000.

Kipling, Rudyard. *From Sea to Sea: Letters of Travel*. Doubleday and McClure, 1899. The Works of Rudyard Kipling, vol. 2.

Kleinberg, Eliot. *Black Cloud: The Deadly Hurricane of 1928*. Carroll & Graf, 2003.

Kline, Benjamin. *First Along the River: A Brief History of the U.S. Environmental Movement*. 3rd ed. Rowman & Littlefield, 2007.

Knights, Pamela. "Kate Chopin and the Subject of Childhood." *The Cambridge Companion to Kate Chopin*, edited by Janet Beer, Cambridge UP, 2008, pp. 44–58.

Kodat, Catherine Gunther. "Unsteady State: Faulkner and the Cold War." *William Faulkner in Context*, edited by John T. Matthews, Cambridge UP, 2015, pp. 156–65.

Kort, Michael. *The Columbia Guide to Hiroshima and the Bomb*. Columbia UP, 2007.

Kropotkin, Peter. *Mutual Aid: A Factor of Evolution*. 1902. Porter Sargent, 2009.

———. "The Sterilization of the Unfit." *Anarchy! An Anthology of Emma Goldman's Mother Earth*, edited by Peter Glassgold, Counterpoint, 2012, pp. 120–23.

Lambert, Darwin. *The Undying Past of Shenandoah National Park*. Roberts Rinehart, 1989.

Larsson, Ulf, editor. *Cultures of Creativity: The Centennial Exhibition of the Nobel Prize*. Rev. ed., Science History Publications, 2001.

LaVoi, Mark. "William Faulkner's 'Speech Accepting the Nobel Prize in Literature': A Language for Ameliorating Atomic Anxiety." *Rhetoric & Public Affairs*, vol. 17, no. 2, 2014, pp. 199–226.
Lawson, Andrew. "Class Mimicry in Stephen Crane's City." *American Literary History*, vol. 16, no. 4, 2004, pp. 596–618.
Lear, Linda. *Rachel Carson: Witness for Nature*. Mariner Books, 1997.
Lears, T. J. Jackson. "From Salvation to Self-Realization: Advertising and the Therapeutic Roots of the Consumer Culture, 1880–1930." *The Culture of Consumption: Critical Essays in American History, 1880–1980*, edited by Richard Wightman Fox and T. J. Jackson Lears, Pantheon, 1983, pp. 1–38.
———. *No Place of Grace: Antimodernism and the Transformation of American Culture, 1880–1920*. Pantheon Books, 1981.
Legler, Gretchen T. "Ecofeminist Literary Criticism." *Ecofeminism: Women, Culture, Nature*, edited by Karen J. Warren, Indiana UP, 1997, pp. 227–38.
Leopold, Aldo. *Report on a Game Survey of Mississippi*. 1929. Edited by Mary P. Stevens, Mississippi Museum of Natural Science, 2010.
———. *The River of the Mother of God and Other Essays by Aldo Leopold*. Edited by Susan L. Flader and J. Baird Callicott, U of Wisconsin P, 1991.
———. *A Sand County Almanac and Sketches Here and There*. Oxford UP, 1989.
Leupp, Francis E. *The Indian and His Problem*. Charles Scribner's Son, 1910.
Levine, George. *Darwin and the Novelists: Patterns of Science in Victorian Fiction*. U of Chicago P, 1988.
Libby, Willard. "Man's Place in the Physical Universe," *Bulletin of the Atomic Scientists*, vol. 21, no. 7, 1965, pp. 12–17.
Lillios, Anna. "'The Monstropolous Beast': The Hurricane in Zora Neale Hurston's *Their Eyes Were Watching God*." *Southern Quarterly*, vol. 36, no. 3, 1998, pp. 89–93.
Limbaugh, Rush H. *The Way Things Ought to Be*. Pocket Books, 1992.
Love, Glen A. *Practical Ecocriticism: Literature, Biology, and the Environment*. U of Virginia P, 2003.
Lowe, John. *Jump at the Sun: Zora Neale Hurston's Cosmic Comedy*. U of Illinois P, 1994.
LuBove, Roy. *The Progressives and the Slums: Tenement House Reform in New York City, 1890–1917*. U of Pittsburgh P, 1962.
Lundblad, Michael. *The Birth of a Jungle: Animality in Progressive-Era U.S. Literature and Culture*. Oxford UP, 2013.
Lutts, Ralph H. "Chemical Fallout: Rachel Carson's *Silent Spring*, Radioactive Fallout, and the Environmental Movement." *Environmental Review*, vol. 9, no. 3, 1985, pp. 210–25.
———. *The Nature Fakers: Wildlife, Science & Sentiment*. UP of Virginia, 1990.
Lutwack, Leonard. *The Role of Place in Literature*. Syracuse UP, 1984.
Lynch, Mike. "Beyond Peak Capacity: A Boom in High Peaks Hikers." *Adirondack Almanac*, 28 Aug. 2016. http://www.adirondackalmanack.com/2016/08/beyond-peak-capacity-boom-high-peaks-hikers.html. Accessed 18 Sept. 2017.

Magoc, Chris J. *Yellowstone: The Creation and Selling of an American Landscape, 1870–1903*. U of New Mexico P, 1999.

Maher, Neil M. *Nature's New Deal: The Civilian Conservation Corps and the Roots of the American Environmental Movement*. Oxford UP, 2008.

Marlon, Jennifer, et al. *Yale Climate Opinion Maps: U.S. 2016*. http://climatecommunication.yale.edu/visualizations-data/ycom-us-2016/. Accessed 9 Oct. 2017.

Marsh, George P. *The Earth as Modified by Human Action*. 1874. Arno, 1970.

Marshall, Robert. *The High Peaks of the Adirondacks*. 1922. *Bob Marshall in the Adirondacks: Writings of a Pioneering Peak-Bagger, Pond-Hopper and Wilderness Preservationist*. Edited by Phil Brown, Lost Pond, 2006, pp. 3–25.

———. "The Problem of the Wilderness." 1930. *The Great New Wilderness Debate*, edited by J. Baird Callicott and Michael P. Nelson, U of Georgia P, 1998, pp. 85–96.

Marx, Leo. *The Machine in the Garden: Technology and the Pastoral Ideal in America*. Oxford UP, 1964.

Matthews, John T. "Touching Race in *Go Down, Moses*." *New Essays on* Go Down, Moses, edited by Linda Wagner-Martin, Cambridge UP, 1996, pp. 21–47.

Mayer, Sylvia, editor. *Restoring the Connection to the Natural World: Essays on the African American Environmental Imagination*. Transaction, 2003.

Maynard, W. Barksdale. *Walden Pond: A History*. Oxford UP, 2004.

Mazel, David. *American Literary Environmentalism*. U of Georgia P, 2000.

———. "Ecocriticism as Praxis." *Teaching North American Environmental Literature*, edited by Laird Christensen, Mark C. Long, and Fred Waage, Modern Language Association of America, 2008, pp. 37–43.

McCally, David. *The Everglades: An Environmental History*. UP of Florida, 1999.

———. "The Everglades and the Florida Dream." *Paradise Lost? The Environmental History of Florida*, edited by Jack E. Davis and Raymond Arsenault, UP of Florida, 2005, pp. 141–59.

McCann, Charles R., Jr. *Order and Control in American Socio-Economic Thought: Social Scientists and Progressive-Era Reform*. Routledge, 2012.

McCombs, W. Douglass. "Therapeutic Rusticity: Antimodernism, Health and the Wilderness Vacation, 1870–1915. *New York History*, vol. 76, no. 4, 1995, pp. 409–28.

McGee, W. J. "Conservation of Natural Resources." *Proceedings of the Mississippi Valley Historical Association for the Year 1909–1910*. Vol. 3, Torch, 1911, pp. 361–79.

McGerr, Michael. *A Fierce Discontent: The Rise and Fall of the Progressive Movement in America, 1870–1920*. Oxford UP, 2003.

McIntosh, Robert P. *The Background of Ecology: Concept and Theory*. Cambridge UP, 1985.

McKay, Nellie. "'Crayon Enlargements of Life': Zora Neale Hurston's *Their Eyes Were Watching God* as Autobiography." *New Essays on* Their Eyes Were Watching God, edited by Michael Awkward, Cambridge UP, 1990, pp. 51–70.

McKibben, Bill, editor. *American Earth: Environmental Writing Since Thoreau*. Library of America, 2008.
McNeill, J. R., and Peter Engelke. *The Great Acceleration: An Environmental History of the Anthropocene since 1945*. Harvard UP, 2014.
Mecklin, John Moffatt. *Democracy and Race Friction: A Study in Social Ethics*. MacMillan, 1914.
Meikle, Jeffrey L. *American Plastic: A Cultural History*. Rutgers UP, 1995.
Mellow, Nicole. "The Democratic Fit: Party Reform and the Eugenics Tool." *The Progressives' Century: Political Reform, Constitutional Government, and the Modern American State*, edited by Stephen Skowronek, Stephen M. Engel, and Bruce Ackerman, Yale UP, 2016, pp. 197–218.
Melosi, Martin V. "The Place of the City in Environmental History." *Environmental History Review*, vol. 17, no. 1, 1993, pp. 1–23.
Melville, Herman. "Bartleby, the Scrivener: A Story of Wall-Street." *Herman Melville: Pierre, Israel Potter, The Piazza Tales, The Confidence-Man, Uncollected Prose, Billy Budd, Sailor*. Library of America, 1984, pp. 635–72.
Merchant, Carolyn. *American Environmental History: An Introduction*. Columbia UP, 2007.
Mighetto, Lisa. *Wild Animals and American Environmental Ethics*. U of Arizona P, 1991.
Millgate, Michael. "The Unity of *Go Down, Moses*." *Bear, Man and God: Eight Approaches to William Faulkner's "The Bear,"* edited by Francis Lee Utley, Lynn Z. Bloom, and Arthur F. Kinney, 2nd ed., Random House, 1971, pp. 222–35.
Milne, Anne. "Ecocriticism." *Contemporary Literary & Cultural Theory: The Johns Hopkins Guide*, edited by Michael Groden, Martin Kreiswirth, and Imre Szeman, Johns Hopkins UP, 2012, pp. 139–43.
Mintz, Steven. *Huck's Raft: A History of American Childhood*. Harvard UP, 2004.
Mitchell, Charles E. *Individualism and Its Discontents: Appropriations of Emerson, 1880–1950*. U of Massachusetts P, 1997.
Mitchell, Lee Clark. "Naturalism and the Languages of Determinism." *Columbia Literary History of the United States*, edited by Emory Elliott. Columbia UP, 1988, pp. 525–45.
———. *Witnesses to a Vanishing America: The Nineteenth-Century Response*. Princeton UP, 1981.
Mitchell, S. Weir. *Doctor and Patient*. J. B. Lippincott, 1887.
———. *Lectures on Diseases of the Nervous System, Especially in Women*. Henry C. Lea's Son, 1881.
———. *Nurse and Patient, and Camp Cure*. J. B. Lippincott, 1877.
Moers, Ellen. *Two Dreisers: The Man and the Novelist as Revealed in His Two Most Important Works,* Sister Carrie *and* An American Tragedy. Viking, 1969.
Montrie, Chad. *The Myth of Silent Spring: Rethinking the Origins of American Environmentalism*. U of California P, 2018.

Morris, Ann R., and Margaret M. Dunn. "Flora and Fauna in Hurston's Florida Novels." *Zora in Florida*, edited by Steve Glassman and Kathryn Lee Seidel, U of Central Florida P, 1991, pp. 1–12.

Morris, Christopher. *The Big Muddy: An Environmental History of the Mississippi and Its Peoples from Hernando de Soto to Hurricane Katrina.* Oxford UP, 2012.

Morris, Matthew J. "The Two Lives of Jurgis Rudkus." *Upton Sinclair's* The Jungle, edited by Harold Bloom, Chelsea House, 2002, pp. 139–55.

Morrison, Toni. "Jim's Africanist Presence in *Huckleberry Finn.*" Adventures of Huckleberry Finn: *A Case Study in Critical Controversy*, 2nd ed., edited by Gerald Graff and James Phelan, Bedford/St. Martin's, 2004, pp. 305–10.

Muir, John. *Our National Parks.* Houghton Mifflin, 1901.

———. *The Story of My Boyhood and Youth. Nature Writings.* Library of America, 1997, pp. 1–146.

Mumford, Lewis. *The Golden Day: A Study in American Experience and Culture.* Horace Liveright, 1926.

———. *Technics and Civilization.* 1934. U of Chicago P, 2010.

Murphy, Earl Finbar. *Governing Nature.* Quadrangle Books, 1967.

Murray, William H. H. *Adventures in the Wilderness.* Edited by William K. Verner, Syracuse UP, 1989.

Myers, Jeffrey. *Converging Stories: Race, Ecology, and Environmental Justice in American Literature.* U of Georgia P, 2005.

Nagel, James. "Donald Pizer, American Naturalism, and Stephen Crane." *Studies in American Naturalism*, vol. 1, nos. 1–2, 2006, pp. 30–35.

Nash, George H. *The Life of Herbert Hoover: The Engineer, 1874–1914.* W. W. Norton, 1983.

Nash, Roderick Frazier. *Wilderness and the American Mind.* 4th ed. Yale UP, 2001.

Newton, Julianne Lutz. *Aldo Leopold's Odyssey.* Island, 2006.

Nigro, Kathleen. "Mr. Emerson Comes to St. Louis: 'Inspiration' and Kate Chopin." *The Concord Saunterer*, vol. 14, 2006, pp. 90–103.

Nolan, Elizabeth. "*The Awakening* as Literary Innovation: Chopin, Maupassant and the Evolution of Genre." *The Cambridge Companion to Kate Chopin*, edited by Janet Beer, Cambridge UP, 2008, pp. 118–31.

Norwood, Vera L. "Heroines of Nature: Four Women Respond to the American Landscape." *The Ecocriticism Reader: Landmarks in Literary Ecology*, edited by Cheryll Glotfelty and Harold Fromm, U of Georgia P, 1996, pp. 323–50.

———. *Made From This Earth: American Women and Nature.* U of North Carolina P, 1993.

Odum, Howard W. "Social and Mental Traits of the Negro: Research into the Conditions of the Negro Race in Southern Towns, a Study in Race Traits, Tendencies and Prospects." Dissertation, Columbia University, 1910.

Oehlschlaeger, Fritz, and George Hendrick, editors. *Toward the Making of Thoreau's Modern Reputation: Selected Correspondence of S. A. Jones, A. W. Hosmer, H. S. Salt, H. G. O. Blake, and D. Ricketson.* U of Illinois P, 1979.

Oelschlaeger, Max. *The Idea of Wilderness: From Prehistory to the Age of Ecology.* Yale UP, 1991.

Olmsted, Frederick Law. *Public Parks and the Enlargement of Towns.* 1870. Arno, 1970.

Olwig, Kenneth R. "Reinventing Common Nature: Yosemite and Mount Rushmore—A Meandering Tale of a Double Nature." *Uncommon Ground: Rethinking the Human Place in Nature*, edited by William Cronon. W. W. Norton, 1996, pp. 379–408.

"O. P. Dexter's Assassination." *The Sun* [New York City], 21 Sept. 1903, p. 1.

Oppenheimer, J. R[obert]. "Atomic Weapons." *Proceedings of the American Philosophical Society*, vol. 90, no. 1, 1946, pp. 7–10.

Outka, Paul. *Race and Nature from Transcendentalism to the Harlem Renaissance.* Palgrave Macmillan, 2008.

Pacyga, Dominic A. *Slaughterhouse: Chicago's Union Stockyard and the World It Made.* U of Chicago P, 2015.

Paris, Leslie. *Children's Nature: The Rise of the American Summer Camp.* New York UP, 2008.

Parmiter, Tara K. "Taking the Waters: The Summer Place and Women's Health in Kate Chopin's *The Awakening*." *American Literary Realism*, vol. 39, no. 1, 2006, pp. 1–19.

Pasinella, Alison. "Becoming (Post) Human: How H. G. Wells, Upton Sinclair, and D. H. Lawrence Tried to Alter the Course of Human Evolution." Dissertation, Boston College, 2014.

Paul, Diane B. *The Politics of Heredity: Essays on Eugenics, Biomedicine, and the Nature-Nurture Debate.* State U of New York P, 1998.

Paul, Eden. "Eugenics, Birth-Control and Socialism." *Population and Birth-Control: A Symposium*, edited by Eden and Cedar Paul, Critic and Guide, 1917, pp. 121–46.

Peterson, Elmer T., editor. *Cities Are Abnormal.* U of Oklahoma P, 1946.

Phillips, Dana. *The Truth of Ecology: Nature, Culture, and Literature in America.* Oxford UP, 2003.

Pickens, Donald K. *Eugenics and the Progressives.* Vanderbilt UP, 1968.

Pierce, Daniel S. *The Great Smokies: From Natural Habitat to National Park.* U of Tennessee P, 2000.

Pinchot, Gifford. *Breaking New Ground.* 1947. Island, 1998.

———. *The Fight for Conservation.* 1910. U of Washington P, 1967.

———. "The Lines are Drawn," *Journal of Forestry*, vol. 17, no. 8, 1919, pp. 899–900.

Pizer, Donald. "Stephen Crane's "Maggie" and American Naturalism." *Criticism*, vol. 7, no. 2, 1965, pp. 168–75.

Prewitt, Wiley C., Jr. "Return of the Big Woods: Hunting and Habitat in Yoknapatawpha." *Faulkner and the Natural World*, edited by Donald M. Kartiganer and Ann J. Abadie, U of Mississippi P, 1999, pp. 198–221.

Prochnik, George. *Putnam Camp: Sigmund Freud, James Jackson Putnam, and the Purpose of American Psychology*. Other, 2006.

Quam-Wickham, Nancy. "'Cities Sacrificed on the Altar of Oil': Popular Opposition to Oil Development in 1920s Los Angeles." *Environmental History*, vol. 3, no. 2, 1998, pp. 189–209.

Ragan, David Paul. "The Evolution of Roth Edmonds in *Go Down, Moses*." *Mississippi Quarterly*, vol. 38, 1985, pp. 295–309.

Raine. Anne. "'The Man at the Sources': Gender, Capital, and the Conservationist Landscape in Mary Austin's *The Ford*." *Exploring Lost Borders: Critical Essays on Mary Austin*, edited by Melody Graulich and Elizabeth Klimasmith, U of Nevada P, 1999, pp. 243–66.

Reagan, Ronald. "Remarks before the American Petroleum Institute." *The Environmental Movement, 1968–1972*, edited by David Stradling, U of Washington P, 2012, pp. 114–18.

Reisner, Marc. *Cadillac Desert: The American West and Its Disappearing Water*. Rev. ed., Penguin Books, 1993.

Renehan, Edward J., Jr. *John Burroughs: An American Naturalist*. Black Dome, 1998.

Rhodes, Richard. *The Making of the Atomic Bomb*. Simon & Schuster, 1986.

Rieger, Christopher. *Clear-Cutting Eden: Ecology and the Pastoral in Southern Literature*. U of Alabama P, 2009.

Riis, Jacob. *Jacob Riis Revisited: Poverty and the Slum in Another Era*. Edited by Francesco Cordasco, Augustus M. Kelley, 1973, pp. 125–298.

Ringe, Donald A. "Romantic Imagery in Kate Chopin's *The Awakening*." *American Literature*, vol. 43, no. 4, 1972, pp. 580–88.

Ringler, Donald P. "Mary Austin: Kern County Days, 1888–1892." *Southern California Quarterly*, vol. 45, no. 1, 1963, pp. 25–63.

Robbins, William G. "The Great Experiment in Industrial Self-Government: The Lumber Industry and the National Recovery Administration." *Journal of Forest History*, vol. 25, 1981, pp. 128–43.

———. *Lumberjacks and Legislators: Political Economy of the U.S. Lumber Industry, 1890–1941*. Texas A&M UP, 1982.

Robertson, Thomas. *The Malthusian Moment: Global Population Growth and the Birth of American Environmentalism*. Rutgers UP, 2012.

Rodgers, Daniel T. *Atlantic Crossings: Social Politics in a Progressive Age*. Harvard UP, 1998.

———. "In Search of Progressivism." *Reviews in American History*, vol. 10, no. 4, 1982, pp. 113–32.

Roosevelt, Franklin D. "Nomination Address. July 2, 1932." *The Public Papers and Addresses of Franklin D. Roosevelt*. Vol. 1, Random House, 1938, pp. 647–59.

Roosevelt, Theodore. "Before the Mothers' Congress, Washington, D.C., March 13, 1905." *A Compilation of the Messages and Speeches of Theodore Roosevelt,*

1901–1905. Edited by Alfred Henry Lewis, vol. 1, Bureau of National Literature and Art, 1906, pp. 576–81.

———. *Hunting the Grisly and Other Sketches*. Review of Reviews, 1904.

———. *Hunting Trips on the Prairie and in the Mountains*. 1885. G. P. Putnam's Sons, 1900.

———. *The Letters of Theodore Roosevelt*. Edited by Elting E. Morison, vol. 5, Harvard UP, 1952.

———. "Opening Address by the President." *Proceedings of a Conference of Governors in the White House, May 13–15, 1908*. Government Printing Office, 1909, pp. 3–13.

———. "A Premium on Race Suicide." *Outlook*, vol. 105, 27 Sept. 1913, pp. 163–64.

———. "Twisted Eugenics." *Outlook*, vol. 106, 3 Jan. 1914, pp. 30–34.

Rosen, Ruth. *The Lost Sisterhood: Prostitution in America, 1900–1918*. Johns Hopkins UP, 1982.

Rosendale, Steven. "In Search of Left Ecology's Usable Past: *The Jungle*, Social Change, and the Class Character of Environmental Impairment." *The Greening of Literary Scholarship: Literature, Theory, and the Environment*, edited by Steven Rosendale, U of Iowa P, 2002, pp. 59–76.

Ross, Andrew. *The Chicago Gangster Theory of Life: Nature's Debt to Society*. Verso, 1994.

Ross, Dorothy. *G. Stanley Hall: The Psychologist as Prophet*. U of Chicago P, 1972.

———. *The Origins of American Social Science*. Cambridge UP, 1991.

Ross, Edward Alsworth. *Social Control: A Survey of the Foundations of Order*. Macmillan, 1901.

Rotundo, E. Anthony. *American Manhood: Transformations in Masculinity from the Revolution to the Modern Era*. Basic Books, 1993.

Round, Phillip H. *The Impossible Land: Story and Place in California's Imperial Valley*. U of New Mexico P, 2008.

Ruffin, Kimberly N. *Black on Earth: African American Ecoliterary Traditions*. U of Georgia P, 2010.

Runte, Alfred. *National Parks: The American Experience*. U of Nebraska P, 1997.

Russell, Edmund. *War and Nature: Fighting Humans and Insects with Chemicals from World War I to* Silent Spring. Cambridge UP, 2001.

Rydell, Robert W. *All the World's a Fair: Visions of Empire at American International Expositions, 1876–1916*. U of Chicago P, 1984.

Sabin, Paul. *Crude Politics: The California Oil Market, 1900–1940*. U of California P, 2005.

Saikku, Mikko. *This Delta, This Land: An Environmental History of the Yazoo-Mississippi Floodplain*. U of Georgia P, 2005.

Scarpino, Philip V. *Great River: An Environmental History of the Upper Mississippi, 1890–1950*. U of Missouri P, 1985.

Scharnhorst, Gary. *Charlotte Perkins Gilman*. Twayne, 1985.

———. *Henry David Thoreau: A Case Study in Canonization*. Camden House, 1993.

———, editor. *Mark Twain: The Complete Interviews*. U of Alabama P, 2006.

Scheffler, William L., and Frank Carey. *Big Moose Lake, New York in Vintage Postcards*. Arcadia, 2000.

Schmitt, Peter J. *Back to Nature: The Arcadian Myth in Urban America*. Johns Hopkins UP, 1990.

Schöberlein, Stefan. "Herman Melville and the International Paper Machine." *ISLE*, vol. 23, no. 4, Autumn 2016, pp. 730–54.

Schulman, Robert. *Social Criticism and Nineteenth-Century American Fictions*. U of Missouri P, 1987.

Schuster, David G. *Neurasthenic Nation: America's Search for Health, Happiness, and Comfort, 1869–1920*. Rutgers UP, 2011.

Scott, Daryl Michael. *Contempt and Pity: Social Policy and the Image of the Damaged Black Psyche, 1880–1996*. U of North Carolina P, 1997.

Seton, Ernest Thompson. *Wild Animals I Have Known*. Charles Scribner's Sons, 1898.

Shabecoff, Philip. *A Fierce Green Fire: The American Environmental Movement*. Hill and Wang, 1993.

Shaler, Nathaniel Southgate. "The Negro Problem." *Atlantic Monthly*, Nov. 1884, 696–709.

———, editor. *The United States of America*. Vol. 2, Appleton, 1897.

Sharp, Paul F. "The Tree Farm Movement: Its Origin and Development." *Agricultural History*, vol. 23, Jan. 1949, pp. 41–45.

Sickels, Amy. "Voices of Independence and Community: The Prose of Zora Neale Hurston." *Zora Neale Hurston*, edited by Harold Bloom, Chelsea House, 2003, pp. 49–71.

Silcox, F. A. "Foresters Must Choose." *Journal of Forestry*, vol. 33, Mar. 1935, pp. 198–204.

Sinclair, Upton. *American Outpost: A Book of Reminiscences*. Kennikat, 1969.

———. *The Autobiography of Upton Sinclair*. W. H. Allen, 1963.

———. *The Book of Life: Mind and Body*. Haldeman-Julius, 1922.

———. *The Jungle*. 1906. Edited by Clare Virginia Eby, W. W. Norton, 2003.

———. *Mammonart: An Essay in Economic Interpretation*. 1924. Simon, 2003.

Singal, Daniel J. *William Faulkner: The Making of a Modernist*. U of North Carolina P, 1997.

Skowronek, Stephen, Stephen M. Engel, and Bruce Ackerman, editors. *The Progressives' Century: Political Reform, Constitutional Government, and the Modern American State*. Yale UP, 2016.

Sloane, David E. E. "The N-word in *Adventures of Huckleberry Finn* Reconsidered." *Mark Twain Annual*, vol. 12, no. 1, 2014, pp. 70–82.

Slosson, Edwin E. *Creative Chemistry*. Century, 1919.

Slovic, Scott. Letter in "Forum on Literatures of the Environment." *PMLA*, vol. 114, no. 5, 1999, pp. 1089–1104.

Smith, David Livingstone. *Less than Human: Why We Demean, Enslave, and Exterminate Others*. St. Martin's, 2011.

Smith, Henry Nash. *Mark Twain: The Development of a Writer.* Harvard UP, 1962.
Smith-Rosenberg, Carroll. *Disorderly Conduct: Visions of Gender in Victorian America.* Oxford UP, 1985.
Smythe, William E. *The Conquest of Arid America.* Harper and Brothers, 1900.
Sobel, David. *Beyond Ecophobia: Reclaiming the Heart in Nature Education.* Orion, 1996.
Sohlman, Ragnar, and Henrik Schück. *Nobel: Dynamite and Peace.* Cosmopolitan Book Corporation, 1929.
Sorrentino, Paul. *Stephen Crane: A Life of Fire.* Harvard UP, 2014.
Spear, Robert J. *The Great Gypsy Moth War: A History of the First Campaign in Massachusetts to Eradicate the Gypsy Moth, 1890–1901.* U of Massachusetts P, 2005.
Spiro, Jonathan Peter. *Defending the Master Race: Conservation, Eugenics, and the Legacy of Madison Grant.* U of Vermont P, 2009.
Spring, Joel. "Education as a Form of Social Control." *Roots of Crisis: American Education in the Twentieth Century*, edited by Clarence J. Karier, Paul C. Violas, and Joel Spring, Rand McNally College, 1973, pp. 30–39.
Stager, Curt. *Your Atomic Self: The Invisible Elements That Connect You to Everything Else in the Universe.* St. Martins, 2014.
State of New York Court of Appeals. *The People of the State of New York vs. Chester Gillette.* Vol. 1, Dussault & Miller, 1906.
Stedman, Edmund Clarence. "Emerson." *Century*, vol. 25, April 1883, pp. 872–86.
Stein, Rachel. *Shifting the Ground: American Women Writers' Revisions of Nature, Gender, and Race.* UP of Virginia, 1997.
Steinberg, Ted. *Acts of God: The Unnatural History of Natural Disaster in America.* 2nd ed., Oxford UP, 2006.
———. *Down to Earth: Nature's Role in American History.* 2nd ed., Oxford UP, 2009.
Stern, Alexandra Minna. *Eugenic Nation: Faults and Frontiers of Better Breeding in Modern America.* U of California P, 2016.
Stewart, David H. "Ike McCaslin, Cop-Out." *Bear, Man and God: Eight Approaches to William Faulkner's "The Bear,"* edited by Francis Lee Utley, Lynn Z. Bloom, and Arthur F. Kinney, 2nd ed., Random House, 1971, pp. 212–20.
Stewart, Randall. "The Growth of Thoreau's Reputation." *College English*, vol. 7, Jan. 1946, pp. 208–14.
St. John, Rachel. *Line in the Sand: A History of the Western U.S.-Mexico Border.* Princeton UP, 2011.
Stoll, Steven. *U.S. Environmentalism since 1945: A Brief History with Documents.* Bedford/St. Martins, 2007.
Stratton-Porter, Gene. *A Girl of the Limberlost.* Doubleday, Page, 1909.
———. "My Life and My Books." *The Ladies' Home Journal*, Sept. 1916, pp. 13, 80–81.
Strayed, Cheryl. *Wild: From Lost to Found on the Pacific Crest Trail.* Vintage Books, 2013.

Sturgeon, Noël. *Ecofeminist Natures: Race, Gender, Feminist Theory, and Political Action*. Routledge, 1997.

Sutter, Paul S. *Driven Wild: How the Fight against Automobiles Launched the Modern Wilderness Movement*. U of Washington P, 2002.

Sweeney, Gerard M. "The Syphilitic World of Stephen Crane's *Maggie*." *American Literary Realism, 1870–1910*, vol. 24, no. 1, 1991, pp. 79–85.

Talkspace. Advertisement. Oprah Winfrey Network. 27 Jan. 2017.

Tallmadge, John and Henry Harrington, editors. *Reading Under the Sign of Nature: New Essays in Ecocriticism*. U of Utah P, 2000.

Tatum, Sophie. "Trump's Border Wall May Be Shorter Than First Advertised." CNN, 9 Jan. 2018. http://www.cnn.com/2018/01/09/politics/donald-trump-border-wall/index.html.

Taylor, Frederick Winslow. *The Principles of Scientific Management*. Harper & Brothers, 1911.

Taylor, Nancy Drew. *Annotations to* Go Down, Moses. Garland, 1994.

Terrie, Phillip. *Forever Wild: A Cultural History of Wilderness in the Adirondacks*. Syracuse UP, 1994.

Thiele, Leslie Paul. *Sustainability*. Polity Press, 2013.

"The Third Republican Debate Transcript, Annotated." *Washington Post*, 28 Oct. 2015. https://www.washingtonpost.com/news/the-fix/wp/2015/10/28/the-third-republican-debate-annotating-the-transcript/?utm_term=.0a5644099a7f. Accessed 23 Dec. 2016.

Thompson, Michael J., editor. *Fleeing the City: Studies in the Culture and Politics of Antiurbanism*. Palgrave Macmillan, 2009.

Todd, Kim. *Tinkering with Eden: A Natural History of Exotic Species in America*. W. W. Norton, 2001.

Torgovnick, Marianna. *Gone Primitive: Savage Intellects, Modern Lives*. U of Chicago P, 1990.

Toth, Emily. *Kate Chopin*. William Morrow, 1990.

Towne, Robert. Chinatown *Screenplay*. 3rd draft. 1973. www.public.asu.edu/~srbeatty/394/Chinatown.pdf. Accessed 2 Jan. 2017.

Traversi, Derek. *T. S. Eliot: The Longer Poems*. Harcourt Brace Jovanovich, 1976.

"Troubled Cities—and Their Mayors." *Newsweek*, Mar. 1967, pp. 38–43.

Tuan, Yi-fu. *Landscapes of Fear*. Pantheon Books, 1979.

Turner, Frederick Jackson. "The Significance of the Frontier in American History." *The Frontier in American History*. Henry Holt, 1920, pp. 1–38.

Tuttle, Jennifer S. "Rewriting the West Cure: Charlotte Perkins Gilman, Owen Wister, and the Sexual Politics of Neurasthenia." *The Mixed Legacy of Charlotte Perkins Gilman*, edited by Catherine J. Golden and Joanna Schneider Zangrando, U of Delaware P, 2000, pp. 103–21.

Twain, Mark. *Adventures of Huckleberry Finn*. Mark Twain Library. Edited by Victor Fischer and Lin Salamo, U of California P, 2010.

———. *A Connecticut Yankee in King Arthur's Court*. Edited by Bernard L. Stein, U of California P, 1983.

———. *Huck Finn and Tom Sawyer among the Indians and Other Unfinished Stories*. Edited by Dahlia Armon, et al., U of California P, 1989.

———. *Life on the Mississippi*. *Mississippi Writings*. Library of America, 1982, pp. 217–616.

———. *Pudd'nhead Wilson: A Tale*. *Mississippi Writings*. Library of America, 1982, pp. 913–1056.

———. *Roughing It*. *Mark Twain:* The Innocents Abroad, Roughing It. Library of America, 1984, pp. 525–986.

US Bureau of the Census. *Historical Statistics of the United States, Colonial Times to 1970*. Part 1, US Government Printing Office, 1976.

Utley, Francis Lee, "Pride and Humility: The Cultural Roots of 'The Bear.'" *Bear, Man and God: Eight Approaches to William Faulkner's "The Bear,"* edited by Francis Lee Utley, Lynn Z. Bloom, and Arthur F. Kinney, 2nd ed., Random House, 1971, pp. 167–87.

Van Dyke, John C. *The Desert*. 1901. Peregrine Smith, 1980.

Vernon, Zackary. "'Being Myriad, One': Melville and the Ecological Sublime in Faulkner's *Go Down, Moses*." *Studies in the Novel*, vol. 46, no. 1, 2014, pp. 63–82.

Vickery, Olga W. "God's Moral Order and Ike's Redemption." *Bear, Man and God: Eight Approaches to William Faulkner's "The Bear,"* edited by Francis Lee Utley, Lynn Z. Bloom, and Arthur F. Kinney. 2nd ed., Random House, 1971, pp. 209–12.

Wade, Louise Carroll. *Chicago's Pride: The Stockyards, Packingtown, and Environs in the Nineteenth Century*. U of Illinois P, 1987.

Waldron, Karen E. "Introduction." *Toward a Literary Ecology: Places and Spaces in American Literature*, edited by Karen E. Waldron and Rob Friedman, Scarecrow, 2013, pp. xv–xxxix.

Walker, Francis A. "Restriction of Immigration. *Atlantic Monthly*, June 1896, pp. 822–29.

Walker, Lawrence. *The Southern Forest*. U of Texas P, 1991.

Wall, Cheryl A. *Women of the Harlem Renaissance*. Indiana UP, 1995.

Walton, John. "Foreword." *The Ford*. U of California P, 1996, pp. ix–xvi.

———. *Western Times and Water Wars: State, Culture, and Rebellion in California*. U of California P, 1992.

Warner, Charles Dudley. *In the Wilderness*. 1878. Syracuse UP, 1990.

Warren, James Perrin. "Contexts for Reading 'Song of the Redwood-Tree.'" *Reading Under the Sign of Nature: New Essays in Ecocriticism*, edited by John Tallmadge and Henry Harrington, U of Utah P, 2000, pp. 165–78.

Warren, Wilson J. *Tied to the Great Packing Machine: The Midwest and Meatpacking*. U of Iowa P, 2007.

Wasik, Bill, and Monica Murphy. *Rabid: A Cultural History of the World's Most Diabolical Virus.* Penguin, 2012.

Waters of Destiny. US Army Corps of Engineers. Ca. 1950s. https://www.floridamemory.com/items/show/232410. Accessed 29 Dec. 2016.

Weingartner, James. "War against Subhumans: Comparisons between the German War against the Soviet Union and the American War against Japan, 1941–1945." *Historian*, vol. 58, no. 3, 1996, pp. 557–73.

Welling, Bart H. "A Meeting with Old Ben: Seeing and Writing Nature in Faulkner's *Go Down, Moses.*" *Mississippi Quarterly*, vol. 55, no. 4, 2002, pp. 461–96.

Wernick, Robert. "Let's Spoil the Wilderness." *Saturday Evening Post*, 6 Nov. 1965, pp. 12, 16.

Wertheim, Stanley. "The New York City Topography of *Maggie* and *George's Mother.*" *Stephen Crane Studies*, vol. 17, no. 1, 2008, pp. 2–12.

———. *A Stephen Crane Encyclopedia.* Greenwood, 1997.

Westling, Louise H. *The Green Breast of the New World: Landscape, Gender, and American Fiction.* U of Georgia P, 1996.

Whicher, Stephen E. *Freedom and Fate: An Inner Life of Ralph Waldo Emerson.* A. S. Barnes, 1953.

Wiebe, Robert H. *The Search for Order, 1877–1920.* Hill and Wang, 1967.

Wieck, Carl F. *Refiguring* Huckleberry Finn. U of Georgia P, 2004.

Will, Barbara. "The Nervous Origins of the American Western," *American Literature*, vol. 70, no. 2, 1998, pp. 293–316.

Williams, Michael. *Americans and Their Forests: A Historical Geography.* Cambridge UP, 1989.

Williams, Raymond. *The Country and the City.* Oxford UP, 1973.

Williams, Vernon J., Jr. *Rethinking Race: Franz Boas and His Contemporaries.* UP of Kentucky, 1996.

Williamson, Joel. *New People: Miscegenation and Mulattoes in the United States.* Free Press, 1980.

Willis, Lloyd. *Environmental Evasion: The Literary, Critical, and Cultural Politics of "Nature's Nation."* SUNY P, 2011.

Wills, John. "'Welcome to the Atomic Park': American Nuclear Landscapes and the 'Unnaturally Natural.'" *Environment and History*, vol. 7, no. 4, 2001, pp. 449–72.

Wilson, Christopher. *Cop Knowledge: Police Power and Cultural Narrative in Twentieth-Century America.* U of Chicago P, 2000.

Winchell, Alexander. *Preadamites.* S. C. Griggs, 1880.

Witschi, Nicolas S. *Traces of Gold: California's Natural Resources and the Claim to Realism in Western American Literature.* U of Alabama P, 2002.

Wittenberg, Judith Bryant. "*Go Down, Moses* and the Discourse of Environmentalism." *New Essays on* Go Down, Moses, edited by Linda Wagner-Martin, Cambridge UP, 1996, pp. 49–71.

Wittkoff, E. Peter. "Brazil's SIVAM: Surveillance Against Crime and Terrorism." *International Journal of Intelligence and Counterintelligence*, vol. 16, no. 4, 2003, pp. 543–60.

Wolcott, Robert H. "Eugenics as Viewed by the Zoologist." *Eugenics: Twelve University Lectures*, Dodd, Mead, 1914, pp. 15–40.

Wolfe, Cary. *Animal Rites: American Culture, the Discourse of Species, and Posthumanist Theory*. U of Chicago P, 2003.

———. *Before the Law: Humans and Other Animals in a Biopolitical Frame*. U of Chicago P, 2013.

Wolff, Cynthia Griffin. "Thanatos and Eros: Kate Chopin's *The Awakening*." *American Quarterly*, vol. 25, no. 4, 1973, pp. 449–71.

Woodward, Susan L., and Joyce A. Quinn. *Encyclopedia of Invasive Species: From Africanized Honey Bees to Zebra Mussels*. ABC-CLIO, 2011.

Worster, Donald. *Nature's Economy: A History of Ecological Ideas*. 2nd ed, Cambridge UP, 1994.

———. *Rivers of Empire: Water, Aridity, and the Growth of the American West*. Oxford UP, 1985.

Wright, Hamilton Bell. *The Winning of Barbara Worth*. Book Supply Company, 1911.

Wrobel, David M. *The End of American Exceptionalism: Frontier Anxiety from the Old West to the New Deal*. UP of Kansas, 1993.

Zahniser, Howard. "Nature in Print." 1945. *The Wilderness Writings of Howard Zahniser*. Edited by Mark Harvey, U of Washington P, 2014, pp. 39–41.

Zender, Karl F. *The Crossing of the Ways: William Faulkner, the South, and the Modern World*. Rutgers UP, 1989.

———. *Faulkner and the Politics of Reading*. Louisiana State UP, 2002.

Index

Adirondacks, 5–6, 12–13, 90–92, 99, 101–103, 149–50, 157, 159, 163 n. 2; in *American Tragedy*, 95–98
agriculture, xvi, 63, 73, 76, 134–35, 141; Austin and, 85–86; in Florida, 106–107; Faulkner and, 135; in *The Ford*, 81–82; in *Go Down, Moses*, 130, 135–39; in *Their Eyes Were Watching God*, 111–12
Alaimo, Stacy, xxiv, xxv, 38, 47, 73–74
animals, 16–18, 57–58, 66–70, 153. *See also* extinction; hunting; race
anthropology, 11, 108–10, 113–14, 117
Antimodernism, 5–6, 9, 69, 127, 145
anti-urbanism. *See* cities
Army Corps of Engineers, 3, 87, 107–108, 119, 150
atomic bomb, xviii, 146–55
Austin, Mary, 73–77, 84–86, 88, 143–44; *The Ford*, 77–84

back-to-nature movement, xvi, 5–6, 33, 38–43, 145, 149–50, 157–59
Bailey, Liberty Hyde. *See* agriculture
Boas, Franz, 109–10, 113, 117
Buell, Lawrence, xv, xxiv, 74, 81, 123
Burroughs, John, xi–xii, 38–39, 66, 157–59, 176 n. 4

Carson, Rachel, 155, 168 n. 1, 175–76 n. 1
Centennial Exhibition, xviii, 15–17
Central Park (New York City), 21, 31, 101
Chopin, Kate, 37, 49, 143–45; *The Awakening* 43–53
cities, xvi, 145; and anti-urbanism, xx, 33–34, 38–39, 73, 100, 145, 150–51; and Austin, 77, 84–86; Chicago, 57–58; and ecocriticism, xix, 21–22; and ecology, 24–25; in *The Jungle*, 61–62; Los Angeles, 74–75, 86–87; in *Maggie*, 25–33; New Orleans, 37–38; New York City, 22–24
Clemens, Samuel. *See* Twain, Mark
conservation, xvii–xviii; xx, 18–19, 128, 150; and Austin, 84, 86; forest, 125–26; and industrial psychology, 82; and irrigation, 73–76, 79, 86; in *The Jungle*, 63; oil, 83–84; and race, 71, 115. *See also* wilderness
Crane, Stephen, 33, 48, 143–45; *Maggie*, 25–34, 41
Cronon, William, xiii, xxiv, xxvi, 57–58, 61, 100, 103, 131, 145

Darwin, Charles. *See* evolutionary theory

Dewey, John, 49–50
Dickey, James, 18, 118, 133
dominance of nature, xvii–xviii, 73, 79–80, 141–42
Dreiser, Theodore, 25, 89, 93, 103, 143–44; *American Tragedy*, 93–99

ecocriticism, xiii–xv, xix, xxiii; and the city, 21–22; and poststructuralism, xxiv–xxv; and praxis, xxv–xxvi. See also discussions of each novel
ecology, 24–25, 55–56, 81; and Leopold, 127–29; in *Maggie*, 28–30
Edison, Thomas, 157–59
Emerson, Ralph Waldo, 39, 44–45, 47–48, 164 n. 15, 166 n. 6
environmentalism, xii–xiii, xx, xxv–xxvi, 139, 141–43, 153–56. See also conservation
environmental justice, xix, xxv, 34–35, 89
eugenics. See race
evolutionary theory, xviii, 24, 51, 59–60, 144, 153, 155; and immigration, 23, 56, 65; in *The Jungle*, 62–63; and Kropotkin, 63, 65
extinction, xvi, xviii, 16–18, 115

Faulkner, William, 122–23, 130, 133, 135, 138–39, 143–44; *Go Down, Moses*, 129–38; Nobel Prize speech, 146–47
feminism. See women
Florida, 106–107
Ford, Henry, 39, 137, 157–59
Foucault, Michel, xxiii, 68, 69–70, 152–53
Freud, Sigmund, 48, 99, 144, 156–57; and *American Tragedy*, 93–99

Gillette (Chester) murder, 89, 95, 96, 101

Hall, G. Stanley, 40–41, 46, 48
Hays, Samuel, xvii, 142, 153–54, 167 n. 8
Hitler, Adolf, 71, 115, 130
Hoover, Herbert, 77, 107, 149, 170 n. 9
Howells, William Dean, 14, 16, 32
Hughes, Langston, 114, 117
hunting, xi–xii, 90–91, 149, 152; Faulkner and, 133, 138; in *Go Down, Moses*, 129, 132–34, 137; Theodore Roosevelt and, 17, 121–22; wildlife management, 126–28. See also extinction
Hurston, Zora Neale, 105–106, 117–18, 133, 143–45; *Their Eyes Were Watching God*, 108, 110–18

immigration, xviii, 22–23, 56–57, 71; in *The Jungle* 60–66, 68. See also race; nonnative species
irrigation. See conservation

Kellogg, John Harvey, 67, 69
Kropotkin, Peter, 63, 65, 66, 80

Leopold, Aldo, 92, 100–101, 127–29, 131, 134, 156
London, Jack, xvii, 48
lumbering, 3, 90–91, 123–26; in *Go Down, Moses*, 129, 137

Marshall, Robert, 92, 100, 102
Marx, Karl. See socialism
Maxwell, Martha, 16–17, 18
Mississippi River, 1–5, 119
Mitchell, S. Weir, 52–53, 167–68 n. 11
Muir, John, 48, 143

Mumford, Lewis 9–10, 39–40

natural disasters, xvi–xvii, 3–4, 37, 105, 107–108, 112, 118–19, 156
Nature Faker controversy, 66–67
New Deal, xiii, xix–xx, xxii, 122–23, 125–26, 128–29, 134–35, 139; in *Go Down, Moses* 130
nonnative species, 21, 55–56, 71. *See also* immigration

Oppenheimer, Robert, 148, 149
Outka, Paul, xxiv, 105–106, 110, 112

Pinchot, Gifford, xvii, xviii, 75, 84, 125
Pizer, Donald, 25–26, 34
preservation. *See* conservation
progressivism, xix–xx, 142; and agriculture, 134–35; Austin and 76–77, 84, 86, 88; and eugenics, 64–65; and the frontier, 9–10; and individualism, 44, 129, 134–35, 139, 143; and industrial psychology, 82; and the lumber industry, 125–26; and the New Deal, xix–xx, 122; and race, 113, 115, 133, 143–44; and social control, xviii, 23–24, 31–32, 48–51, 53, 71, 90–92, 101–102, 143; and urban reform, 23–24, 31–32. *See also* conservation
psychology, 50, 52–54, 100, 144; industrial, 81–82; nature therapy, 5, 38, 48–49, 52–54, 149; recapitulation, 40–42. *See also* Freud

race, xviii, 108–10, 139, 152–53; assimilation, 10–15, 56, 62, 109–10, 113–15, 143–44; and conservation, 71, 115, 133; eugenics, 46, 51, 56–57, 64–66
Raine, Anne, 73, 78, 79

Riis, Jacob, 22, 23
Roosevelt, Franklin, 2, 126, 129, 130, 150. *See also* New Deal
Roosevelt, Theodore, 17, 59, 66, 75, 121–22, 124; and eugenics, 46, 56–57

scientific control of nature, xi–xii, xvii–xviii, 59–60, 73, 88, 106, 109, 144, 156–57, 158–59, 161 n. 2; atomic bomb, 148–50, 154; Mississippi River, 3–4; and ecology, 24–25; in *The Ford*, 81–82; and Hurston, 117–18; in *The Jungle*, 63; wildlife management, 127
Seton, Ernest, 66–67
Sinclair, Upton, 58–59, 67, 70, 143–45; *The Jungle*, 60–70
socialism, 58–60, 65, 69–70, 77, 80, 82, 125; in *The Jungle*, 62–64, 68–69
sociology, 25, 49, 109–10

Thoreau, Henry David, 39
Truman, Harry, 147, 151, 153
Trump, Donald, 71, 142
Turner, Frederick Jackson, 9, 10–11
Twain, Mark, 18, 133, 143–45; *Huckleberry Finn*, 1–2, 6–15, 17–19; *Life on the Mississippi*, 3–5, 18

Van Dyke, John C., 87–88

Walker, Francis, 46, 56
Warner, Charles Dudley, 5–6, 7, 163 n. 8
Water Wars, California, 74–76, 86–87
wilderness, 31, 38, 48, 99–103, 135; in *Go Down, Moses*, 129–34, 136–38; in *Huckleberry Finn*, 6–9; nostalgia, 15–19, 117–18, 133,

wilderness *(continued)* 144–45; protection of, 92, 141, 154–55. *See also* Adirondacks; conservation

Wolfe, Carey, 68, 153

women, xiii–xiv, 117; in *The Awakening*, 43–48, 51–52; control of, 49–51, 143–44; ecofeminism, xiv–xv, 38, 47, 73–74, 79, 81, 88; in *The Ford*, 79–80; and motherhood, 43, 46, 56–57; and nature, 41–43; and therapy, 50–54

Worster, Donald, 76, 82, 87, 154, 171 n.13

www.ingramcontent.com/pod-product-compliance
Lightning Source LLC
Chambersburg PA
CBHW030648230426
43665CB00011B/1005